DATE DUE

DEC 2 0'04			

DEMCO 38-296

SHAPING THE FUTURE OF
FEMINIST PSYCHOLOGY

PSYCHOLOGY OF WOMEN
BOOK SERIES

CHERYL B. TRAVIS, Series Editor

Bringing Cultural Diversity to Feminist Psychology: Theory, Research, and Practice
   Hope Landrine, Editor
Shaping the Future of Feminist Psychology: Education, Research, and Practice
   Judith Worell and Norine G. Johnson, Editors

SHAPING THE FUTURE OF FEMINIST PSYCHOLOGY

EDUCATION, RESEARCH, AND PRACTICE

EDITED BY

JUDITH WORELL AND NORINE G. JOHNSON

American Psychological Association

Washington, DC

Published by
American Psychological Association
750 First Street, NE
Washington, DC 20002

Copies may be ordered from
APA Order Department
P.O. Box 92984
Washington, DC 20090-2984

In the UK and Europe, copies may be ordered from
American Psychological Association
3 Henrietta Street
Covent Garden, London
WC2E 8LU England

Typeset in Goudy by EPS Group Inc., Easton, MD

Cover designer: Minker Design, Bethesda, MD
Printer: Data Reproductions Corp., Auburn Hills, MI
Technical/production editor: Ida Audeh

Library of Congress Cataloging-in-Publication Data
Shaping the future of feminist psychology: education, research, and
    practice / Judith Worell and Norine G. Johnson, editors.
        p.   cm. — (Psychology of women book series)
    Includes bibliographical references and index.
    ISBN 1-55798-448-4 (alk. paper)
    1. Feminist psychology.   I. Worell, Judith, 1928–
II. Johnson, Norine G.   III. Series.
BF201.4.S53   1997
150′.82 — dc21
                                                                97-17947
                                                                CIP

British Library Cataloguing-in-Publication Data
A CIP record is available from the British Library

Printed in the United States of America
First edition

We would like to dedicate this volume to our six feminist daughters:

Amy, Beth, and Wendy Worell
and Cammarie, Kathryn, and Margaret Johnson

CONTENTS

CONTRIBUTORS

Mary Brabeck, Department of Counseling and Developmental
Psychology, Boston College
Laura Brown, Private Practice, Seattle, WA, and Department of
Psychology, University of Washington
Jean Lau Chin, South Cove Community Health Center, Boston, MA
Mary Ann Dutton, Department of Emergency Medicine, George
Washington University Medical Center and Domestic Violence
Advocacy Project, George Washington University Law Center
Nancy P. Genero, Psychology Department, Wellesley College
Lucia A. Gilbert, Women's Studies and Department of Educational
Psychology, University of Texas at Austin
Beverly Greene, Department of Psychology, St. John's College
Frances K. Grossman, Department of Psychology, Boston University
Susan E. Hawes, Department of Clinical Psychology, Antioch New
England Graduate School and Private Practice, Amherst, MA
Janet S. Hyde, Women's Studies and Department of Psychology,
University of Wisconsin—Madison
Norine G. Johnson, ABCS Psychological Resources, Quincy, MA
Ellen Kimmel, Psychological and Social Foundations of Education and
Department of Psychology, University of South Florida
Jeanne Marecek, Department of Psychology, Swarthmore College
Natalie Porter, California School of Professional Psychology,
Berkeley/Alameda
Pamela Remer, Department of Educational and Counseling Psychology,
University of Kentucky
Joy K. Rice, Department of Psychiatry, University of Wisconsin Medical
School and Psychiatric Services, SC, Madison, WI
Nancy Felipe Russo, Psychology Department, Arizona State University
Janis Sanchez-Hucles, Psychology Department, Old Dominion
University

Maryann Santos de Barona, Division of Psychology in Education, Arizona State University

Melba Vasquez, Vasquez and Associates Mental Health Services, Austin, TX

Judith Worell, Department of Educational and Counseling Psychology, University of Kentucky

Karen Fraser Wyche, School of Social Work, New York University

PREFACE

This book is the collective outcome of the first National Conference on Education and Training in Feminist Practice, held at Boston College on July 8–11, 1993. The need for such a conference emerged from our increasing awareness that most undergraduate, graduate, and postdoctoral programs in psychology provide little, if any, attention to the many issues related to gender and the lives of women. Educational programs should recognize two facts: Women are the major consumers of mental health services, and women are entering the field in record numbers. In organizing this conference, our aim was to gather the foremost scholars and practitioners in feminist psychology to address the mental health needs of girls and women, particularly in the prevention of emotional disturbances and intervention to promote mental health.

The broad goals of the conference were to explore, integrate, and create a cohesive agenda for training and educating in feminist practice for the next decade. For the purposes of this conference, we defined *feminist practice* very broadly to include activities related to all relevant areas of psychology. Feminist practice may include research, teaching, clinical practice and supervision, scholarly writing, leadership, and any of the other activities in which psychologists currently participate. Of the many outcomes anticipated from the conference, we envisioned this book as a summation of the best in current perspectives on feminist approaches to the practice of psychology, with a proactive forecast of future directions in feminist education, research, and practice.

CONFERENCE PLANNING

To organize and plan the conference, a committee of nine members of the American Psychological Association's Division of the Psychology of

Women (Division 35) volunteered to meet for a series of four planning meetings in Boston and Albuquerque. In these planning meetings, we developed a mission statement, topical areas to be included, a broad structure for the conference, and a set of detailed plans for implementation. We structured the conference as an extended working meeting to discuss the nine topical areas—theory, assessment, therapy, curriculum, pedagogy, research, diversity, supervision, and postdoctoral training—we regarded as essential to our goals. For each topic, we developed a set of critical questions to be considered and discussed.

To meet our goals for the outcomes of the conference, we aimed to collect and integrate the contributions of the diverse community of feminist psychologists into a set of working papers. During the planning stages, we selected the nine topics listed above and agreed that cross-cutting topics would include diversity and ethics. The cross-cutting topics were intended to infuse each chapter with some content that we deemed essential to the practice of feminist psychology. We anticipated that the outcomes of this conference would point the way for education and training in feminist practice for the remainder of the 20th century and beyond.

Participants for the conference were solicited through various channels, including announcements in academic and professional newsletters and personal communication by members of the planning committee to colleagues in the feminist psychology community. The criteria for participation included a doctoral degree in any area of psychology and a commitment to promoting the goals of feminist education, research, and practice. Seventy-seven psychologists representing a range of areas of academia, research, and practice attended the 4-day conference. We also invited 12 psychology graduate students as participant–observer workers; they were distributed among the nine topical groups. One additional graduate student, Peggy Bell, served as a conference organizer throughout the months of planning and the 4-day conference sessions. These students liberally contributed their time and expertise to the proceedings, and they volunteered at the end of the conference to write a collective chapter for the book.

The conference meetings were held at Boston College, which graciously lent us space and resources and housed and fed our attendees in relative comfort. Mary Brabeck was the on-site coordinator; she did a magnificent job of keeping us organized and functional while mentoring and supporting the students. She was assisted throughout the planning and registration process by the very efficient Peggy Bell, who enabled us to proceed with our work without worrying about conference details.

CONFERENCE STRUCTURE AND PROCEDURES

The final group of 77 conference attendees were all doctoral-level psychologists. Prior to the start of the conference, they joined one of the nine working groups according to their expressed interests on the application form. To ensure that group size was relatively equal, each participant joined either her first or second group choice. Participants were then sent a list of questions and suggested readings that might be addressed by their group and were invited to submit their own questions. These combined sets of questions became the starting point for small-group discussions.

The conference proceeded in a three-stage rotating process. First, members met for a full day in one of the nine 6- to 8-person "home groups" for intense small-group working interactions. For each group, two members served as facilitators throughout the conference and were responsible for ensuring that group process was implemented and that group goals were met. Student participant–observers attended each home group and took running notes, providing typed feedback to their group members at the end of each day regarding major topics discussed and group decisions concluded that day. During the last hour of each day, all nine groups convened for a communal plenary session. In these plenary sessions, each working group reported its progress to the full conference on a draft set of principles related to its topical area and planned for the activities on the following day.

On the second and third days, the home groups met for one session and then separated, with members moving to "triads" composed of representatives from two other groups. These triads were designed to encourage cross-group communication and feedback. Half of each working group met with different sets of rotating triads from the other working groups. In this manner, part of each working group met with parts of all other working groups, mutually providing information and receiving feedback. In one session, for example, the pedagogy working group might meet in a triad with curriculum and therapy. Sharing and discussing their deliberations with members of these two other groups enabled the pedagogy group members to reconsider their interim product in the light of the work and feedback from others. The nine working groups then reconvened to process the feedback and to adjust their principles as required. Working notes were collated, and each group constructed a final set of principles related to its topic.

On the fourth day of the conference, all nine groups convened to arrive at a final consensus about which principles of feminist education, research, training, and practice were common across groups. Each group displayed its essential principles and compared these across the principles developed by other groups. Agreement on the adoption of each principle was accomplished through total group consensus rather than by majority vote. Disagreements were discussed until consensus was reached. To accommodate individual group perspectives, we identified as unique concerns those principles identified as important for one group but not common across groups. Through dialogue, dissent, and final consensus, we articulated common themes across the nine topical areas and included and honored unique themes. In this manner, all voices were heard, equally valued, and integrated into the final set of conference principles. Through a feminist process, we completed our task within the structured time frame and effectively achieved our goals.

MULTIPLE OUTCOMES OF THE CONFERENCE

The outcomes of the 4-day conference were multiple. At the process level, we discovered and confirmed that a feminist approach to problem generation and solution can indeed produce a body of knowledge that promises to move the discipline forward. Here, consensus meant integrating diverse viewpoints into a cohesive set of principles that reflected the collective thinking of all participants. At the product level, we had many plans for implementation. These plans included a handbook of the conference proceedings (Chin, 1994) and the publication of this book.

As a final consummation of the conference, this book covers the nine topic areas in depth. Most of the chapters were written by the two facilitators for each group, with the remaining members providing feedback and commentary. Several groups divided their chapters into sections, with each member taking responsibility for writing a section. All chapters follow a structured format, however, that generally begins with a section describing the process generated by group members, followed by a survey of relevant literature on the topic, a discussion and summary of the principles developed by that group, and a proposal for future directions. Thus, the book reflects the content and process of the conference, but each chapter moves beyond the topic and embeds it within the context of current literature and future directions.

The 12 student participants, along with coordinator Peggy Bell, requested to collaborate on a final chapter reporting on their experiences of the conference. The enthusiasm and hard-working approach to the chapter of the student group resulted in an exciting and original addition to the volume. Aside from the contribution of their astute and thoughtful comments, the struggles and successes of these students in completing a successful "group-write" project represents an outstanding example of feminist process in action.

Additional implementation projects were volunteered from more than 35 participants. These included presentations on feminist education and practice at national and regional meetings, curriculum revision projects, resource bibliographies related to the topical areas, a videotape resource bank, and planning for the next conference. These projects were coordinated through a continuing task force to ensure that tasks were accomplished and support received where needed. We anticipate that as the distribution and circulation of the conference outcomes increase, educational and training programs will take note and will begin to integrate many of the ideas proposed here.

REFERENCE

Chin, J. L. (Ed.). (1994). *Proceedings of the national conference on education and training in feminist practice*. Washington, DC: Office of Women's Affairs, American Psychological Association.

ACKNOWLEDGMENTS

The enthusiasm, dedication, and sense of community generated by the participants in this conference continue to lighten our hearts and guide our efforts. As the primary conveners of the conference and editors of this collated volume, we want to extend our deepest appreciation and admiration for all the women who participated in the conference and its follow-up activities. In particular, we celebrate the vision and efforts of the other seven members of the planning committee, whose sage guidance energized us throughout: Mary Brabeck, Jean Chin, Lucia Gilbert, Beverly Greene, Natalie Porter, Maryann Santos de Barona, and Karen Wyche. The successes of the conference were certainly furthered by their hard work and commitment to advancing our feminist visions. Sisters, we thank you all and we honor each of you.

We extend our gratitude and appreciation to many sectors of the American Psychological Association (APA): The Division of the Psychology of Women (Division 35), the Women's Programs Office, the Education Directorate, and the Board of Directors, whose generous support and encouragement made this conference possible. We wish to acknowledge the contributions of those individuals who worked with us to bring this book to fruition: Natalie Porter, who as president of Division 35 initiated the brain-storming session that birthed this project; the members of the Executive Committee of Division 35, who continued to support the conference and the book in innumerable ways; and our APA colleagues Cynthia Baum, Joanne Callan, Frank Farley, Gwen Keita, and Jeanie Kelleher, who gave generously of their time and resources to enable the conference to succeed. Finally, we would like to thank Cheryl Travis, senior editor of the Division 35 book series; Cheryl was always there for us with sage counsel and calm support as we worked our way through the editorial and publication process.

1

INTRODUCTION: CREATING THE FUTURE: PROCESS AND PROMISE IN FEMINIST PRACTICE

JUDITH WORELL AND NORINE G. JOHNSON

CURRENT STATUS OF FEMINIST PSYCHOLOGY

In the past 25 years, feminist psychologists have seen their discipline expand from relative obscurity to a position of healthy growth and expansion. Emerging from the revitalization of earlier women's movements, feminist psychology now claims a space of its own in the context of scholarship, research, professional practice, educational programs, community activism, leadership, and policy implementation (O'Connell & Russo, 1991; Worell & Etaugh, 1994). Each of these activities meets the broad feminist goals of (a) making visible and improving the lives of all girls and women and (b) fostering the healthy and equitable functioning of families and communities.

Feminist psychologists now represent these goals in practice areas specific to their interests and expertise, including such areas as basic cognitive and learning processes, social and interpersonal relationships, psychobiological factors, multicultural issues, health and well-being, career development, organizational management, education, and sexuality and reproductive processes. Feminist psychologists also explore and intervene in the darker side of women's lives: discrimination, harassment, violence, illness, and poverty.

Feminists from all theoretical persuasions are well aware, however, that their efforts and contributions are underrepresented in the mainstream literature, in the practice of psychology, in business and professional organizations, and in academia. The challenges to contemporary feminist psychologists are many: how to influence mainstream psychology without losing our unique perspective; how to challenge the academy without being dismissed as hostile or political; how to further our research efforts without becoming marginalized into specialized journals; and how to assert our values without being dismissed as unscientific. For all of us, however, a primary goal is to extend the boundaries of our influence so that feminist psychology becomes channeled in multiple ways into the discipline as a whole. These inroads into traditional psychology encompass all aspects of education, training, research, practice, and leadership.

Integration of feminism into mainstream psychology can be accomplished through many formats. For some, inclusion in the traditional structure and content of psychology is a desirable goal (e.g., Bronstein & Quina, 1988). For others, the problems inherent in the dominant discourse of traditional psychology cannot be remedied by simple arithmetic addition of topics and courses (Anderson, 1987). Instead, a complete transformation of the teaching and practice of psychology is considered essential (e.g., Diller, Houston, Morgan, & Ayim, 1996; Landrine, 1995; Paludi & Stuernagel, 1990). For either position, however, a cohesive body of tenets and principles is required that represents the collective wisdom of contemporary feminism. To this end, we sought to merge the diverse strands of feminist psychological thought to form a common braid that weaves together the collective consciousness of the discipline. This book represents this new vision for psychology.

The challenge of convening contemporary feminist psychologists to arrive at consensus across a range of topics is a formidable one. Although common threads unite us, feminist psychologists are as varied in their approach to the content and practice of the discipline as are members of the United Nations with respect to international unity. Feminist psychologists represent a range of geographical areas, professional commitments, theoretical persuasions, and beliefs about the locus of women's subordination and the possible solutions. The need is evident for a broad representation of feminist psychologists to carve out an educational agenda that represents contemporary understandings and forecasts directions.

DEVELOPING AN AGENDA FOR FEMINIST PRACTICE

In this introductory chapter, we address three questions about the development of an agenda for the future of education and training in feminist practice: Why it is necessary, how it might happen, and what direction it might take. We have already addressed why it is necessary, and throughout this book we address the marginal status of feminist psychology and ways in which to integrate it within the mainstream of the discipline. We examine how a feminist agenda may be developed by presenting an overview of how we developed and used the feminist process of decision making and consensus to carve out the themes and principles that form the chapters of this book. The direction of that agenda is approached with a broad road map that overviews the topics that form the substance of this book. The outcomes of group dialogue and the accumulated wisdom and expertise of 90 authors are collected in this volume. Each topical chapter integrates in unique ways the process of feminist decision making and collaboration with creative proposals that reflect current knowledge and foretell future directions for the discipline.

FORMULATING A FEMINIST PROCESS

There are many ways to move a field forward. Among these are scholarly writing and development of ideas, empirical research to test these ideas, and conferences at which new concepts and research findings are presented to professional colleagues. Another means of discovering the present and inventing the future is the working conference. At a working conference, group goals are identified and questions are raised that address these goals. These questions are discussed and processed among many participants. The outcomes of an effective working conference emerge from a cohesive group process in which all persons have had the opportunity to deliberate, speak, challenge, and contribute. The contents of this volume represent the collective wisdom of the 90 participants at a national working conference organized to assess the present and future status of feminist practice.

From the start of the planning sessions for the working groups, implementing a "feminist process" was paramount. How did each of the nine working groups articulate their process of formulating critical questions and arriving at recommendations? Can commonalities across the working groups be identified? In what ways were the attributes of small-group dynamics reflected in these feminist groups?

Discourse and research related to group process and group decision making is well established in psychology (e.g., Brown, 1988; McGrath, 1984). In contrast, less has been written about a feminist approach to decision making in small groups and its role in defining the feminist vision in psychology. Most of the discourse related to feminist process appears in the literature on feminist pedagogy (e.g., Briskin, 1990; Bunch & Pollack, 1983; Culley & Portuges, 1985; Deats & Lenker, 1994; Romney, Tatum, & Jones, 1992). In developing a working model of feminist process for small groups, literature was considered from research on small-group dynamics as well as from the teaching-learning process represented by feminist pedagogy.

To understand the feminist process within the context of small task-oriented groups, we looked first at the literature on small-group dynamics. We asked several questions. What are the characteristics of an effective task-oriented group? How do small groups change over time? Did the nine working groups demonstrate these characteristics in their decision-making process, or did they invent novel ways of addressing critical issues in their task?

DEFINING GROUPS AND GROUP PROCESS

A small working group is characterized by members who are inter-dependent and interactive and who are likely to exert an influence on one another. Would the small working groups develop this interdependency during the 4 days they were together? We looked to the literature on small-group process for direction. Group process encompasses the formation and development of the group, how effectively the group functions, and the procedures by which it accomplishes its goals (Sears, Peplau, & Taylor, 1991). If feminist-oriented groups function in some unique ways, what attributes of the groups facilitate their process?

Attributes of Small Groups

According to the psychological literature, three important attributes of small groups influence group process: structure, cohesiveness, and communication (Brown, 1988). In terms of structure, group members adopt or are assigned roles, rules, and tasks. Group structure influences the development of cohesiveness and communication patterns. *Cohesiveness* describes the degree of mutual commitment to the group members or goals. Cohesive groups interact effectively and use conflict constructively to accomplish group goals. In cohesive groups, members also have positive feelings toward one another (Ridgeway, 1983). In our working groups, we aimed to establish a collaborative group structure that would invite open dialogue to include both agreement and dissent and that would facilitate cohesiveness and mutuality. An overarching goal of each group was to accomplish their task through collaboration and consensus rather than through competition and rivalry.

Groups exhibit communication patterns that define the types and degree of activity produced by each member. For example, in most groups, certain members contribute more "talk time" than do others (Ridgeway, 1983). Talk time in turn encourages group members to regard the person who talks the most as the leader, who may then exert a disproportionate influence over group decisions (Mullen, Salas, & Driskell, 1989). Communication among and between members of a group also is affected by a number of other factors, including the size of the group, its purposes and goals, the types of tasks to be accomplished, the reward structure, and the nature of its leadership. In our working groups, effective communication was facilitated by controlling group size, honoring self-selected topic assignments, structuring for a diffusion of leadership, and encouraging an ethic that valued the expression of every voice.

Feminist groups are particularly sensitive to the issues surrounding leadership and hierarchy. Leadership styles influence not only group communication but also group productivity, task effectiveness, and member satisfaction (Fiedler, 1981). Fiedler identified two types of leaders: those who are task oriented and those who are relationship oriented. He concluded that either style of leadership may be effective, depending on the extent to which the leader matches her or his style to the requirements of the situation. The success of differing styles, for example, may depend on the nature of the task and the amount of leader control required to accomplish it. In the nine working groups, we wanted to integrate both leadership styles. We wanted to use an equity-relationship model that encompassed feminist egalitarian values through shared responsibility. We also wanted sufficient task orientation to achieve goals and outcomes that articulated feminist principles of education and training.

Stages of Group Development

We anticipated some changes in group process as our working groups developed over time. Models for group development have emerged from the psychological literature on groups with therapeutic goals and from the business–management literature on groups with task-oriented goals. As small groups evolve from formation to termination, changes occur in structure, cohesiveness, and communication that may resemble a stagelike progression. Are these stagelike qualities useful in understanding process within a feminist working group?

One model that appears useful outlines five stages of group development: pre-affiliation, power and control, intimacy, differentiation, and separation (Garland, Jones, & Kolodny, 1965). Each of these stages describes an element of group process that may be applicable to our working groups.

The pre-affiliation stage is characterized by exploration and preliminary commitment. Each member has an individual perspective. The power and control stage involves status jockeying and power struggles among members. Each member competes to propose ideas to others. In the intimacy stage, mutuality and interdependency emerge, with increased interpersonal involvement. There is a growing ability to coordinate disparate ideas and carry the group project forward. The differentiation stage describes the formation of group cohesion, free expression of ideas, mutual support, and a high level of communication. Cooperative activity toward group goals is prominent and members develop a sense of group identity. Finally, the separation stage covers review and evaluation of the group's accomplishments and a movement toward dissolution.

Within the working groups that developed the chapters in this book, we observed characteristics of all five stages. In particular, we observed the emergence of a strong in-group identity within each working group, whereby the sense of "we" gradually assumed precedence over the assertion of "me." Certain issues, such as those of power and control or of similarity versus difference among members, were more evident in some groups than in others. However, the specific processes by which these groups approached their task and the interactions that facilitated their task accomplishment reflected a feminist format.

Group Process in Feminist Perspective

The perspectives explored by researchers, therapists, and feminist pedagogues on group process came together in the design and functioning of the nine working groups. Seven process themes provided the foundation for the development of these chapters.

A FRAMEWORK OF FEMINIST PROCESS

As we envisioned a conference to articulate principles of feminist practice, it was essential to promote consistency between process and outcome. Toward that goal, we developed and followed a framework of feminist process, whose principles are presented in the Appendix, that was intended to be universal in its application to all activities and persons in the conference. We judge our success in this effort to the extent that our process was consistent with our principles. Each theme is described briefly below.

1. Structure for Diversity
   A document that represents all women should be created by representatives of all women. To the extent that it was fea-

sible, we structured for diversity. Diversity included not only participants but also viewpoints, meeting formats, group size, opportunities for participation, and procedures. The planning group included women of varied color and ethnicities, age, national distribution, sexual orientation, religion, and professional identities in psychology. Although these diversities were not specifically explored within the process of the planning group, it was anticipated that they would serve to frame in unique ways the perspectives of each member. The working group participants were selected according to the same criteria, although limitations were imposed by who elected to attend. The inclusion of student participant–observers as recorders integrated the education and training aspects of the conference and provided for the perspective of a younger generation. Although we planned a specific working group on diversity, each of the other groups was asked to apply its principles as well to the various layers of identity that are represented in diverse populations of women.

2. Distribute Leadership

The issue of power and authority is fundamental to all feminist concerns. The diffusion of leadership was intended to distribute the power of decision making across planners, facilitators, and participants (Roffman, 1994; Schneidewind, 1983). At the same time, the planning committee, which assumed initial and continuing leadership, did not relinquish its role to provide structure and direction for effective task accomplishment. Here, leadership integrated both task and relationship types of orientations (described by Fiedler, 1981) into one cohesive style. Each working group was also assigned two facilitators to convene and lead the discussions. In no sense, however, were these persons to serve as "leaders" in terms of determining the scope and direction of the discussions. Rather, their major purposes were to facilitate discussion, to assist all participants in gaining an equitable share of talk time, and to monitor the time limitations.

3. Distribute Responsibility

Responsibility should not be relinquished when power and authority are diffused. All participants were expected to take responsibility for contributing ideas and assisting in modifying the structure and procedures as needed. The conference was designed to be "everyone's show," in that each person would serve at times as both leader in initiating ideas and collaborator in facilitating in their development. All participants were accepted as experts with particular areas of expertise to contribute. To meet these goals, working groups were kept small, and cross-fertilization of ideas was encouraged. Although each working group was responsible for developing its own set of principles, the rotating triads met for mutual feedback with triads from all other groups, preparing all participants to assume an active role in contributing ideas across the topical areas.

4. Value All Voices

   The principle that all voices must be valued is a cornerstone of feminist theory and ethics. It is aimed at breaking the silences to which women traditionally have been relegated. It is intended to send a message to speakers and listeners alike that all ideas are to be heard and respected. Dissent is encouraged and resistance is regarded as a sign for further discussion (Briskin, 1990). The choice to remain silent is also honored as a personal decision to withhold one's voice.

5. Honor Personal Experience

   Women's subjective experiences have been suppressed in the academic community in favor of the objective and "rational." We encouraged participants to express their "intuition" as well as their intellect and to bring their personal experiences to bear in considering ideas and arriving at decisions. Exploring feelings about a topic should be as relevant as exercising cognitive abilities (Briskin, 1990). Within the working groups, personal experiences were shared as participants carved out the landscape of their tasks.

6. Decide Through Consensus

   Collaboration requires that all views are considered before they are integrated into a decision. The challenge becomes to coordinate individual voices with a final group consensus on each issue. For consensus to occur, decisions are negotiated through mutuality rather than through competition. There should be no winners or losers in decision making. Disagreements are mediated through discussion and compromise rather than through power assertion. Everyone becomes an expert in the process of problem solving.

7. Promote Social Change

   A fundamental goal of all feminist theory and practice is to disrupt the status quo and to move toward the betterment of women's status and well-being (Weiler, 1988). We aim to be reflexive in considering our process and whether our process moves us toward the goal of productive social change.

These seven principles formed both the implicit and explicit working basis for the development of the ideas that framed these chapters. The process for each working group was unique, however, because it was constructed and implemented by the group itself. For example, one group challenged the time structuring of the planning committee and continued at its own task rather than joining in the daily plenary session. Some groups reported considerable conflict and dissent; others appeared to merge their perspectives with little disagreement. The "honoring of all voices" was experienced with some difficulty by those who saw themselves having less power or authority in their group. Issues of inclusion and exclusion in a few groups were articulated with particular poignancy because expectations were initially high for an ethic of inclusiveness. Some student observers expressed this discomfort with being "less than equal" in their assigned groups, although others felt welcomed and integrated as regular players at the table. In each group, members struggled to match their ideals and beliefs about a feminist process with the enactment of these principles in reality.

Individual working groups practiced their unique interpretation of a feminist process. Every chapter of this book includes a section describing the experiences of the participants in implementing their group process. For many of us, the challenge became to mediate the collaborative feminist process with our individual life experiences. We live in a society that typically uses more traditional top–down decision-making models and rewards individual rather than group accomplishment. The struggles, problems, and pleasures of engaging in a feminist process were articulated by each of the working groups. Their stories tell of a deep appreciation of the feminist process that framed the heart of their deliberations.

From the perspective of the research working group, we quote the following:

> Perhaps the most important conclusion we reached was how immensely heartening and energizing it was to meet with a group of psychologists committed to the same goals. We were clear we wanted to do it again, with each other and with groups at our home institutions/communities. We would encourage this as a model for all feminist[s].

From the theory working group:

> Our discussions . . . were wide-ranging and animated. This brief summary captures the essential points of agreement in our discussions; unfortunately, it does not capture the joy of the process, the energy of the women engaged in this endeavor, and the pleasure of honest, open thinking about ideas that define who we are . . . we spoke frankly, sometimes passionately, and we listened attentively . . . we were each changed collectively and individually by the process . . . our collective work was an instance of feminism in action.

A ROAD MAP FOR THE FUTURE

Three observations should be made from the outset. First, the reader should note how each working group integrated process with content, using its method of negotiating agreement and dissent with the outcomes of its determinations. Second, the reader should consider the extent to which the contributions of the chapters are unique in their relationship to current feminist psychology. These chapters were intended to reflect contemporary scholarship and to reach into the future with new insights and provocative suggestions. Finally, the reader should observe the common threads of feminist thought that are woven throughout the text, revealing a synchrony of principles and themes that merges the chapters into a cohesive whole. Indeed, feminist practice covers the range of topics included in this volume and exists wherever feminists raise their voices.

What do these chapters tell us? The theory working group (chapter 2) offers a foundation for considering the role of theory in every aspect of feminist practice. Their eight tenets of feminist theory provide guiding principles for the central task of theory building for feminist practice. In concert, the assessment working group (chapter 3) asserts that theory must be the foundation for psychological assessment. This chapter provides a thorough discussion of the role of assessment in feminist practice and develops five principles for a feminist model of the assessment process. With so many diverse approaches and definitions of feminist therapy, the therapy working group (chapter 4) struggled to decide among competing models. Their 14 tenets of feminist therapy are intended to cover the core of these approaches, which is the analysis of women's experience within both social and individual context.

Moving to other aspects of feminist practice, chapters 5, 6, and 7 address the concerns of research, scholarship, and education. The research working group (chapter 5) asked some cutting questions: What makes a research paradigm feminist? How can feminist research transform psychology? What are some ethical concerns in feminist research? How do we legitimize feminist research within traditional institutional settings? In this provocative chapter, the authors collaborate to offer insights into the possibilities for helping those who do feminist research find their way through the land mines that lay in their path.

Within the academy, feminists have forged additional new inroads through transformations in curriculum and strategies of instruction. The curriculum working group (chapter 6) asked how psychologists can be educated to apply feminist principles in their work. The group identified eight principles for curriculum design, reflecting a network of assumptions, values, knowledge, and skills. It relates these four factors creatively to each of the eight principles, forming an elegant model that is then applied to undergraduate, graduate, and postgraduate settings. Following the curriculum, the pedagogy working group (chapter 7) offers a complex matrix of strategies that link the feminist teacher to a range of feminist principles and goals, including issues related to power and authority, process, content, and outcomes. In chapter 8, the supervision working group continues the discussion by exploring the process of teaching through the relationship of the feminist supervisor and trainee. Central to feminist supervision are issues of ethics, a collaborative process, personal disclosure, power and authority, and advocacy.

The diversity working group (chapter 9) stands alone in its unique concern for the cross-cutting issue of inclusiveness. The members of this group present a passionate appeal for the inclusion of multiple perspectives throughout the practice of psychology to provide a realistic view of the realities of all women's lives. From these multiples perspectives on the values and principles of feminist practice, the postdoctoral working group (chapter 10) carves out a proposal for a specialty in feminist practice that may be implemented at the graduate, internship, or postdoctoral levels.

As a final tribute to the intensity of the feminist process, the 13 student observers ("Baker's Dozen") volunteered to collaborate on a chapter of their own, "Feminist Student Voices" (chapter 11). The Baker's Dozen provide us with insights into the ways in which traditional psychology programs can stifle and intimidate the student with feminist values and beliefs. Their analysis of their experiences with their respective working groups and the ways in which they experienced the process as feminist or not-so-feminist provides an invaluable lesson to us all about inclusion and the authority of power dynamics.

Our final chapter, "Afterword," provides a summary of the outcomes of the collected working groups and ties together the major consensus themes as well as those that were unique to some groups. In this epilogue, we hope to communicate the excitement, passion, and inspiration that permeated our work together. Throughout this volume, the importance of dialogue and reflective experiencing is critical to the work of building consensus about the future of feminist psychology. If we have not yet revolutionized the practice of psychology, then perhaps tomorrow?

CONCLUSIONS

A key concern for the feminist goal of implementing social change is to maintain consistency between process and outcome. As the discussion in this chapter suggests, implementing and maintaining a feminist process are not easy tasks. The research on small groups provides many guidelines, suggesting that successful group process includes the dimensions of structure, cohesiveness, and communication. The stages through which groups move as they develop over time likewise implicates common issues of conflict, intimacy, and identity.

In applying these criteria to the committed work of these feminist groups, we see that our carefully designed structure encouraged both group cohesiveness and interpersonal communication. The 4-day intensive interaction format promoted both conflict and intimacy, leading to a continuing sense of identity in each working group. This identity is expressed eloquently in the following chapters, which expand on the creative process within each group and suggest guidelines for the future.

These broad characteristics of group process, however, become reinterpreted in differing contexts. For the implementation of feminist process, we outlined a 7-point framework that articulates additional concerns. We emphasize in particular a diffusion of status and leadership demands, the honoring and integration of diverse voices, a collaborative group effort leading to consensus, and an ethic of policy making toward the goal of social change on behalf of women everywhere. We look to the feminist community of the 21st century to fulfill our visions.

APPENDIX
A MODEL OF FEMINIST PROCESS

1. Structure for diversity
2. Distribute leadership
3. Distribute responsibility
4. Value all voices
5. Honor personal experience
6. Decide through consensus
7. Promote social change

REFERENCES

Anderson, M. L. (1987). Changing the curriculum in higher education. *Signs: Journal of Women in Culture and Society, 12,* 222–254.

Briskin, L. (1990). *Feminist pedagogy: Teaching and learning liberation.* Ottawa, Ontario: CRIAW/ICREF.

Bronstein, P., & Quina, K. (1988). *Teaching a psychology of people: Resources for gender and sociocultural awareness.* Washington, DC: American Psychological Association.

Brown, R. (1988). *Group process: Dynamics within and between groups.* New York: Basil Blackwell.

Bunch, C., & Pollack, S. (1983). *Learning our way: Essays in feminist education.* New York: Crossing Press.

Culley, M., & Portuges, C. (1985). *Gendered subjects: The dynamics of feminist teaching.* Boston: Routledge & Kegan Paul.

Deats, M., & Lenker, L. T. (1994). *Gender and academe: Feminist pedagogy and politics.* Lanham, MD: Rowman & Littlefield.

Diller, A., Houston, B., Morgan, K. P., & Ayim, M. (1996). *The gender question in education: Theory, pedagogy, and politics.* Boulder, CO: Westview Press.

Fiedler, F. E. (1981). Leadership effectiveness. *American Behavioral Scientist, 24,* 619–632.

Garland, J., Jones, H., & Kolodny, R. (1965). A model for stages of development in social work groups. In S. Bernstein (Ed.), *Explorations in group work.* Boston: Boston University Press.

Landrine, H. (1995). Cultural diversity, contextualism, and feminist psychology. In H. Landrine (Ed.), *Bringing cultural diversity to feminist psychology: Theory, research, and practice* (pp. 1–20). Washington, DC: American Psychological Association.

McGrath, J. E. (1984). *Groups: Interaction and performance.* Englewood Cliffs, NJ: Prentice-Hall.

Mullen, B., Salas, E., & Driskell, J. E. (1989). Salience, motivation, and artifact as contributors to the relationship between participation rate and leadership. *Journal of Experimental Social Psychology, 25,* 545–559.

O'Connell, A. N., & Russo, N. F. (1991). Women's heritage in psychology: Origins, developments, and future directions. *Psychology of Women Quarterly, 15*(4).

Paludi, M., & Stuernagel, G. A. (1990). *Foundations for a feminist restructuring of the academic disciplines.* New York: Harrington Park Press.

Ridgeway, C. L. (1983). *The dynamics of small groups.* New York: St. Martin's Press.

Roffman, E. (1994). The personal is professional is political: Feminist praxis in a graduate school counselor training program. In S. M. Deats & L. T. Lenker (Eds.), *Gender and academe: Feminist pedagogy and politics* (pp. 79–90). Lanham, MD: Rowman & Littlefield.

Romney, P., Tatum, B., & Jones, J. (1992). Feminist strategies for teaching oppression: The importance of process. *Women's Studies Quarterly, 20,* 95–110.

Schneidewind, N. (1983). Feminist values: Guidelines for teaching methodology in women's studies. In C. Bunch & S. Pollack (Eds.), *Learning our way: Essays in feminist education* (pp. 261–271). New York: Crossing Press.

Sears, D. O., Peplau, L. A., & Taylor, S. E. (1991). *Social psychology* (7th ed.). Englewood Cliffs, NJ: Prentice-Hall.

Weiler, K. (1988). *Women teaching for change: Gender, class, & power.* South Hadley, MA: Bergin & Garvey.

Worell, J., & Etaugh, C. (1994). Transformations: Reconceptualizing theory and research with women [Special issue]. *Psychology of Women Quarterly, 18*(4).

2

FEMINIST THEORY AND PSYCHOLOGICAL PRACTICE

MARY BRABECK AND LAURA BROWN

WITH LOUISE CHRISTIAN, OLIVE ESPIN, RACHEL HARE-MUSTIN,
ALEXANDRA KAPLAN, ELLYN KASCHAK, DUSTY MILLER,
ELAINE PHILLIPS, THERESA FERNS, AND ALICE VAN ORMER

For at least the last two decades, models of feminist practice and feminist theories have been available, but the defining characteristics of a feminist theory of psychological practice have not been fully described. In this chapter we describe the work of the conference group charged with defining the characteristics or guiding principles of a feminist theory of psychological practice. We present a summary of the sociohistorical realities that have affected the articulation of feminist theories of psychological practice and discuss the reasons that such an articulation is timely. We place this current effort to evolve feminist theory in historical context and note the paradoxes inherent to our endeavor. We describe the defining

The authors are listed in alphabetical order. The first two authors assumed major responsibility as scribes for the discussion held by the theory working group. The last two authors are student participant–observers who greatly facilitated the group discussion (and the writing of this chapter) through their careful and insightful summaries of the discussion. Members of the larger group of conference participants contributed comments; others read earlier drafts. To all we acknowledge our gratitude for their encouragement and ideas.

characteristics and tenets of a feminist theory of practice that emerged from our group discussions. Throughout this chapter we acknowledge that no theory is static; feminist theory of practice is evolving, and the process of feminist work itself is building theory. Thus, we invite reflection, modification, and extension of the ideas presented here. We end the chapter with recommendations for using the work of the theory working group to change the education, scholarship, and practice of psychology.

THEORY WORKING GROUP

Members of the theory working group who worked to articulate the general principles of a feminist theory of practice are university-based researchers; professors of women's studies; clinical, counseling, and developmental psychologists; theorists and practitioners in university counseling centers and private practice; and doctoral-level counseling psychology students. For 3½ days we struggled to describe what marks feminist theory as unique and to articulate the defining characteristics of feminist theories of practice. Our goal was not to develop a single feminist theory but to identify defining principles that could be used to generate and to evaluate a feminist theory of practice.

Our discussions at the conference were wide ranging and animated. This brief summary captures the essential points of agreement in our discussions; unfortunately, it does not capture the joy of the process; the energy of the women engaged in this endeavor; and the pleasure of honest, open thinking about ideas that define who we are. We drew from existing theory and research; our own past experiences; and our present feelings, thoughts, and reactions. We challenged and quizzed one another and encouraged the ideas that were tentative and emerging in each of us and collectively within the group. We put everything on newsprint and each night Theresa Ferns and Alice Van Ormer typed it all up for us to critique, revise, amend, and change the next day. We spoke frankly, often passionately, and we listened attentively. We tried to reach consensus as a group and to convince one another of the right-ness of our individual ideas. We were each changed individually and collectively in the process. We were doing feminist theory; we were practicing our feminist theory of psychological practice, and our collaborative work was an instance of feminism in action.

LACK OF GUIDING THEORY OF FEMINIST PRACTICE

Feminist psychological practice has grown and developed over the past two decades in an astonishingly wide range of settings. Although feminist practice often has been characterized as constituting psychotherapy practice alone, the reality is that feminist psychological principles are applied in many ways. Psychotherapy, supervision and consultation, forensic psychology, psychological assessment, research, training, social action, teaching, community organization, organizational consultation, and political practice in formal structures (psychological organizations, university, legislature) are a few of the varied forms taken by feminist psychological practice. In this chapter we use *practice* broadly to encompass all these activities. A burgeoning literature, often developed through "grassroots" work, describes these modalities of practice (Brown & Root, 1990; Dutton-Douglas & Walker, 1988; Kaschak, 1976, 1992; Rosewater & Walker, 1985; Worell & Remer, 1992). Nevertheless, until recently, the feminist literature has lacked a strong statement regarding the theory guiding such practice. This absence of theory is due to several factors, some of which reflect the strengths of feminist psychological practice. The theory working group identified four reasons for the relative lack of theory to guide feminist psychological practice.

1. Feminist practice, like other aspects of feminism, does not have a founding mother, teacher, or guru who served as the "official" authority for our theories. There is no feminist psychological equivalent of Freud, Skinner, or Rogers. Feminist practice has developed in a grassroots manner, responding to felt and emergent needs arising from the insights and strategies of the feminist revolution (Brown & Brodsky, 1992) and from listening to women through a feminist filter.

2. Feminist practice has focused on the solution of practical problems facing women: discrimination, violence, oppression, marginalization. Concern about the appropriate action to relieve suffering (and sometimes the threat of death) has taken precedence over reflection and theory building. Theory was considered interesting, but it was also time-consuming. Members of the theory working group noted that practical, action oriented, hands-on advocacy work is prerequisite for a feminist theory of psychological practice. Hannah Lerman, one of the first among us to propose criteria for a feminist theory, suggested that, for a theory to be feminist, it must arise from and be true to the data of lived, clinical experience (Lerman, 1986). Moving from practice to theory, drawing from grassroots experience rather than from experts in the absence of models for such a process of theory building, has been and remains challenging. To a large degree, the past two decades of feminist psychological practice have created the necessary, if not sufficient, conditions for feminists to engage in theo-

rizing. Without practice, our theories would violate feminist precepts; without theory, our practice lacks explanatory power. The capacity to create theory comes from experience and human connections, which take a variety of forms, and psychological practice in feminist theory is embraced in all its great variety of these forms. Human communication, written word, political action, administration, group solidarity, and community organization and action are all sources of individual and group behavior and are matter for feminist theorizing, and all are matters that require theory.

3. The development of theory in feminist psychological practice has been impeded by the location of the practitioners. Theory building traditionally has been confined to academic psychologists, and many feminist practitioners have been situated outside settings that reward the work of theory development. Feminist psychologists are increasingly breaking down obstacles to inclusion in the academy. We have recently begun to carve out the physical and phenomenological room of one's own necessary for discourse that leads to development of theory (Leaska, 1984). In psychology this has been most pronounced in theories of feminist therapeutic practice (e.g., Brown, 1994; Kaschak, 1976; Lerman, 1986). However, this work has not specifically addressed the broader question, "What makes a theory feminist?" As we break down the barriers of academic–practitioner, theory becomes a greater part of the work of all of us than in the past.

4. The relative recency of a feminist intellectual heritage in psychology has constricted theory building. As feminist historian Gerda Lerner (1993) noted, White men, as members of the dominant cultures of Western civilization, have been able intellectually and metaphorically to stand on the shoulders of the dominant culture's theorists and scholars. For example, in Western psychotherapy theory, almost every perspective has either derived from or been positioned in rebellion against psychoanalytic theory. As numerous feminist theorists have pointed out (e.g., Flax, 1990; Karshak, 1992; Lerner, 1993; Stiver, 1991), psychoanalytic theory has assumed male experience as central. As women have developed feminist consciousness and attempted to theorize their lives within the social and political context of patriarchy, these psychological models have not been fruitful traditions on which to stand. In fact, the theories and intellectual heritage of psychology that developed out of patriarchy at best obscured, and at worst have been destructive to, feminist the-

orizing (Kaschak, 1992; Lerner, 1993). Whereas feminist political theories developed over the past several hundred years,
the infusion of feminist consciousness into psychological
practice is a relatively recent phenomenon (Eisenstein, 1983;
Tong, 1989); almost every psychologist who has contributed
to the development of theory in feminist practice is still alive
and actively working. This is not to say that there were no
distinguished women in psychology; rather, few of these foremothers applied feminist analysis to the problems of psychological practice until the past two decades because of the
absence of feminist consciousness in psychology (Marecek &
Hare-Mustin, 1991).

NEED FOR A FEMINIST THEORY OF PSYCHOLOGICAL PRACTICE

Feminist practice has emerged in the absence of feminist psychological theory, yet it appears to be flourishing. Why, one might wonder, is
feminist theory even necessary? The theory working group's discussion was
formed out of the assumption of the value of theory. Several cogent arguments can be made for the value of theory in feminist practice. First, an
articulation of what constitutes feminist theory would help clarify the parameters of feminist practice. Feminist practice is frequently perceived as
having something to do with women therapists working with women clients on so-called women's issues (e.g., abuse, eating problems, depression,
dual career issues). This approach has led to an interesting and sometimes
problematic confusion of identities. Is a feminist practitioner a women who
serves women? Does a woman who works with women have to be a
feminist? What about her clients? How do we understand feminist practitioners who depart from this stereotypic notion and work, for example,
with male clients (Ganley, 1988) or in forensic practice (L. E. A. Walker,
1989) or those who see no clients at all but practice as trainers, consultants,
or applied researchers (Fine, 1992) or act collectively in political action
against psychological abuse (Lykes, Brabeck, Ferns, & Radan, 1993)? Without an articulated theory, no clear conceptual threads tie together the diverse work of feminist practitioners, and no clear parameters are available
to determine what is or is not feminist practice.

Furthermore, the absence of theory poses serious risks. For example,
some (Kitzinger & Perkins, 1993) have argued that there are no criteria
by which the "real" feminist therapist can be identified at this time. This
assumed absence allows for broad, over-arching, and incorrect assumptions

about who can be called a feminist therapist. Without criteria, anyone choosing to call herself a feminist therapist can do so with impunity; neither the public nor members of the profession of psychology can ascertain the difference between a feminist therapist and "a woman therapist working with women." Such an assumption also belies the existence of male feminists (Jardine & Smith, 1987). Such definitional problems emerge when there is no theory to delineate the parameters of a field; it is the purpose of this chapter to present the work of the theory working group, which attempted to reach consensus on the parameters and to identify the defining tenets of a feminist theory of psychological practice.

The efforts of the theory working group are important for another reason. A feminist theory of psychological practice supports liberation from dependence on the theoretical models emerging from dominant patriarchal cultures. Lacking feminist theories, we have often taken theories based on male models of psychological development and attempted to modify or otherwise reshape them to fit a feminist enterprise and feminist goals. This approach leads to some rather odd intellectual marriages in which feminist practitioners speak in the language and concepts of flagrantly misogynist psychological traditions, or feminist political analyses of our practice become little more than a parenthetical comment to dominant, White Eurocentric or patriarchal psychological traditions (Lerman, 1986).

Theory is necessary if we are to move beyond the familiar, male-dominated, and male-defined psychological theories in which we were trained, to start fresh from our own beginnings in feminist consciousness. In the theory working group and in our own practice, we struggled to think as feminists. That deliberate struggle led us to understand how each act that we take in our practice, however mundane and banal, must be feminist; we must learn even to set the fee as feminists (Luepnitz, 1988), to develop informed consent as feminists (Lykes et al., 1993), and to conduct psychological research as feminists (Fine, 1992). This can happen consistently, across settings, practitioners, and practices, only when we have been able to define ourselves conceptually, when we have described a feminist epistemology and feminist methodology of psychological practice. To do this, theory is necessary.

To illustrate this point, we use the example of informed consent to treatment, assessment, or research participation. The concept of informed consent is a basic ethical norm for all psychological practitioners. Informed consent reflects the ethical principles of client autonomy and respect for each individual's right to make informed choices about participation with a therapist, evaluator, or researcher. How would this simple procedure, almost a routine part of the work of most psychologists working with people, be transformed by a feminist theory of practice? We return to this question after we describe the tenets of feminist psychological practice.

PARADOXES INHERENT TO FEMINIST THEORY BUILDING

Paradoxes are inherent to our endeavor. We identified at least three paradoxes in developing feminist theory: connecting with patriarchal systems while rejecting patriarchal ideas; using language that both liberates and stereotypes; and affirming diversity, empowerment, and equality without becoming unreflectively relativistic. We describe our discussions about each of these paradoxes. Although we were unable to resolve the paradoxes we identified, we assert the value of acknowledging and examining them.

We feel a responsibility to connect feminist theory with existing patriarchal theories both to establish its rightful place in professional psychology and to transform mainstream psychology. However, while envisioning changes in psychology that are informed by feminist thinking, we inevitably must engage with hierarchy and authority to have an effect. This endeavor is problematic. On the one hand, feminist theory must be developed separate from what is the established canon of psychological knowledge; if our critique is not detached it may not be transformative and may, as noted above, be destructive. For example, feminists have applied a feminist analysis to the third and fourth editions of the *Diagnostic and Statistical Manual of Mental Disorders* (American Psychiatric Association, 1980, 1994; Caplan, 1995; Kaplan, 1983; Lerman, 1995). The power of such feminist critiques in part depends on an "outsider's" perspective to evaluate critically the errors of "the canon" of psychological theory. On the other hand, we must immerse ourselves in discussions of mainstream concepts and theories and be "at the table" of discussion of mainstream organizations to transform ideas in the direction of feminist principles. Such immersion can change one, rather than retain what Rachel Hare-Mustin (1994) described as "a special vision that can challenge the assumptions of dominant discourses rather than merely going along with them" (p. 33). Members of the theory working group asked, "How do we challenge the system while being paid and rewarded by it?"

We wrestled with another example of this insider–outsider paradox: Feminism conceptualizes change as systemic and contextual, and most dominant psychology conceptualizes change as individualistic; most interventions are designed to change individuals. How does feminist practice, which is a liberating and emancipatory process directed at systemic change, connect with existing psychological theories that focus on the individual and often ignore context? Is it possible to effect social transformation at the individual or micro level? We concluded that to resolve these tensions we need a better understanding of the concept of self as formed within the social context (Kaschak, 1992). We also need a better understanding of what it means to work as psychologists when the client is society and a fuller acceptance of the responsibilities and risks of social transformation for the feminist practitioner (Lykes, 1989).

Language creates other paradoxes. The language that we need to use for our own integrity is the language that may alienate us from those whom we want to influence. Terms such as "patriarchy" and "social revolution," for example, are often problematic for people and can become buzzwords that trivialize or dismiss complex problems. Our language is problematic for ourselves as well: Do we want to use words that imply violence ("revolution") or invoke the "helper" role of caregiver that paradoxically feeds into the stereotype of "the good woman" (Brabeck, 1996)? The language that we need to use to maintain our own integrity may alienate us from those whom we most want to influence and change. Subtle distinctions are of critical importance. For example, feminist theory celebrates a woman-centered analysis (Einsenstein, 1983) and considers that what is experienced by women as women is important to the formation of feminist theory. However, feminist theory does not essentialize masculinity or femininity, maleness or femaleness. For example, feminists (Chodorow, 1978; Russo, 1979) have argued against simplistic theories of maternal instinct or gender-based dichotomies such as feeling–thinking and emotional–rational as validly describing any essential or defining quality of women or men (Brabeck, 1983, 1989; Lott, 1990).

Other paradoxes lie within feminist psychological theory. Feminist theory of psychological practice empowers individuals, but it is not without evaluation, discrimination, or judgment; it embraces diversity but is not relativistic. Radical relativism, the view that all opinions are of equal merit, allows no adjudication between conflicting claims; no way of arguing that regardless of context, torture, rape, or other gross acts that harm individuals are wrong; no way of resolving disputes over interpretations of reality (Bohan, 1994). For example, feminist theory tries to break the silencing of women's voices but at other times advocates silencing some voices to privilege the marginalized or to prevent damage to someone. In doing so, we establish moral standards (if not truth standards) by which we authorize some voices and privilege some experiences and knowledge claims. Efforts to articulate feminist criteria for such standards, which avoid radical relativism, are underway (Bohan, 1994).

We acknowledge these paradoxes as we attempt to describe the work of the theory working group in defining the characteristics of a feminist theory of psychological practice. There is one final paradox. Each of us struggled to retain our voice and articulate our vision, and what emerged was consensus and a voice for this chapter that was more than the individuals who shaped it.

FOUNDATIONAL CONCEPTS OF A FEMINIST THEORY OF PSYCHOLOGICAL PRACTICE

After 3½ days of discussion; four walls of newsprint, summaries, and revisions; many plenary sessions; and much feedback and reworking, we brought the following statement to the plenary session:

> Feminist theory of practice is unique. It can be defined, promotes social transformation, embraces diversity as a requirement of feminism and a foundation for practice, and recognizes that the person is political. Feminist practice includes an analysis of power and the multiple ways people are oppressed and oppressing.

The above statement was endorsed by the entire group at the conference. Behind these 48 words are nine tenets that members of the theory working group agreed were foundational for and defining of feminist theory of feminist practice. These tenets are listed in the Appendix.

Goal of Feminist Practice: Social Transformation Toward Development of Feminist Consciousness (Tenets 1 and 2)

We begin with what is central to feminism, the development of feminist consciousness in support of feminist social and political transformation. Our understanding of feminist consciousness follows Lerner's (1993) definition:

> the awareness of women that they belong to a subordinate group; that they have suffered wrongs as a group; that their condition of subordination is not natural, but is societally determined; that they must join with other women to remedy these wrongs; and finally, that they must and can provide an alternate vision of societal organization in which women as well as men will enjoy autonomy and self-determination. (p. 14)

One of the problems of feminist psychological practice, in its second decade, has been its drift away from feminist political theories toward dominant psychological models (Tong, 1989). We assert that a theory of feminist psychological practice emerges from within feminist political theories. It both refers to and expands meanings and applications of political and psychological feminist thought. A feminist theory conceptualizes psychological practice as a strategy for advancing feminist social action and social transformation. A feminist theory of psychological practice situates that practice within the larger feminist revolution, de-privatizing the actors and making connections to the political forces and the social contexts that shape and affect both the psychologist and those who receive her services.

Because of our rootedness in feminist political theories, feminist psychological practitioners are concerned with oppression and liberation; our theories must support liberation strategies that undermine oppressive realities. Feminist theories of practice serve to raise feminist consciousness, to sensitize the psychologist to issues of power and hierarchies of domination, in all of our dealings as practitioners and as human beings (Hare-Mustin, 1991a). Any theory of feminist psychological practice must lead to and support ways of being and working that are consistently liberating. The goal of feminist practice is the creation of a state of being and knowing in which feminist consciousness is the disruption of patriarchal hegemony over ways of knowing, with its claims to "objectivity" and sole authority over "truth." It will be replaced with feminist consciousness, which proposes a diversity of ways of knowing and authorities. A theory of feminist psychological practice functions to put feminist consciousness at the center of understanding. Our goal is the creation of "another mother tongue" (Grahn, 1984) to give voice to feminist consciousness.

Feminist Theory Develops out of Experience (Tenet 3)

As we sought to define feminist theory, we found ourselves returning again and again to our own experiences. We described the insights about women and our clinical practice that our clients revealed to us; we described our own experiences with exclusion because we are women or because of misguided attempts to name our experience. We came to realize that our theories of feminist psychological practice reflect lived experiences, and such experiences emerge from the relationships that develop between practitioners and colleagues, clients, students, and research participants, and our communities and their social structures and political realities. Such relationships may not take place face-to-face or one-on-one. For the practitioner who is a writer, relationships may take the shape of written communication with the reader. For the feminist forensic expert, they may be embodied in the form of expert testimony. Feminist connections may happen on a computer bulletin board, or through a special interest group on the Internet, and in several other ways. Thus, our theories are experientially founded and are not locked into the structures of a specific place and time. Feminist theories envision and reflect these lived experiences that take place in the changing social worlds in which feminist psychologists work.

Power Imbalance in Gender and Diversity (Tenets 4 and 5)

Feminist theories begin with gender (Unger, 1989) as a locus for understanding oppression and power imbalance. However, we assert that gender cannot be the sole site for our understandings of oppression and liberation because it is not the variable on which all people experience these dynamics of interpersonal and sociopolitical power (Brown, 1994; Brown & Root, 1990; Espin & Gawelek, 1992).

One of the most problematic aspects of feminist practice in the past two decades has been the centrality of White women's voices in defining the categories and meanings of feminist analyses. Internalized domination (Pheterson, 1986) has led many women to exclude the experiences of those for whom ethnicity, class, culture, sexual orientation, age, spiritual practice, and ability are the most salient aspects of their experience of oppression and liberation. However, there have been attempts by White feminists to proclaim the primacy of gender, instead of being open to the multiple interactions of gender with other variables that are important to the lived experiences of women who are not members of the dominant class (hooks, 1981, 1984, 1989, 1993; Spelman, 1988). A feminist theory of practice recognizes that any theory that does not acknowledge the diversity of experiences is greatly limited in its validity and usefulness.

As feminist practitioners, we attend to hierarchies of power and dominance among and between people in all practice settings. We notice the ways in which we are both oppressed and oppressor, dominant and marginal, as well as the interactive relationships that emerge from these different positions of power. One of the challenges of feminist practice is to theorize a liberation model of relating within a larger social and political context. This model encourages and sometimes appears to demand the imposition of hierarchies of dominance and submission between practitioners and those practiced with (or, one might say, "practiced on"). We are seeking ways to change this power imbalance as a step toward the creation of a feminist consciousness.

A theory of feminist psychological practice illuminates for practitioners their position in a varied and complex social and political matrix. Such theory derives from an awareness of the various interactive and additive possibilities that emerge from the intersections of gender with other social factors (Sieber & Cairns, 1991). Within the theory working group we were constantly reminded of the manner in which our positions in dominance hierarchies potentially undermine the authorization of the voices of those who are less powerful than we. We came to the realization that acknowledgment of positions of power is particularly important for psychologists. Feminist consciousness is a process of becoming; a way of seeing, sensing, and responding to the world in a more egalitarian manner, open to the experience of multiple subgroups of women; and recognition that one's own power status changes within different groups.

Feminist Theory Authorizes Voices of the Oppressed (Tenet 6)

Another important aspect of feminist theorizing of psychological practice concerns what is considered authoritative knowledge. Feminist epistemologies are not solely derived from the experiences of the dominant or privileged group. We have been challenged to recognize that, because of ethnicity and class, some of us constitute a dominant group within some social settings. Yet, acknowledging this reality enables us to broaden within psychological practice an understanding of what constitutes valid sources of information. To recognize dominant or "mainstream" knowledge as authoritative constitutes founding another, parallel, "feminine" dominant paradigm and discourse, rather than a feminist and liberating one.

Socialization into our discipline privileges information arising from empirical, logical positivist epistemologies and methodologies and marginalizes information that is qualitative, intuitive, or nonrational in its sources. To define the "data of experience" (to quote Hannah Lerman, 1986, p. 176) as being equivalent in their value to the charts and tables of statistical analysis and large sample sizes disrupts the relationship between feminist psychology and the mainstream of the discipline. Yet it is a necessary disloyalty if we are to theorize in a manner that advances feminist re-voicing and de-silencing of those on the margins. It can also be uncomfortable to those who are dominant, as we learned when our student helpers asserted their voice in the conversation of the theory working group and brought with it a critique of the way our group did not work actively to support their marginalized voices.

The mandate of feminist theory to value diverse experiences and voices of women becomes an important corrective to our training in "the canon" of psychology. From a feminist perspective, the voices of the oppressed are specifically theorized as authoritative, valued, and valuable sources of knowledge. The role of the practitioner and the expertise deriving from this role are theorized as being simply another source of information, rather than the best or most "objective" of such sources. Authorization of the voices of the oppressed leads to a de-silencing of them. A feminist practice theory supports and enables the recovery of voice. It values native emotional language, a capacity to speak one's self, and the possibility of "hearing ourselves into speech" (Morton, 1985, p. 54) without relying on patriarchal terms, consciousness, or understandings. We are rewriting the canon through feminist consciousness.

Feminist Theory Leads to Expanded Notions of Identity and Multiple Subjectivities (Tenet 7)

Because the practice that we are theorizing has to do with human beings and human behavior, theories of feminist practice also posit models of the person. This aspect of theory is problematic for feminists because we recognize that the notions of "identity," "self," and "person" are social constructs that reflect certain belief systems, rather than descriptions of phenomena that exist universally and across cultures (Kaschak, 1992).

Much of dominant psychological theory is essentialist and individualistic (Sampson, 1993). Such theories carry the intellectual and epistemological baggage of concepts profoundly disruptive to the feminist objective of diversity and pluralism of voice. The language with which we can accurately and respectfully describe the various ways in which people come to understand and recognize who they are is sparse and inadequate. Identity language is limited by the assumptions and social constructions of the discourse in which feminist practitioners speak and write (Hare-Mustin, 1994). Thus, we find feminists theorizing about the "self-in-relation" (Jordan, Kaplan, Miller, Stiver, & Surrey, 1991), the "indexical and referential self" (Landrine, 1992), and "social individuality" (Lykes, 1985). These efforts reflect attempts to bend American English to describe felt and embodied experiences of self-knowledge. Ideally, feminist theories of psychological practice use and support the development of new language to describe the phenomenology of knowing and naming experience. Development of new language may move feminist practice away from the concept of "self" to capture more fully the collective and the individual experiences of women (Lykes, 1993).

As theorized within feminist paradigms the person is one who is an active participant in personal definition. She or he possesses the capacity to change and to produce change. However, members of the theory working group recalled instances in which society had labeled them *incompetent* or *helpless*. We believe that competence at interpersonal relatedness, moral agency in the face of opposition, and the capacity to resist patriarchal training and maintain feminist consciousness, one's voice, and vision are all aspects of agency and competence. We recognize, however, that these images of women's activity and agency are subversive views and values about women and, thus, distrusted and condemned by many.

Our model also theorizes the manner in which the feminist practitioner relates to herself and challenges the patriarchal image of woman-as-selfless-caregiver. Consequently, a feminist theory of psychological practice promotes the practitioner's capacity for response-ability. *Response-ability* is the ability to respond to one's own self as well as others. Response-ability makes caring for self of equal importance to caring for others.

Feminist theories of psychological practice replace the notion of objectivity of knowledge claims with a multiplicity of subjectivities, no one consistently more valid than another. We reject the notion that any one single perspective is "the objective view." As discussed above, feminist theory does not support the practitioner as the only, or even the most important, authorized voice of knowledge. At the same time, we recognize the risks to knowledge inherent in the dominance hierarchies that emerge within feminist practice. Feminist theory supports self-awareness and reflectiveness on the part of feminist psychological practitioners as a corrective that is necessary because of hierarchical power relations and the inevitable inequities they bring.

Reformulated Understanding of Psychological Distress From Feminist Theory (Tenet 8)

Feminists struggle to achieve a better world that reflects the lived realities and truths of the diversity of people that inhabit that world. Transformation of the canon of psychology to reflect these realities leads to a profound de-centering of the experiences of the dominant as "normal," "right," or "healthy." It changes our theories about distress and our understanding of feminist strategies for healing and empowerment through psychological practice. Embracing knowledge arising from the experience of marginality and viewing life through the oppositional gaze of the oppressed (hooks, 1984; Kaschak, 1992) re-positions the meaning of experiences of pain and dislocation. Paradigms for understanding human behavior that flow from such a reconfiguration of value are those in which pain is not defined as evidence of deficit or defect but as evidence of resistance and the skill and will to survive.

For psychological practice this re-ordering of meanings has especially subversive implications because it leads feminist practitioners to an additional disloyalty. The dominant paradigms reflect dichotomized thinking and infer illness and deficit rather than distress or difficulties in psychosocial functioning or learned ways of coping. The "dis-ease" (experienced as something wrong or out of joint) embedded in the norms of dominant culture is ignored. For example, submission of women in families is taken for granted in patriarchal theories of family therapy. The loss of voice and sense of self in White adolescent girls is assumed to be normal female development in many mainstream models of personality. We reframe distress, not as disease, but as a communication about unjust systems. Thus, dis-ease may be indicative of health and the capacity to resist patriarchy, even at a cost. This reframing is a distinctly revolutionary development that derives from feminist theorizing when applied to psychological practice (e.g., Brown, 1994; Hare-Mustin, 1991b).

In many mainstream models of psychological practice, *resistance* is a descriptor for clients' unwillingness to accept the authoritative interpretation of the practitioner. Feminist theory transforms *resistance* into a term describing the person's ability to remain alive and powerful in the face of oppression (Brown, 1994). Such resistance can be observed on a number of dimensions: spiritual, social, emotional, intellectual, creative. It may be individual or collective. It allows the person to break through noise and distractions to attend to one's self and to discover what Audre Lorde (1978) described as the "many kinds of power, used and unused, acknowledged or otherwise" (p. 1).

The transformative function of feminist theory lends itself to a new model of the roots or factors affecting human behavior. Psychology traditionally concerns itself with the individual in a decontextualized manner or, at best, within the context of the immediate family of the individual. Feminist theory observes the development of human behavior across a wide range of interpersonal, social, and political dimensions. All behavior is theorized as deriving from multiple sources and as expressed within a given social context. Persons and behaviors are not fixed or invariant across situations. However, we recognize that all experiences are profoundly shaped by the contexts within which each of us lives.

This insight regarding the power of social context to transform behavior and meaning has particular salience when applied to attempts to understand characteristics that are typically ascribed to gender. Feminist psychologists have found that gender is a far less potent variable for the expression of behaviors than is position in social hierarchies of dominance and submission (Hare-Mustin & Marecek, 1990). The development of the person is perceived as occurring because of the constant interplay of internal, phenomenological experience and external sociopolitical realities that inform, and in turn are informed by, the internal experiences of each person. In this way, the personal is defined as political because the meaning of any human experience must be understood within the context of what is a patriarchal system.

The model of human development arising from feminist theory of psychological practice supports a broad-ranging, bio-psycho-social formulation of behavior. In a feminist bio-psycho-social model, the meanings of the body (Miller, 1994) and the interaction of internal, phenomenological experience with external observable reality are all important. We agree that both normative and distressed ways of being are a focus of inquiry. Our model assumes that the etiology of all behavior is complex and multidetermined and that the politics of the social milieu always and profoundly influence the expression and meaning of human behavior.

Because behavior is multiply determined and contextually situated, feminist theory building is not static. Our final tenet (Tenet 9) is this: Feminist theory of psychological practice is evolving and in process. This articulation is an attempt to capture the most current thinking about feminist theory; we expect others to build on this work and to broaden our understanding of feminist theory of practice through their research, theorizing, and practice in all its various forms.

APPLICATION OF FEMINIST THEORY OF
PSYCHOLOGICAL PRACTICE

When feminist principles of psychological practice are applied to a familiar concept such as informed consent, the result is profoundly transformative because feminist consciousness attends to some very different factors regarding informed consent than would a dominant conceptualization. Rather than being the establishment of a contract between two parties assumed to be of equal status and value, which is an illusion, feminist theorizing of informed consent would lead us to inquire into the power differences and dynamics inherent in the situation. Such feminist theorizing might ask about the kinds of information given and the ways in which such information would either support or undermine the cultural status quo. For example, feminist theory would lead us to analyze what the consent means not simply in terms of this one narrowly defined transaction but also within the larger social and political milieus in which this transaction is situated (Lykes, 1989). It would examine the meaning of consent within the cultural and socioeconomic reality of the consenting person. Feminist theorizing of informed consent might lead to offering different sorts of information than what is usually contained in the consent form of a nonfeminist practitioner. It might necessitate changing the time frames commonly allotted for obtaining consent. Perhaps nothing would change on the surface; perhaps the changes would be subtle, attitudinal in the direction of a more feminist consciousness of the practitioner and the participant, client, or patient regarding how consent to engage in practice is given (Brown, 1994).

The work of feminist theorizing is relatively recent and arises out of feminist grassroots work, courageous departures from the mainstream canon: It developed out of feminist practice in all its various forms. The tenets outlined here are abstractions and generalizations arising from that experience. These tenets represent a departure from lived experiences, and we acknowledge the difficulty feminist practitioners may encounter with this chapter. The chapters that follow represent attempts of other groups to apply the tenets to specific arenas of feminist practice—therapy, supervision, teaching, research—and thus present additional examples of doing feminist theorizing and applying theory to practice.

RECOMMENDATIONS

We recognize that the tenets of feminist theory of psychological practice described here must be tested in the real world of practice, and we invite application across settings. Following Lerman's (1986) criteria that a feminist theory should be useful, we must apply the theoretical concepts to practice and determine their usefulness. Feminist practitioners—in individual or collective practice, teaching, or research, with an individual or community focus—are invited to apply these tenets to their practice and to help reform and revise feminist theory. We hope that the inquiry into the tenets of feminist theory of practice is continued through published dialogue and response to what is begun here.

At the structural level of psychology, we recommend that the tenets of feminist theory of practice described here be formally discussed by the professional boards responsible for educating and training psychologists. We have written to some of these groups and requested that they respond with plans for disseminating our ideas to training directors and psychology departments.

In an attempt to be self-reflective, we ask the executive committee of Division 35 to discuss the advantages and disadvantages to changing the name of the Division from Division of Psychology of Women to the Division of Feminist Psychology. We ask that the principles articulated here form the basis of that conversation. This discussion must be informed by the recognition that the word *feminist* has different meanings for different women. Some women of color, for example, noting the exclusionary practice in the name of some feminist theorizing, prefer the word *womanist* (A. Walker, 1983).

CONCLUSION

The members of the theory working group affirm the need for the creation of feminist consciousness in the work of psychological practice. For this reason, we assert that feminist theory of psychological practice is not a luxury but is central and foundational. Feminist theory clarifies our definitions of feminist practice and lays bare every facet of psychological practice to feminist questions, analyses, and ways of knowing. Because feminist knowledge and scholarship are in a continuous state of development, feminist theories of psychological practice cannot be static. They are evolving and in the process of being invented and recreated in response to the growth of feminist politics and scholarship. A diversity of theories and methodologies is a hallmark of feminist theorizing (Brown & Ballou, 1992). Because an inherent principle of feminist thought is respect for the diversity of epistemologies, feminist theories of psychological practice are inclusionary by supporting such diversity. Thus, we invite readers to respond to our work and to extend our ideas presented here so as to enlarge the theory and improve the practice.

APPENDIX
SUMMARY OF TENETS OF FEMINIST THEORY OF PSYCHOLOGICAL PRACTICE

1. Feminist theory of psychological practice is consciously a political enterprise, and its goal is social transformation in the direction of feminist consciousness.
2. We are trying to change women's understanding of their reality to include the oppression of the patriarchal society and to create feminist consciousness. *Feminist consciousness* is a process of becoming, a way of seeing and sensing the world, a familiar lens, "another mother tongue." Feminist consciousness leads one to be response-able to self and others, attend to one's own and collective well-being; it is unnumbing and re-integrating of all experiences and leads to social transformation. A goal of feminist practice is the creation of a feminist consciousness that becomes as unconscious as patriarchal consciousness is currently.
3. The capacity to create theory comes from experience and human connections through any form or medium: human communication, written word, political action, group solidarity, community activism. In this way, the personal is political because experience is connected to transformation and change.
4. Gender is an important locus of women's oppression and intersects with other important loci of oppression including but not limited to ethnicity, culture, class, age, sexual orientation, ability, and linguistic status. The practitioner of feminist theory is self-reflective regarding her positions in these various hierarchies.
5. Feminist theory of feminist practice embraces human diversity as a requirement and foundation for practice. Diversity (ethnicity, sexual orientation, ablebodiness, religion, language) not only is a goal in its own right but also is necessary for feminist theory to be complete and reflective of the total range of human experience.
6. Feminist theory affirms, attends to, and authorizes the experience of the oppressed in their own voices. This is an interactive process in which our role as oppressor must be considered a part. Feminist therapists—psychologists are self-reflective about their own experience, which informs this process.
7. Feminist practitioners expand the parameters of conceptions of identity or personhood. Feminist theorists and practitioners seek models of human growth and development that describe a variety of ways that people have a sense of identities and multiple subjectivities.
8. Feminist theory of practice leads to an appreciation of the complex and multidetermined causations of distress, with particular attention to the sociopolitical context. Within this context, persons are viewed as capable of acting (response-able) to effect change, and each person is viewed as responsible for participating in the process of change. As part of the process of change, those practicing a feminist theory contextualize behavior as occurring within a patriarchal system. Women are viewed as agentic and powerful but not entirely responsible for the pathology of sexism. Feminist theory of practice challenges assumptions of men as whole and center and women as broken and marginalized.
9. Feminist theory building is not static. Feminist theory of psychological practice is evolving and in process.

REFERENCES

American Psychiatric Association. (1980). *Diagnostic and statistical manual of mental disorders* (3rd ed.). Washington, DC: Author.

American Psychiatric Association. (1994). *Diagnostic and statistical manual of mental disorders* (4th ed.). Washington, DC: Author.

Bohan, J. (1994, August). *Every answer is a question.* Paper presented at the 102nd Annual Convention of the American Psychological Association, Los Angeles, CA.

Brabeck, M. M. (1983). Moral judgment: Theory and research on differences between males and females. *Developmental Review, 3,* 274–291.

Brabeck, M. M. (Ed.). (1989). *Who cares? Theory, research and educational implications of the ethic of care.* New York: Praeger.

Brabeck, M. M. (1996). The moral self, values, and circles of belonging. In K. F. Wyche & F. J. Crosby (Eds.), *Women's ethnicities: Journeys through psychology* (pp. 145–165). Boulder, CO: Westview Press.

Brown, L. (1994). *Subversive dialogues: Theory in feminist therapy.* New York: Basic Books.

Brown, L., & Ballou, M. (Eds.). (1992). *Personality and psychotherapy: Feminist reappraisals.* New York: Guilford Press.

Brown, L., & Brodsky, A. M. (1992). The future of feminist therapy. *Psychotherapy: Theory, Research, Practice and Training, 9,* 51–57.

Brown, L., & Root, M. P. P. (Eds.). (1990). *Diversity and complexity in feminist therapy.* New York: Haworth.

Caplan, P. (1995, August). *The DSM–IV and gender issues.* Paper presented at the 103rd Annual Convention of the American Psychological Association, New York.

Chodorow, N. (1978). *The reproduction of mothering.* Berkeley: University of California Press.

Dutton-Douglas, M. A., & Walker, L. E. A. (Eds.). (1988). *Feminist psychotherapies: Integration of therapeutic and feminist systems.* Norwood, NJ: Ablex.

Eisenstein, H. (1983). *Contemporary feminist thought.* Boston: G. K. Hall.

Espin, O., & Gawelek, M. A. (1992). Women's diversity: Ethnicity, race, class and gender in theories of feminist psychology. In L. S. Brown & M. Ballou (Eds.), *Personality and psychopathology: Feminist reappraisals* (pp. 88–107). New York: Guilford.

Fine, M. (1992). *Disruptive voices: The possibilities of feminist research.* Ann Arbor: University of Michigan Press.

Flax, J. (1990). *Thinking fragments: Psychoanalysis, feminism, and postmodernism in the contemporary west.* Berkeley: University of California Press.

Ganley, A. (1988). Feminist therapy with male clients. In M. A. Dutton-Douglas & L. E. A. Walker (Eds.), *Feminist psychotherapies: Integration of therapeutic and feminist systems* (pp. 186–205). Norwood, NJ: Ablex.

Grahn, J. (1984). *Another mother tongue: Gay words, gay worlds*. Boston: Beacon Press.

Hare-Mustin, R. T. (1991a). Changing women, changing therapy: Clinical implications of the changing role of women. *Journal of Feminist Family Therapy, 4*(3/4), 7–18.

Hare-Mustin, R. T. (1991b). Sex, lies, and headaches: The problem is power. In T. J. Goodrich (Ed.), *Women and power: Perspectives for family therapy* (pp. 63–85). New York: Norton.

Hare-Mustin, R. T. (1994). Discourses in the mirrored room: A postmodern analysis of therapy. *Family Process, 33*, 19–35.

Hare-Mustin, R. T., & Marecek, J. (1990). *Making a difference: Psychology and the construction of gender*. New Haven, CT: Yale University Press.

hooks, b. (1981). *Ain't I a woman? Black women and feminism*. Boston: South End Press.

hooks, b. (1984). *Feminist theory: From margin to center*. Boston: South End Press.

hooks, b. (1989). *Talking back: Thinking feminist, thinking Black*. Boston: South End Press.

hooks, b. (1993). *Sisters of the yam: Black women and self-recovery*. Boston: South End Press.

Jardine, A., & Smith, P. (Eds.). (1987). *Men in feminism*. New York: Methuen.

Jordan, J. V., Kaplan, A. G., Miller, J. B., Stiver, I. P., & Surrey, J. (1991). *Women's growth in connection: Writings from the Stone Center*. New York: Guilford Press.

Kaplan, M. (1983). A woman's view of DSM–III. *American Psychologist, 38*, 786–792.

Kaschak, E. (1976). Sociotherapy: An ecological model for psychotherapy with women. *Psychotherapy: Theory, Research and Practice, 13*, 16–63.

Kaschak, E. (1992). *Engendered lives: A new psychology of women's experience*. New York: Basic Books.

Kitzinger, C., & Perkins, R. (1993). *Changing our minds: Lesbian, feminism and psychology*. New York: New York University Press.

Landrine, H. (1992). Clinical implications of cultural differences. *Clinical Psychology Review, 12*, 481–416.

Leaska, M. A. (Ed.). (1984). *The Virginia Woolf reader*. San Diego: Harcourt Brace Jovanovich.

Lerman, H. (1986). *A mote in Freud's eye: From psychoanalysis to the psychology of women*. New York: Springer.

Lerman, H. (1995, August). *A critical look at the DSM–IV*. Symposium presented at the 103rd Annual Convention of the American Psychological Association, New York.

Lerner, G. (1993). *The creation of feminist consciousness*. New York: Oxford University Press.

Lorde, A. (1978). *The Black unicorn: Poems*. New York: Norton.

Lott, B. (1990). Dual natures or learned behaviors: The challenge to feminist psychology. In R. T. Hare-Mustin & J. Marecek (Eds.), *Making a difference: Psychology and the constriction of gender* (pp. 65–101). New Haven, CT: Yale University Press.

Luepnitz, D. A. (1988). *The family interpreted.* New York: Basic Books.

Lykes, M. B. (1985). Gender and individualistic versus collectivist notions about the self. *Journal of Personality, 53,* 356–383.

Lykes, M. B. (1989). Dialogue with Guatemalan Indian women: Critical perspectives on constructing collaborative research. In R. K. Unger (Ed.), *Representations: Social constructions of gender* (pp. 167–185). Amityville, NY: Baywood.

Lykes, M. B., Brabeck, M. M., Ferns, T., & Radan, A. (1993). Human rights and mental health among Latin American women in situations of state sponsored violence: Bibliographic resources. *Psychology of Women Quarterly, 17,* 525–544.

Mareck, J., & Hare-Mustin, R. T. (1991). A short history of the future: Feminism and clinical psychology. *Psychology of Women Quarterly, 15,* 521–536.

Miller, D. (1994). *Women who hurt themselves.* New York: Basic Books.

Morton, N. (1985). *The journey is home.* Boston: Beacon Press.

Pheterson, G. (1986). Alliances between women: Overcoming internalized oppression and internalized domination. *Signs, 12,* 146–160.

Rosewater, L. B., & Walker, L. E. A. (Eds.). (1985). *Handbook of feminist therapy: Women's issues in psychotherapy.* New York: Springer.

Russo, N. F. (1979). Overview: Sex roles, fertility, and the motherhood mandate. *Psychology of Women Quarterly, 4,* 7–15.

Sampson, E. (1993). *Celebrating the other: A dialogic account of human nature.* Boulder, CO: Westview Press.

Sieber, J. A., & Cairns, K. V. (1991). Feminist therapy with ethnic minority women. *Canadian Journal of Counselling/Revue Canadienne de Counseling, 25,* 567–580.

Spelman, E. (1988). *Inessential woman: Problems of exclusion in feminist thought.* Boston: Beacon Press.

Stiver, I. P. (1991). Beyond the Oedipus complex: Mothers and daughters. In J. V. Jordan, A. G. Kaplan, J. B. Miller, I. P. Stiver, & J. Surrey (Eds.), *Women's growth in connection: Writings from the Stone Center* (pp. 97–121). New York: Guilford Press.

Tong, R. (1989). *Feminist thought.* Boulder, CO: Westview Press.

Unger, R. K. (Ed.). (1989). *Representations: Social constructions of gender.* Amityville, NY: Baywood.

Walker, A. (1983). *In search of our mothers' gardens: Womanist prose.* San Diego: Harcourt Brace Jovanovich.

Walker, L. E. A. (1989). Psychology and violence against women. *American Psychologist, 44,* 695–702.

Worell, J., & Remer, P. (1992). *Feminist perspectives in therapy: An empowerment model for women.* New York: Wiley.

3

FEMINIST PERSPECTIVES ON ASSESSMENT

MARYANN SANTOS DE BARONA AND MARY ANN DUTTON

WITH ROSALIE J. ACKERMAN, MARY BALLOU,
FRANCES CULBERTSON, TERRESA PECK,
AND ANNA MARIA LAURENTI

Assessment and evaluation are important functions in the practice of psychology. Both the underlying assumptions and methods of psychological assessment are driven by theory; for example, behavioral assessment relies on behavioral and social learning theories, family assessment relies on theories of family and interpersonal processes, educational assessment relies on theories of cognitive development, and assessment in behavioral medicine relies on theories of physiological self-regulation. Thus, "[t]he nature of data, and of admissible procedures for gathering and interpreting them, cannot be discussed very long in theory-free terms" (Ericsson & Simon, 1981, p. 16).

The purpose of this chapter is to discuss psychological assessment from a feminist theoretical perspective. Before presenting our analysis, we briefly describe the process used by the assessment working group to provide a context within which to understand our work. We then briefly discuss current feminist theory, followed by a summary of the literature on feminist assessment. Finally, we review substantive areas of consensus derived from the group process and present recommendations for implementation.

PROCESS OF THE ASSESSMENT WORKING GROUP

The assessment working group consisted of seven women, including the facilitator and a recorder. One of the first process issues that developed within the group was the role of the student recorder. Whereas the role had been previously defined as one of "observer," the group unanimously invited her to join the group as a full participant. Even though the student was required to engage in a specific task of recording the sessions, her equal input to the discussion was invited.

However, a couple of factors maintained students in a more subordinate role. The demands of the task of recorder interfered with the opportunity to participate fully as a discussant. Thus, the dual role (e.g., recorder and participant) constituted a barrier to full and equal participation. Including students as participants in a manner equal to that of other conference attendees would have maximized the possibility that students' participation was solicited as equally valuable. Second, although the student's active participation as a discussant was eventually invited (in this group and others), the "historical" context of having been identified as an "observer" only was not erased. Parallels to other situations in which persons of lower status based on social power eventually attain equal status are apparent (e.g., when a student marries a professor or an employee marries a boss).

Near the end of the conference, another possibility for inclusion arose within the assessment working group. A new person, arriving late to the conference, asked to join our working group. There was no intragroup conflict about her inclusion, and the group proceeded with one additional member for the remainder of the final session.

Throughout the course of the group discussions, consensus generally was not difficult to achieve. Although the group engaged in lively discussion at times, there was little overt or expressed conflict. The process involved consensus building through discussion. When differences emerged, discussion eventually resulted in an alignment among views.

UNDERSTANDING ASSESSMENT

The initial discussion of the assessment working group focused on the definition of *assessment*. We derived a working definition: *Assessment* is the act of identifying and naming human experience relevant to the questions asked, and to that end it integrates the theory, science, and practice of psychology.

We identified six necessary underlying assumptions as central to the concept of assessment but acknowledged that some of these assumptions should be questioned from a feminist perspective. First, identifiable phenomena are perceptible, observable, or measurable in some way, although the methods of detecting or knowing these phenomena vary. Second, assessment is a process that occurs in a sociopolitical, legal, and economic context. It occurs within a hierarchical power relationship; the assessment process may be helpful, or alternatively, it may be harmful. A third assumption is that, as a result of the assessment process, the assessor comes to understand some aspect of the client's experience better than the client. Some feminist psychologists take exception to this assumption and believe that the client's empowerment and increased self-awareness need not be accompanied by a concomitant understanding on the part of the assessor. Fourth, decision making in assessment is based on comparison to some standard, either group membership or the client's own behavior in another context or at another time. A fifth assumption is that sufficient information may be obtained to guide the assessment process. Finally, the assessment process may rely on ways of knowing other than those derived exclusively from the scientific model.

None of these assumptions is particularly unique to feminist assessment; each can be found in reference to other approaches to psychological assessment. Several features, however, lend themselves as characteristics of feminist assessment:

1. The assessment process is overtly recognized as one that inevitably involves the use of power between the client and the professional, parallel to that of feminist therapy (Douglas, 1985; Smith & Douglas, 1990). As with feminist therapy, assessment within a feminist paradigm strives to empower the client (Smith & Douglas, 1990).

2. Placement of the client's assessment within the multifaceted social, political, and economic context within which she or he lives is a hallmark characteristic of both feminist (Brown & Root, 1990) and ethnic or multicultural (Fulani, 1988; Ramirez, 1991) psychologies.

3. Different ways of knowing (Ballou, 1990; Belenky, Clinchy, Goldberger, & Tarule, 1986; Gilligan, 1982) that rely not only on the rational and objective, but also on the intuitive and subjective, can be used. One of the biggest challenges to a feminist model of assessment is to incorporate these differences into the process of assessment and into an understanding of that which is assessed.

RELEVANT MULTIDIMENSIONAL PERSPECTIVES

A feminist perspective on assessment necessarily is influenced by the prevailing state of feminist theory. Current feminist theory has been criticized as being "neither diverse nor complex" (Brown, 1990, p. 3), and efforts to develop a unifying theory applicable to all women should be continued. Feminist theory has been influenced primarily by White feminists who often do not incorporate the experiences of women of color, women from non-Western societies, or women from poor or working classes into their view of women. Such an approach generates a knowledge base that does not accurately reflect reality for all women and in fact represents only a narrow segment of the female population. As such, this knowledge should not be considered as a universal truth but as only a "form of socially negotiated understanding" (Crawford & Marecek, 1989, p. 480).

The power of racial and cultural identity certainly cannot be ignored in feminist theory, particularly vis-à-vis the role of gender. Many women of color perceive racism to be a more powerful oppressor than sexism; these women also must continuously deal with the impact of class, culture, and sociopolitical forces (Comas-Díaz, 1991). These forces are significant influences in women's lives. Consequently, a multicultural model of feminist psychology that draws on the experiences of women of varying ages, social classes, sexual orientations, and cultures is needed to achieve greater relevance for all women (Santos de Barona & Reid, 1992).

Several basic points are important in facilitating progress toward a multicultural model of feminist psychology and are presented because of their relevance to our subsequent discussion on assessment.

- Aspects of work from other disciplines as well as non-North American behavioral sciences should be incorporated to create greater flexibility in how we define and acquire knowledge (Ballou, 1988; Brown, 1990).
- Gender should not be considered the only determinant of women's experiences. For many women, the complex and ongoing interaction of gender, race, ethnicity, culture, class, sexual orientation, religion, and sociopolitical forces shape their life experiences. The proportional influence of such factors is fluid and subject to change. The sociocultural context of women's lives is extremely important, and multicultural feminist theory should develop paradigms that acknowledge the influence of such contexts and interactions (Comas-Díaz, 1991; Mahoney, 1993).
- Differences are not necessarily deficiencies or indicative of pathology but may reflect the uniqueness of diverse groups (Comas-Díaz, 1991).

- Each person has the right to equal personal power in relationships. This requires that interventions based on a feminist perspective both enable a more egalitarian relationship and strive for empowerment (Comas-Díaz, 1991).

As feminist psychology as a whole moves toward this multicultural model, the subdiscipline of feminist assessment must also embrace a multifaceted approach to accommodate the many sociocultural factors that affect testing. Before specifically addressing these factors, however, we examine some of the more fundamental critiques of "traditional" psychological assessment.

FEMINIST CRITIQUE OF PSYCHOLOGICAL ASSESSMENT

Assessment targets diverse aspects of an individual's functioning, among them performance in the cognitive, educational, vocational, and personality realms. Assessment takes many forms. It is a process that may be undertaken formally or informally. It may involve use of a variety of strategies, such as clinical observation, interviews, standardized measures, qualitative strategies, and functional analyses. (See Hackett & Lonborg's, 1994, discussion of feminist considerations in using these techniques.)

Epistemology

One of the first issues in a critique of traditional psychological assessment is that of epistemology. We refer to methods of knowledge generation that are appropriate for psychological assessment. Ballou (1990) articulated five basic epistemological positions relative to knowledge generation and validation that are applicable to the practice of assessment: (a) the scientific method based on logical positivism; (b) phenomenology or experiential methodologies; (c) reasoning; (d) appeals to authority; and (e) nonrational knowledge generation based on intuition, spiritualism, personal or tacit knowledge, or "revealed truth." Ballou asserted that feminist principles suggest a multimethod approach as the epistemological standard for feminist assessment. Although she argued for an equal weighting of the five methods, she did not suggest whether inclusion of each is essential in the "nexus of convergency" (p. 35) among them. However, she does suggest that a feminist approach to practice in psychology incorporates diverse methods that derive knowledge from multiple sources through varying methods of inquiry.

Contextual Concerns

Among the criticisms directed at assessment procedures is the concern that their use may reinforce existing barriers for women rather than provide new options and opportunities (Hackett & Lonborg, 1994). In this section, we identify some of the ways this occurs.

Rosewater (1988) provided a feminist critique of psychological testing. Her concern regarding sex bias in testing is based on the use of biased items, inappropriate norm groups for interpreting an individual's score, and constructs that reflect the sexist structure of society. To illustrate the latter, in a study of battered women, Rosewater expressed concern that psychiatric labels applied to victims of violence further victimized them because many of the behaviors inherent in the diagnostic criteria reflected female cultural conditioning.

Recently, Worell and Remer (1992) critiqued traditional approaches to psychological assessment. They list four ways in which sex bias occurs: "(a) disregarding or minimizing the effect of the environmental context on individuals' behavior; (b) different diagnoses being given to women and men displaying similar symptoms; (c) therapists' misjudgments in selection of diagnostic labels due to sex-role-stereotyped beliefs; and (d) using a sex-biased theoretical orientation" (p. 151).

Others also have elaborated on these points in the feminist literature and in other arenas. Numerous authors (Barona & Santos de Barona, 1987; Comas-Díaz, 1991; Dutton, 1995; Hackett & Lonborg, 1994; Sattler, 1993) have commented on the problems inherent in examining a narrow area of functioning separate from the broader context of the individual's life. Indeed, in the area of education, the United States federal government (Education for All Handicapped Children Act of 1975) has mandated a multidimensional approach to the assessment and diagnostic process: Prior to determining that an educational disability exists, it is necessary to conclude that socioeconomic and educational disadvantage have not contributed to existing learning problems.

Procedural and Psychometric Concerns

Lewin and Wild (1991, pp. 582–583) addressed psychometric and procedural issues in assessment from a feminist perspective. Noting that a basic problem in approaching measurement issues lies in determining how to approach "truth," they summarized the reasons that tests and other assessment measures have been criticized by feminists:

- the unfairness of some measures for girls and women. One example involves assessing skills and characteristics from a stereotypical male perspective, such as asking whether the individual had a paper route as a child to determine whether responsibility had been accepted early in life (Sackett & Wilk, 1994);

- failure to consider alternate interpretations when women's scores differ from those of men. As an example, when women's average group scores are lower on a particular measure, it is not uncommon to conclude that women are less skilled, or deficient, on a particular dimension rather than considering that the measure taps the dimension less effectively for women than for men;
- the traditional conceptualization of a number of psychological variables, such as masculinity and femininity;
- the dubious appropriateness of using operational definitions derived from psychological constructs that themselves are ambiguous or otherwise problematic, such as masochism, femininity, and masculinity;
- the inappropriate or biased way in which test results can be used to diagnose inaccurately or prevent access to programs or jobs (Lewin & Wild, 1991). One example involves the use of test scores as selection criteria when performance on the test has not been established as a good predictor of future job performance.

Concerns Related to Personality Instruments

A major concern regarding the use of projective testing involves the assumption that "similar psychological processes account for all aspects of human behavior" (Barona & Hernandez, 1990, p. 298). This assumption has been challenged (Diaz-Guerrero, 1981; Kaplan, Rickers-Ovsianka, & Joseph, 1956). In addition, projective techniques have been hampered by their lack of predictive validity, especially for individuals whose backgrounds vary from those on whom the instrument was developed. As an example, Costantino and Malgady (1983) found that ethnic minorities were more expressive and elaborative when evaluated with an instrument containing culturally relevant themes and symbols. Similarly, responses to clinical interviews were considered more bizarre and deviant when clients were not evaluated in their native language (Malgady, Rogler, & Costantino, 1987).

Sociocultural Factors Affecting Test Performance

We cannot overemphasize the critical need for the assessor to be familiar with the sociocultural context of the client. This is especially pertinent to women of color, whose cultural upbringing may present a reality to which the assessment situation may not be sensitive. Differences in communication styles, health beliefs, and variations in learning are specific areas that should receive attention to avoid misdiagnosis or ambiguous findings. We address each and discuss its implications for the assessment process.

Styles of Communication

Assessors may be unfamiliar with specific cultural characteristics that influence the test performance of women of color. They may not be aware that nonverbal means of communication, such as the use of silence, eye contact, facial expression, gestures, and body language, are not universal in their meaning (Cheng & Clark, 1993), and they may interpret these behaviors relative to the reference group with which they typically interact. This lack of awareness may increase the possibility of inaccurate interpretation and misdiagnosis.

Although some research findings suggest that particular ethnic groups rely heavily on nonverbal communication cues (Langdon & Clark, 1993; Wallace, 1993), all cultural and ethnic groups probably rely on nonverbal communication cues and rely less on what is said than how it is said (Barnlund, 1968). However, assessors must understand that nonverbal cues often are used and interpreted differently by different ethnic groups and therefore should make an effort to ensure that they do not attribute such cues incorrectly. For example, directness in communication in the Hispanic culture often is viewed as indicative of rudeness or immaturity (Langdon & Clark, 1993); some members of the dominant American culture mistakenly consider the more poetic speech patterns of African American and Hispanics to be reflective of thinking or communication problems (Grossman, 1995). Similarly, a woman of ethnic origin may appear verbally reticent and unresponsive, resulting in some negative diagnostic impressions by an assessor from the dominant American culture. However, depending on the culture, it may be culturally appropriate to appear humble and not seek attention or praise. Alternatively, it may be acceptable in some cultures (e.g., Hispanic) to reveal only positive emotions. The assessor must be aware of these cultural nuances to arrive at appropriate conclusions and recommendations.

Health Beliefs

Disability is perceived differently by cultures. As an example, a physical, emotional, or developmental disability is considered a stigma to many Asians (Cheng & Clark, 1993). As a result, the assessor may need to be especially sensitive to this cultural perspective during the assessment process and work closely with the client to optimize the success of any recommendations.

Variations in Learning

In contrast to American society where learning is viewed as an active experience, some cultures encourage passive learning. For example, many Asian students learn through observation and imitation rather than discovery learning or critical thinking activities (Cheng, 1991). Similarly, Gallegos and Gallegos (as cited in Langdon & Clark, 1993) indicated that many Hispanics are taught not to challenge a person of authority but rather to listen and obey. Consequently, they may seek information in a less overtly active manner and be less likely to clarify or contradict a perceived authority figure.

Different cultures reinforce different skills. Whereas American culture tends to reinforce a more linear style of thought, some Asian and Pacific Island cultures support a more circular model. This style, which involves the simultaneous development of many parallel and related points, may be perceived by an assessor unfamiliar with the culture as indicative of "reflective, incomplete, or disorganized thoughts" (Cheng & Clark, 1993, p. 127).

Individual Versus Collective Orientation

Individuals raised in traditional Asian, Hispanic, and Native American families may be less concerned than those raised in dominant culture American families with individual achievement and place greater importance on group goals and needs. As such, they may be more concerned with social norms than individual pleasure and may place greater value on group cooperation than individual success (Pipes, Westby, & Inglebert, 1993).

Implications

An assessor who is unfamiliar with such basic cultural differences may be ineffectual in producing accurate findings and recommendations. First, the female client either may not understand the rationale underlying the recommendation or may feel that compliance creates greater dissonance within the culturally embedded social network within which she lives. Second, it may not be culturally appropriate for women who are not fully acculturated into mainstream America to disagree with or challenge the findings of the assessor, who may be regarded as an expert. For example, Chinese individuals may remain silent rather than voice disagreement or anger (Cheng & Clark, 1993), and Hispanics often do not reveal negative thoughts or feelings (Langdon & Clark, 1993). Many women of color, particularly those with limited finances, may be less sophisticated regarding assessment procedures and their use; thus, they may not fully understand the ramifications that test findings may have for them in terms of access to, exit from, or denial of services.

Concerns Related to Diagnoses

Rosewater (1987, 1990) offered a critique of personality disorder diagnoses, with specific focus on self-defeating personality disorder (previously referred to as masochistic personality disorder) in the third revised *Diagnostic and Statistical Manual of Mental Disorders* (*DSM–III–R*; American Psychiatric Association, 1987). According to *DSM–III–R*, predisposing factors include "having been physically, sexually, or psychologically abused as a child" (p. 373). Although guidelines regarding differential diagnosis indicate that behaviors that otherwise meet the criteria for the diagnosis may actually be "coping strategies to avoid . . . threats to her life" (p. 373), further discussion suggests that the diagnosis may be appropriate for a person who "has been (or is being) physically, sexually, or psychologically abused" (p. 373). Rosewater (1987) argued that the diagnosis "implies that the abuse is the victim's, not the perpetrator's fault" (p. 190). Furthermore, she argued that the diagnosis excludes only current victims, whereby long-term abuse may result in patterns of behavior similar to short-term abuse and "many individuals have yet to deal with ongoing or past victimization" (p. 191). She also argued that the diagnostic category of self-defeating personality disorder reflects sexist bias. This category does not appear in the latest version of the *Diagnostic and Statistical Manual of Mental Disorders* (4th ed.; *DSM–IV*; American Psychiatric Association, 1994). The argument concerning women's tendency toward self-defeating behavior or masochism is not a new one. Caplan (1984) critiqued the psychoanalytic concept of masochism and credited feminism for calling attention to the social basis of what has been termed *masochism*.

Worell and Remer (1992) further critiqued *DSM–III–R*, the predominant diagnostic system in the United States. They voiced the concern held by many professionals that it is the most sexist of existing diagnostic systems (p. 153), and they enumerated the ways in which sex bias is incorporated into the nomenclature. Few *DSM–III–R* diagnoses identify a problem's source in environmental stressors; instead, they tend to locate pathology within the individual. Moreover, clinicians' diagnoses may be affected by their personal value system and theoretical orientation (Brown, 1990; Worell & Remer, 1992). Investigators suggested that the therapist's view of a client may influence outcome (Vannicelli, 1984) and that gender-role stereotypes may be reinforced in therapeutic settings (Cuskey, 1982). Indeed, in a study that examined gender differences in treatment outcomes for adolescents referred to drug abuse prevention programs, it was found that although male clients had more severe problems at intake, counselors rated female clients more negatively during program participation and at the time of discharge (Santos de Barona, 1992).

A third criticism involves the use of sexist categorical descriptions. Worell and Remer (1992) cited evidence (Hamilton, Rothbart, & Dawes,

1986) that "diagnostic categories that have a higher prevalence rate for males have clear behavioral descriptors" (p. 157), whereas several personality disorder categories with higher prevalence rates for women contain trait descriptors that require more clinical interpretation, thus rendering them susceptible to bias. They also expressed concern over the lack of empirical research to validate numerous diagnostic categories. Unfortunately, *DSM–IV* is not a significant improvement over previous editions as far as sex bias is concerned.

Over time, some test developers have acknowledged the negative impact of unfair practices and have initiated changes in the test development process to achieve greater equity (Lewin & Wild, 1991). Modifications include (a) using sensitivity reviews, a process that strives both to eliminate sexist, racist, or otherwise offensive language and to obtain greater balance in the numbers of items referring to female and male individuals; (b) using differential item functioning (a statistical procedure that can identify items that function differently for two groups of people during test development) to decide whether the item should be retained in the final version; and (c) increasing the percentage of feminists serving as experts on test committees, where test content is defined, written, and critiqued. Inclusion of feminists on test committees has led to a gradual redefinition of test content (Lewin & Wild, 1991).

These much-needed advances gradually are being infused into the test development process. However, older tests as well as more recent measures that have not undergone bias-minimizing procedures should be evaluated to determine whether problems exist. An evaluation of a measure for gender balance should consider whether the test is an equally good predictor for both female and male clients. Also important is knowing what the test score is purported to reflect. Does the score indicate past achievement or future potential performance? Finally, a determination of whether the test measures similar abilities for male and female clients alike should occur.

These changes in the test development process gradually will help to move the field forward and to bring it closer to a feminist approach toward assessment. We recognized that many assumptions underlie a feminist approach to assessment. Thus, our working group set out to identify and examine the assumptions underlying assessment and to understand the principles of a *feminist* analysis before developing a model of and future directions for assessment from a feminist perspective.

A FEMINIST ANALYSIS OF PSYCHOLOGICAL ASSESSMENT

The assessment working group identified the following principles as informing a feminist analysis or critique of psychological assessment.

1. The realities of people's lives should be incorporated into each stage of the assessment process. Does the assessment process incorporate, either as the focus of assessment or as contextual factors, all relevant domains of a person's life? Pertinent factors to be considered include but are not limited to developmental issues, life history (including experiences with oppression as well as privilege), socioeconomic status, physical condition (e.g., medical, neurological), ethnic and cultural factors including acculturation, sexual orientation, geographical influences, spiritual or religious influences, physical strengths and challenges, age, social support (and barriers to support or social obstructionism), kinship grouping, and household arrangements. Unless the influences of these comprehensive factors are considered, assessment decisions may not capture an adequate understanding of the client.

2. An additional consideration for a feminist analysis of assessment is collaboration. Combining the client's knowledge with the assessor's area of expertise can generate more effective choices and strategies (Hansen, Himes, & Meier, 1990). To accomplish this goal, it must be determined (a) whether the assessor and client are working together on mutually agreed on goals and (b) whether they have jointly agreed on the problem and developed a plan for assessment. Unless these two conditions are met, collaboration is unlikely. An assessor with a feminist perspective is then faced with evaluating the situation to make the best possible decision with regard to proceeding. Collaboration does not mean that the assessor must operate outside appropriate professional boundaries, meet all of the client's (or therapist's) needs, or betray her or his own professional values and ethical considerations. However, collaboration does require that both assessor and client accept joint responsibility for the process, which may involve a delineation of roles and delegation of tasks.

   Clients can become actively involved in the assessment process in a number of ways. In addition to investing appropriately and in a forthcoming manner on direct assessment tasks, they can identify others who may be able to provide additional information regarding their particular situation and provide ways to contact them. Furthermore, in some situations clients may obtain the information themselves through clearly delineated data collection strategies. This procedure may involve using a variety of data collection techniques to document the occurrence of well-defined behaviors and the circumstances under which they occur (Parsons & Meyers 1984). This data can be reviewed with the client to determine whether the behavior's occurrence warrants special attention. For example, a client may be asked to record his or her daily consumption of alcohol to consider with the client the role of alcohol in mood fluctuations.

3. Although a scientifically based method using standardized instrumentation and procedures is the dominant way of knowing, other means (e.g., personal knowledge, intuition) may be equally valuable. Does the assessment acknowledge information gained through various means? Does the assessor use diverse ways of gaining information and acknowledge the basis on which various decisions are made? A central issue in this regard is one of accountability—to ensure that the assessment decisions are recognized for the process through which they were derived. We recognize that issues of validity may be raised, particularly in those instances where legal or other binding decisions are involved. This possibility may require the assessor to be extremely thorough in documenting the process of data collection and interpretation.

4. Social, political, professional, or personal action is taken when assessment processes are misused. Some examples of misuse include not taking a victimization history into account when assessing psychological condition or disregarding the presence of a history of violent behavior when determining parental fitness. Social action is a central component of the professional role involved in assessment from a feminist perspective. Social action may be necessary to facilitate a wider recognition of feminist concerns in psychological assessment practices. Such action may involve refusing to accept or act on the assessment report, becoming involved in the revision of professional and ethics codes, facilitating changes in education and training guidelines, or endorsing legislative reform.

5. A feminist analysis of assessment recognizes that the assessment process can, at best, provide a "best fit" description of a particular client within a given set of circumstances (e.g., child custody, forensic, employment, pretreatment evaluation) at a given point in time that reflects the complex context of an individual's life. In other words, conclusions and the formulations about them must be considered as a snapshot of the client derived at the time of the assessment, not necessarily as enduring "realities." Furthermore, the sociopolitical and ethical implications of an assessment process

cannot be understood outside of the context in which it occurs. That is, a feminist analysis understands assessment as a strategic act within the relevant context.

MODEL OF ASSESSMENT FROM A FEMINIST PERSPECTIVE

We describe a general model from which feminist assessment can proceed. Because feminist assessment per se is not based on a comprehensive theory of human behavior, our model integrates existing assessment methodologies and feminist principles to develop a process for feminist assessment. What follows is an outline of the stages at which one may consider the various issues of feminist analysis described above.

The definition of these stages of assessment rests on the basic assumption that assessment is a process that attempts to capture continuous, ongoing, and shifting phenomena while recognizing the practical reality that an assessment procedure typically must be conducted within a finite time frame. We consider five stages at which one can apply a feminist analysis of assessment.

1. Develop hypothesis collaboratively. During the initial stage the assessor works with the client to come to an understanding about the purpose for the assessment and to agree on the referral question. Together they determine the information that is needed to answer the referral question.
2. Develop strategies jointly to obtain information. This stage involves determining the methods to be used in gathering the assessment information. Data should be obtained using multiple techniques and, where appropriate, multiple sources. It is extremely important that the assessor shape the data collection strategies to fit the referral question and that such strategies not resemble a recipe or cookie cutter format (whereby each client, regardless of presenting problem or background, is assessed in the same manner). Therefore, the information for two clients with similar referral questions might be obtained in entirely different ways because of the unique characteristics of each individual as well as the differences in the potential impact the assessment process may have in the clients' sociopolitical milieu. For this reason, client input at this stage is vital.

   The assessor should consider whether any physical, medical, emotional, or cognitive factors limit the client in the assessment process. Other important factors are the client's literacy and language fluency and the cultural appropriateness of involving the client's family or social network in the process. This list is not exhaustive; it serves only to demonstrate a few of the many issues that should be considered at this stage.

3. Collect data. The necessary information should be obtained in the manner previously determined. In situations where formal instruments are used, deviations from standard administration procedures should be documented along with the rationale for such modifications. Data that have been collected from informal instruments or through the use of techniques unfamiliar to many in the profession should be identified, and the process used in such situations should be specified.

    As stated earlier, the client may be able to participate in the gathering of assessment data. As an example, the client may be instructed to provide anecdotal information about specific life events or taught to document the frequency or duration of particular behaviors along with its antecedent and consequent conditions. The client and the assessor can then use this information in the analysis phase to determine the degree of severity and to develop joint action strategies.

4. Analyze the data. The assessment information should be synthesized within the framework of the referral question and in the context of the client's life. The assessor must integrate knowledge about the client with the obtained data. It may be appropriate in some instances to ask the client to clarify the data.

    The assessor should consider pertinent sociocultural variables and other factors in analyzing the data. As an example, the assessor should not view a nonnative English speaker who does not speak English with a high degree of elaboration as limited in verbal skills or in abstract thought unless additional corroborating data are provided. Ideally, this information should be provided through the native language. Similarly, the assessor should not interpret differences in affect or in interactions from a strict Eurocentric perspective unless the client's background clearly is consistent with such an interpretation. Finally, the assessor should closely examine the assessment data of a medically or physically challenged client for performance decrements. It is possible that decreased performance over time is related to the length of the assessment procedure rather than difficulty in the area being evaluated. These examples are not exhaustive but merely suggest some ways to ensure that feminist principles are considered at this stage of the assessment process.

5. Derive a formulation. After the information has been collected and analyzed, the assessor reaches a conclusion regarding the referral question. This formulation may take several forms. Depending on the referral question, it may culminate formally or informally, be tied to a diagnosis that may aid access to specific services, or result in a set of recommendations designed to optimize the client's situation.

The assessor should work closely with the client to ensure an understanding of the implications of any recommendations or action strategies. Ideally, the client should participate in shaping such strategies, which should build on her individual strengths. The client's involvement in this process also increases the probability that such strategies are viable within the sociocultural context of her life. In some instances, the assessment process may identify additional questions that both client and assessor agree must be examined. These questions should be approached using the above process, with careful consideration of the client's state and circumstances at each stage.

FUTURE DIRECTIONS IN FEMINIST ASSESSMENT

Feminist psychology has progressed in stages (Walker & Dutton-Douglas, 1988). The first generation of feminist practice in psychology provided a critique of sexism in the theory and practice of assessment and psychotherapy. The second generation has provided an integration of feminism with other theoretical approaches, primarily modifying them to include an understanding of women and girls. The third generation creates new models that more effectively address the realities of women's and men's lives.

One of the realities that has yet to be addressed adequately, even within most approaches to feminist theory and practice, is a full integration of the multiple contexts in which people live their lives. The assessment working group recognized the importance of the contextual analysis but acknowledged that a universal, or even common, understanding of its implications had yet to be realized. One example is the tension between the context of gender and the contexts of ethnicity and race. Although both of these contexts have inevitable influences on lived experience, one may dominate in its influence over the other in particular situations.

A recognition within feminist theory and practice that the context of gender may not supersede all others remains controversial. Women, in particular, may be more committed to their ethnic identity than they are to their identity as women (Comas-Díaz, 1988). Although one's identity as female is likely to be important, it may not be experienced as primary in the social construction of dominance because of other contextual markers, especially race (see Mahoney, 1993, for a general discussion of this issue within a legal framework). A crucial challenge for feminist assessment is to incorporate contextual variables beyond that of gender that define women's lives (e.g., race, culture, sexual orientation, age, immigration status) in a manner that reflects the meaning of that context for the particular woman for whom an assessment is being conducted.

We acknowledged that feminist approaches to assessment are evolving and so chose to emphasize a best practices approach that involves the client throughout the assessment process. This approach allows the client to become a more active participant in the process and to gain a fuller understanding of the implications of the assessment activities. Examples of how elements critical to a feminist perspective may be incorporated into the psychological assessment process were provided. These examples illustrate how the principles of feminism, regardless of the assessor's theoretical orientation, may be applied to a wide range of assessment situations.

REFERENCES

American Psychiatric Association. (1987). *Diagnostic and statistical manual of mental disorders* (3rd ed., rev.). Washington, DC: Author.

American Psychiatric Association. (1994). *Diagnostic and statistical manual of mental disorders* (4th ed.). Washington, DC: Author.

Ballou, M. (1988, May). *Building feminist theory through feminist principles.* Paper presented at the meeting of the Advanced Feminist Therapy Institute, Seattle, WA.

Ballou, M. B. (1990). Approaching a feminist-principled paradigm in the construction of personality theory. In L. S. Brown & M. P. P. Root (Eds.), *Diversity and complexity in feminist therapy* (pp. 23–40). New York: Harrington Park Press.

Barnlund, D. (1968). *Interpersonal communication: Survey and studies.* Boston: Houghton Mifflin.

Barona, A., & Hernandez, A. E. (1990). Use of projective techniques in the assessment of Hispanic school children. In A. Barona & E. E. Garcia (Eds.), *Children at risk: Poverty, minority status, and other issues in educational equity* (pp. 297–304). Washington, DC: National Association of School Psychologists.

Barona, A., & Santos de Barona, M. (1987). A model for the assessment of limited English proficiency students referred for special education services. In S. H. Fradd & W. J. Tikunoff (Eds.), *Bilingual education and bilingual special education: A guide for administrators* (pp. 183–210). San Diego, CA: College Hill Press.

Belenky, M. F., Clinchy, B. M., Goldberger, N. R., & Tarule, J. M. (1986). *Women's ways of knowing: The development of self, voice, and mind*. New York: Basic Books.

Brown, L. S. (1990). The meaning of a multicultural perspective for theory-building in feminist therapy. In L. S. Brown & M. P. P. Root (Eds.), *Diversity and complexity in feminist therapy* (pp. 1–22). New York: Haworth Press.

Brown, L. S., & Root, M. P. P. (Eds.). (1990). *Diversity and complexity in feminist therapy*. New York: Haworth Press.

Caplan, P. J. (1984). The myth of women's masochism. *American Psychologist, 39*, 130–139.

Cheng, L. L. (1991). *Assessing Asian language performance*. Oceanside, CA: Academic Communication Associates.

Cheng, L. L., & Clark, L. W. (1993). Profile of Asian and Pacific Island students. In L. W. Clark (Ed.), *Faculty and student challenges in facing cultural and linguistic diversity* (pp. 114–136). Springfield, IL: Charles C Thomas.

Comas-Díaz, L. (1988). Feminist therapy with Hispanic/Latina women: Myth or reality? In L. Fulani (Ed.), *The psychopathology of everyday racism and sexism* (pp. 39–62). New York: Harrington Park Press.

Comas-Díaz, L. (1991). Feminism and diversity in psychology. *Psychology of Women Quarterly, 15*, 597–609.

Costantino, G., & Malgady, R. G. (1983). Verbal fluency of Hispanic, Black, and White children on TAT and TEMAS, a new thematic apperception test. *Hispanic Journal of Behavioral Sciences, 5*, 199–206.

Crawford, M., & Marecek, J. (1989). Feminist theory, feminist psychology: A bibliography of epistemology, critical analysis, and applications. *Psychology of Women Quarterly, 13*, 477–481.

Cuskey, W. R. (1982). Female addiction: A review of the literature. *Journal of Addictions and Health, 3*(1), 3–33.

Diaz-Guerrero, R. (1981). El enfoque cultural-contracultural de desarollo humano social: El caso de las madres en cuatro subculturas mexicanas [The cultural–countercultural focus of human and social development: A case study of mothers in four Mexican subcultures]. *Revista de la Association Latinoamericana de Psicologia Social, 1*, 75–92.

Douglas, M. A. (1985). The role of power in feminist therapy: A reformulation. In L. B. Rosewater & L. E. A. Walker (Eds.), *Handbook of feminist therapy: Women's issues in psychotherapy* (pp. 241–249). New York: Springer.

Dutton, M.A. (1995, March). *Understanding context in battered women's response to violence: Intervention, research and policy implications*. Paper presented at the International Study Group on the Future of Intervention with Battered Women & Their Families, Haifa, Israel.

Education For All Handicapped Children Act of 1975, Pub. L. No. 94–142, 20 U.S.C. §1401 (1975).

Ericsson, K. A., & Simon, H. A. (1981). Sources of evidence on cognition: A historical overview. In T. V. Merluzzi, C. R. Glass, & M. Genest (Eds.), *Cognitive assessment* (pp. 16–51). New York: Guilford Press.

Fulani, L. (Ed.). (1988). *The psychopathology of everyday racism and sexism.* New York: Harrington Park Press.

Gilligan, C. (1982). *In a different voice: Psychological theory and women's development.* Cambridge, MA: Harvard University Press.

Grossman, H. (1995). *Teaching in a diverse society.* Boston: Allyn & Bacon.

Hackett, G., & Lonborg, S. D. (1994). Career assessment and counseling for women. In W. B. Walsh & S. H. Osipow (Eds.), *Career counseling for women* (pp. 43–85). Hillsdale, NJ: Erlbaum.

Hamilton, S., Rothbart, M., & Dawes, R. M. (1986). Sex bias, diagnosis, and DSM–III. *Sex Roles, 15,* 269–274.

Hansen, J., Himes, B. S., & Meier, S. (1990). *Consultation: Concepts and practices.* Englewood Cliffs, NJ: Prentice-Hall.

Kaplan, B., Rickers-Ovsianka, M. A., & Joseph, A. (1956). An attempt to sort Rorschach records from four cultures. *Journal of Projective Techniques, 20,* 172–180.

Langdon, H. L., & Clark, L. W. (1993). Profile of Hispanic/Latino American students. In L. W. Clark (Ed.), *Faculty and student challenges in facing cultural and linguistic diversity* (pp. 88–113). Springfield, IL: Charles C Thomas.

Lewin, M., & Wild, C. L. (1991). The impact of the feminist critique on tests, assessment, and methodology. *Psychology of Women Quarterly, 15,* 581–596.

Mahoney, M. R. (1993). Whiteness and women, in practice and theory: A reply to Catharine MacKinnon. *Yale Journal of Law and Feminism, 5*(2), 217–251.

Malgady, R. G., Rogler, L. H., & Costantino, G. (1987). Ethnocultural and linguistic bias in mental health evaluation of Hispanics. *American Psychologist, 42,* 228–234.

Parsons, R. D., & Meyers, J. (1984). *Developing consultation skills.* San Francisco: Jossey-Bass.

Pipes, M. A., Westby, C. E., & Ingleberrt, E. (1993). In L. W. Clark (Ed.), *Faculty and student challenges in facing cultural and linguistic diversity* (pp. 137–172). Springfield, IL: Charles C Thomas.

Ramirez, M., III. (1991). *Psychotherapy and counseling with minorities: A cognitive approach to individual and cultural differences.* New York: Pergamon Press.

Rosewater, L. B. (1987). A critical analysis of the proposed self-defeating personality disorder. *Journal of Personality Disorders, 1*(2), 190–195.

Rosewater, L. B. (1988). Battered or schizophrenic? Psychological tests can't tell. In K. Ylló & M. Bograd (Eds.), *Feminist perspectives on wife abuse* (pp. 200–216). Newbury Park, CA: Sage.

Rosewater, L. B. (1990). Diversifying feminist theory and practice: Broadening the concept of victimization. *Women and Therapy, 9,* 299–311.

Sackett, P. R., & Wilk, S. L. (1994). Within-group norming and other forms of score adjustment in preemployment testing. *American Psychologist, 49,* 929–954.

Santos de Barona, M. (1992, April). *Differential effects of counseling programs for male and female adolescents in drug abuse prevention programs*. Paper presented at the Rocky Mountain Psychological Association Convention, Boise, ID.

Santos de Barona, M., & Reid, P. T. (1992). Ethnic issues in teaching the psychology of women. *Teaching of Psychology, 19*(2), 96–99.

Sattler, J. M. (1993). *Assessment of children* (3rd ed.). San Diego, CA: Author.

Smith, A. J., & Douglas, M. A. (1990). Empowerment as an ethical imperative. In H. Lerman & N. Porter (Eds.), *Feminist ethics in psychotherapy* (pp. 43–50). New York: Springer.

Vannicelli, M. (1984). Barriers to treatment of alcoholic women. *Substance and Alcohol Actions/Misuse, 5*, 29–37.

Wallace, G. (1993). Profile of African American student. In L. W. Clark (Ed.), *Faculty and student challenges in facing cultural and linguistic diversity* (pp. 63–87). Springfield, IL: Charles C Thomas.

Walker, L. E., & Dutton-Douglas, M. A. (1988). *Feminist psychotherapies: Integration of therapeutic and feminist systems*. Norwood, NJ: Ablex.

Worell, J., & Remer, P. (1992). A feminist approach to assessment. In J. Worell & P. Remer (Eds.), *Feminist perspectives in therapy: An empowerment model for women* (pp. 143–168). New York: Wiley.

4

FEMINIST THERAPY: FROM DIALOGUE TO TENETS

KAREN FRASER WYCHE AND JOY K. RICE

WITH DOROTHY CANTOR, BARBARA CLASTER,
IRIS FODOR, COLLEEN GREGORY, JANE HASSINGER,
GWENDOLYN PURYEAR KEITA, HANNAH LERMAN,
EDNA RAWLINGS, LISA ROCCHIO, LYNNE BRAVO ROSEWATER,
LOUISE SILVERSTEIN, AND LENORE WALKER

The therapy working group consisted of 12 women who were clinicians and academics with many years of experience in teaching, writing, research, and practice with and about women. We engaged in a very active, intense dialogue for 4 days and struggled to develop a document that would reflect our collective opinions regarding the definitions and tenets of feminist therapy. We had various theoretical orientations (cognitive–behavioral, humanistic, gestalt, crisis intervention, psychodynamic), types of practices (individuals, families, groups, couples), and specializations (abused women, older women, adolescents, minorities, etc.). Unique to this process was the experience of coming together in the spirit of mutual trust and respect for the endeavor. Student observers enriched this experience by asking questions, focusing us when necessary, and (most important) recording our deliberations. What follows in this chapter is our attempt to recapture the spirit of our lively and exciting discussions and to articulate the tenets of feminist therapy that were generated during our meeting. We hope that all who engage in feminist therapy with their clients find our thoughts useful in their own professional development.

This chapter is written for feminist therapists at the beginning of their careers and for seasoned veterans. We hope to engage our readers in a dialogue that inspires them to reflect on their own practice. First, we review briefly some of the literature that helped inform our process and structure our framework for defining feminist therapy. All of our participants have been active contributors to the body of literature regarding the process and context of feminist therapy. Our intention is not to reiterate that literature in this chapter but rather to give the reader a general overview of our efforts. We then discuss our group process and how we addressed five thematic core questions. We conclude the chapter with a summary of our discussion that resulted in a preamble and 16 tenets of feminist therapy.

FEMINIST THERAPY LITERATURE: IMPORTANT THEMES

Over the past several decades, the literature on feminist therapy has expanded in both the description of the therapeutic process and the articulation of the philosophy of feminist therapy. Feminist writers, including members of this group, have provided many excellent books and articles on the subject. Early writings on psychotherapy for women (e.g., Rawlings & Carter, 1977) and the influence of the women's movement on psychotherapy (e.g., J. D. Rice & Rice, 1973) helped lay the groundwork for the expansion of feminist therapy to focus more broadly on issues relating to women. For example, feminist ethics in psychotherapy (Contratto & Hassinger, 1995; Lerman & Porter, 1990), women as victims of violence (Rosewater, 1993; Walker, 1989), cultural contexts of therapy (Comas-Díaz & Greene, 1994; Wyche, 1993), and women as therapists (Cantor, 1990) are some of the areas that feminist psychologists have begun to examine. Feminist analysis was extended to important issues in women's emotional well-being such as the psychological and therapeutic factors in women's occupational stress (Keita & Sauter, 1992), social policy implications of maternal employment (Silverstein, 1991), and public policy issues for women's mental health (Claster & Towns, 1988). Recently, applications of feminist theory, approaches, and epistemological critique have also been applied to the field of family research and family therapy (J. K. Rice, 1994).

In addition to an expansion of feminist theory and therapy relating to the contexts of women's lives, scholarly journals developed that focused on feminist issues in psychotherapy and practice. *Psychology of Women Quarterly*, *Journal of Feminist Family Therapy*, and *Therapy, Feminism and Psychology* are a few examples. Moreover, journals with a mental health focus have devoted special issues to the topic of feminist therapy (e.g., *The Counseling Psychologist*, Vol. 21, January 1993).

Whereas the literature on feminist therapy has grown, there are no set definitions of feminist therapy, but rather multiple and varied approaches to its practice. Fodor (1993) noted that feminist therapy is more of an approach, a framework, or a way of analyzing therapy than an actual system of therapy. According to Brown (1992), many therapists erroneously define themselves as feminist therapists simply because they support the general ideals of the feminist movement; however, they do not incorporate feminist methods of therapy into their research and practice. Thus, feminist therapy is not simply about women therapists working on women's issues such as eating disorders or sexual abuse with women clients (Greenspan, 1983). There is agreement in the literature that feminist therapy encompasses core concepts, a feminist analysis of one's therapeutic intervention, and a philosophy of psychotherapy. These elements relate to concepts of power, advocacy, and social and contextual variables that influence women's lives (Brown & Brodsky, 1992). Feminist writers and practitioners describe these elements in varying ways. Current writings incorporate women's culturally diverse life experiences as positive and essential to the therapeutic process.

Feminist therapists are seen as highly sensitive to issues of advocacy, power, and inherent power imbalances in therapy; they strive for an egalitarian relationship with clients. Power is viewed in the therapeutic relationship as egalitarian and collaborative, rather than as linear and patriarchal (Hawes, 1993). The feminist therapist maintains a heightened awareness of power relationships so as not to abuse or restrict unduly a client's choices. Laidlow and Malmo (1990) called for a reinterpretation of traditional (patriarchal) power structures in favor of those that allow for more reciprocal interaction and support of clients. This reinterpretation of power redefines the therapist–client relationship as a less rigid power structure, allowing for an analysis of power as it affects women's lives.

Over the years the following major themes have recurred in the feminist therapy literature: (a) the assumption of the centrality of gender and its salience to the therapeutic process, outcome, and evaluation; (b) the understanding of women clients through a sociocultural as well as an intrapsychic lens; and (c) the empowerment and enlightenment of women clients as a critical goal of therapy. The resulting therapeutic relationship and the power within it is seen as shared by client and therapist.

Centrality of Gender

Gender is salient in the way in which interpersonal transactions are represented in belief systems and power relationships (Worell, 1993). The feminist therapist thus integrates the new conceptions about women's psychology and the goals of the women's movement into the therapeutic process (Espin, 1994).

Although early feminist writers viewed gender as a basis of oppression, more recent literature on feminist therapy has presented gender-related issues in a historical, political, racial, class bound, and sexual context. Enn (1993) noted that, as the field emerged, feminist therapy was applied to specific problems of women (e.g., abuse, sexual assault, rape, aging). Less understood were women of diverse ethnicity or sexual orientation. As a result, less attention was given to these issues in the early literature. Today feminists understand the importance of recognizing the multifaceted aspects of women's lives. The current literature explores the intersection of gender and ethnicity with other social context or ecological variables and discusses how a White, middle-class perspective framed the dialogue; however, the degree to which this critique has been put into practice is still debated (see chapter 9, "Diversity: Advancing an Inclusive Feminist Psychology").

Sociocultural and Intrapsychic Perspectives

For the feminist therapist, it is important to integrate the social, historical, political, class, and sexual aspects of a woman's life. The client and the feminist therapist work collaboratively to challenge and transform the societal beliefs and values that have been experienced by the client as destructive. In doing this, the therapist helps the client to distinguish between the situations in her life for which she is personally responsible and social circumstances, societal bias, attitudes, and conditioning that reflect broader social problems (Espin, 1994). A feminist therapist helps a client appreciate the socialization processes and the societal and cultural context that defines what is normative from what is deviant behavior for a woman, a man, or a "healthy adjusted adult" (Broverman, Broverman, Clarkson, Rosenkrantz, & Vogel, 1970). How the resulting stereotypes impinge on and limit her options are explored.

Empowerment and Enlightenment as Goals of Therapy

Gender relations are viewed historically as being asymmetrical in any power relationships that involve personal and societal resources, with the net result that men are privileged over women (Hare-Mustin & Marecek, 1990). The feminist therapist helps women to explore and understand the dynamics of gender relationships and to engage her inner resources for nurturance and self-healing. The goal of therapy is personal empowerment, that is, helping the woman to become more independent and assertive about attaining her goals and achieving change and psychological growth.

To come up with an agenda that would guide our work for 4 days, we began by brainstorming about several questions: What is feminist therapy and practice? How is it defined? How do therapists engage in the process of feminist therapy? Can feminist therapy be demonstrated empirically? From these questions arose other related themes such as the role of advocacy in feminist therapy and the limitations of feminist therapy. Can a feminist framework be integrated with other therapeutic approaches, or is feminist therapy something completely different and separate? We debated whether feminist therapy had a core of tenets that could be integrated with other therapeutic orientations and methods or whether feminist therapy is a distinct entity. There was no consensus on this topic, and we knew that we would return to it.

We agreed on many issues. Empowering women to get in touch with their individual and collective power as women and to expand their alternatives, opinions, and choices was seen as an important component of feminist therapy. We discussed the key tenet that the "personal is political" in therapy: that power arrangements in society are reflected in our personal experience and in our interpersonal behavior. We also (a) called for an end to victim blaming (i.e., those in power taking advantage of and blaming those who are not in power) and (b) agreed that recognizing the client's behaviors as adaptive survival responses to unhealthy, oppressive societal conditions represented a move away from a pathological view of women. The feminist therapist looks actively for positive adaptations made by clients and emphasizes support for those adaptations to help clients regain self-esteem. To operationalize this value, the feminist therapist focuses on the clients' strengths, not deficits. "Symptoms" then are viewed as adaptive strategies in the face of oppression and adversity.

We embraced the need to recognize and to appreciate diversity among and between women. We recognized, however, that the feminist therapist who wants to serve as an effective role model may encounter difficulties when working with clients whose culture, history, and traditions are different. We acknowledged that gender affects development, behavior, and cognition but that gender is only one of the many variables that may cause oppression. Other variables include race, ethnicity, class, age, sexual identity, and ablebodiness. Oppression experienced by women on the basis of any of these variables can cause a figure–ground situation that becomes fluid with whatever foreground needs validation for the woman at a particular moment. For example, at any given moment race may be a more significant attribute than gender for women of color in terms of eliciting discrimination or oppression. The feminist therapist must pay particular attention to these variables when helping female clients.

We devoted a great deal of time to discussing the relationship between the feminist therapist and the client. Part of this discussion focused on the active demystification of the therapeutic process and language. The direction and pace of therapy is mutually negotiated by the client and therapist and is within the client's control. The therapist must pay continuous attention to the process of therapy and to the validation of the woman's experience. The relationship between client and therapist should be nonauthoritarian, and there should be an explicit acknowledgment of mutual respect. Despite attempts to minimize power differentials between therapist and client, however, power differences do exist and must be acknowledged. Part of this acknowledgment involves constant monitoring by the therapist of the power balance between therapist and client. Attention must be given to the potential abuse of power within the therapeutic relationship; the client's welfare and needs must always predominate.

These considerations led to a discussion of the limitations to feminist therapy. Some techniques (e.g., confrontational therapy) are not compatible with feminist therapy. Ethnic, religious, or class values may influence a women's view of feminist psychotherapy as inappropriate for her and may be incompatible with her personal values or cultural norms. Furthermore, a client may come to therapy during an intense crisis, and the feminist therapist's attempts to reduce power differentials by self-disclosure or joint goal setting may be experienced as unhelpful or cause for discomfort. Those who do not want to change old patterns of dominance, develop new ways of coping, and engage in a collaborative process will experience this therapy as limiting. These are the issues for any therapeutic orientation when the therapist gives up some power in the relationship. At the same time, the therapist must recognize her or his own power as an inherent force still present within the relationship.

We did not always agree. One topic on which no consensus could be reached involved the role of self-disclosure by the therapist. This complex topic generated the following questions: When is self-disclosure appropriate, and with which types of clients? How can one be sure that self-disclosure is in the client's best interest and not simply meeting the needs of the therapist? In what ways can standards and checks and balances be implemented and monitoring of feminist therapists be done? Is it possible (even with the best of intentions) to use therapeutic approaches that have been used in the past to oppress women by omitting aspects of development relevant to them? How should supervision be conducted (see chapter 8, "Covision: Feminist Supervision, Process, and Collaboration")? How can research inform and validate our work? What is the integration or lack of integration of feminist therapy with other theoretical orientations and philosophies of treatment? That is, are we using feminist theory and only borrowing techniques from other therapy theories, or are we actually integrating feminist theory with other theories? Are there feminist principles and techniques that are inappropriate with particular clients or in particular situations?

These issues framed our discussions. It was interesting to note the extent of our agreement on philosophical beliefs and practices regarding feminist therapy. Our view was that feminist therapy is concerned with exploring, recognizing, and understanding new perspectives and then working together with our clients to re-appraise those values, beliefs, and feelings. Throughout our discussions, we found ourselves appraising and reappraising the content, process, and limitations of feminist therapy, the role of advocacy and power, and the need for empirical research and integration with other orientations.

The many themes that emerged during our deliberations can be organized around five central questions.

Question 1. Does feminist therapy offer a coherent system of concepts and practices, and how is it different from or compatible with other schools of therapy? Is it possible to integrate a feminist framework with other therapy theories, or is it a distinctly separate approach? Are we using feminist theory and only borrowing techniques from other therapeutic systems, or are we actually integrating feminist theory with other theories?

We felt it important to acknowledge the historical context in which feminist therapy evolved. Feminist therapy developed in reaction to the invisibility of women in psychological theory and in recognition of the oppression of women in society. It has moved from a more reactive posture to a more proactive stance that is rooted in an understanding of the role of societal power imbalance that negatively affects women's lives. The development of feminist therapy was spurred by the recognition that women were virtually invisible in existing psychological theories. Laidlaw and Malmo (1990) posited that feminist therapy evolved from the realization that "the oppression of women was as present and as damaging in our own profession as it was in society at large" (p. 1). Thus, the commitment to address women's subordination and disadvantaged status in society serves as unifying thread linking all feminist psychologists.

Through a feminist lens, we use various techniques as necessary, but in doing so these techniques become transformed. A therapist or counselor can have a theoretical orientation that is cognitive–behavioral, family therapy, psychodynamic, or gestalt, but basic feminist tenets may be integrated into that framework. It is the feminist lens that is the value system, the philosophy that transforms practice regardless of theoretical orientation. A feminist therapist adheres to the principles of feminist therapy, a philosophical approach to how practice is conducted and how the client is viewed. It is this interaction which is important.

We identified three possible models of feminist therapy intervention:

1. Separate model: Feminist therapy is seen as a separate, unique model of psychotherapy that simultaneously deals with the cognitive, affective, interpersonal, and spiritual concerns of women. Such a core model of feminism is holistic in approach.
2. Integrative model: Multiple techniques and practices deriving from many systems of therapy are embedded in feminist approaches to therapy. Through a feminist lens, we understand how the world oppresses women, and this understanding transforms the theoretical orientations and practices.
3. Hybrid model: A particular system of psychotherapeutic thought, such as psychoanalytic theory and practice, is applied through a feminist lens.

It is important to note, however, that in all of these approaches, the core of feminist therapy (and what makes it unique) is the analysis of the women's experience as it is affected by the social and the psychological context.

Question 2. What is the role of self-disclosure in feminist therapy?

Feminist therapy involves appropriate types of self-disclosure. Self-disclosure can be client initiated or therapist initiated. There are different levels and kinds of self-disclosure, such as those relating to class and cultural issues or semipublic knowledge (e.g., a death in the family that is reported in the newspaper). The term *self-disclosure* has so many different meanings that there is no consensus on its appropriate use. However, because self-disclosure may be ill-advised, it must be both value and theory driven and always in the client's best interest. As a result, therapists must develop methods of continually monitoring their level of self-awareness. The Feminist Training Institute's Code of Ethics states that the therapist is responsible for the use of self-disclosure in a purposive and discretionary manner and always in the best interest of the client (Lerman & Porter, 1990).

Self-disclosure is one key tenet of feminist therapy because feminist therapy is a demystification process that validates and affirms the shared and diverse experiences of women. Feminist therapy writings first defined the concept and its possible excesses. Field-based research is needed to describe, operationalize, and evaluate empirically the many varieties of feminist self-disclosure to help us better articulate its place as a key tenet of feminist therapy and to inform practice. Because of the potential for misuse, it is very important that the therapist ensures that any self-disclosure is under constant self-scrutiny. The chapter on supervision in this volume (chapter 8) addresses self-disclosure as an issue of supervision with clients and trainees.

Question 3. What are some key questions for feminist therapy researchers?

The therapy working group met with the research working group. Our dialogue was productive, and our brainstorming resulted in the following questions, which represent key issues for further discussion and investigation:

1. How can we generate and provide a database for process and outcome research in feminist therapy? Would a national or regional pool of therapy tapes, ethnographic accounts, or field observations of self-disclosure or analogs of feminist therapy promote more feminist therapy dissertations, further research, and eventually a larger knowledge base?
2. How can we deal with ethical considerations that may arise as a result of the dual role we play as researchers and therapists?
3. What feminist methods (e.g., process-oriented, qualitative methods) can we identify that would be useful in research on feminist therapy?
4. How do we integrate the psychological research literature on self-schema, self-esteem, and feminist identification that has bearing on feminist therapy?

Question 4. What are some key questions related to teaching feminist therapy?

Our meeting with the pedagogy working group focused on the interface between feminist therapy and feminist pedagogy. We identified the following key questions:

1. What would be the basic ingredients and components of a feminist therapy curriculum?
2. What are some logical sequences of practicums, courses, and seminar experiences from a feminist perspective?
3. What is a valuable structure for mainstreaming, infusing, or separating feminist therapy training in the curriculum?
4. When articulating and teaching how feminist therapy and other systems of therapy might interact, how can we best deal with faculty resistance to such curricular change?

Question 5: Is there a core of theory and practice in feminist therapy in terms of content, process, limitations, advocacy, and power issues?

The parts of this question dominated our general discussion for 4 days. Despite our disparate orientations, we reached consensus on a core of 16 tenets of feminist therapy and a philosophical preamble to those tenets. The context for this preamble is an antipathology model where differences among women are not viewed as deviant and where the norm is not assumed to be the White, middle class, and heterosexual woman. All women are seen as unique. The oppression of women is seen as filtered through the multiple lenses of historical, social, political, economic, ecological, and psychological realities. Recognition of these multiple perspectives is critical if feminist therapy is to become truly comprehensive. Feminist therapists can have multiple theoretical orientations, but feminist tenets are always integrated into these therapeutic orientations which thereby transforms them. Therefore, feminism as a value system and philosophy transforms our practice.

After 4 days of discussions, we outlined a preamble and 16 core tenets of feminist therapy (see the Appendix). The preamble sets the stage for the tenets; taken together, they reflect our shared philosophy regarding feminist therapy. These core tenets are the heart of what feminist therapists do, the lens through which they view their work with their clients, and the philosophical framework in which clients' problems are conceptualized.

PREAMBLE

Feminist therapy is based on an empirical and qualitative knowledge base that comes from a psychology of women, drawing on interdisciplinary feminist scholarship. It deals with the examination and understanding of the cognitive, affective, spiritual, and behavioral dimensions of girls' and women's experiences, and it can be practiced with individuals, couples, families, and groups. A basic principle of feminist therapy is that the personal is political. This principle acknowledges that power arrangements in society are reflected in personal experiences and in interpersonal relationships. Feminist therapy uses a dual focus that simultaneously highlights and examines the interconnectedness of the personal and the political.

Feminist therapists value and respect diversity among women, which become the lens through which to understand both theory and practice in feminist therapy. Feminist therapists conceptualize their work in terms of the tenets of feminist therapy. The techniques they use may vary but must be consistent with the tenets. The therapy process is always mediated by clients' experiences, stories, and narratives because these are affected by the cultural, social, political, economic, and historical context and by their intrapsychic experiences.

CORE TENETS OF FEMINIST THERAPY

The core tenets of feminist therapy—the basic structures and distinguishing characteristics we felt epitomize feminist therapy—are outlined in the Appendix. We hope these tenets are helpful to both the beginning feminist therapist and the more experienced clinician. These core tenets are the foundation of the feminist therapeutic process, which are organized into four areas: (a) the social and ecological context of women's lives, on which feminist therapy focuses; (b) the analysis of the client's problem; (c) the goals of therapeutic outcome; and (d) the role of the feminist therapist.

Tenets 1 and 2 describe the ecological context in which to view women's lives. These tenets argue that being female can be understood only within the therapeutic process which evaluates the social context, both recent and historical, of a woman's life and how that context interacts with intrapsychic factors. Gender is not the only category of analysis; each woman's uniqueness is influenced by a multiple set of factors (cultural, social, political, economic, and historical) that shape the ways in which she lives her life.

In analyzing the client's problem, the feminist therapist investigates how the ecological, social, and political forces shape her life (Tenets 3–6). This includes an analysis of power and the multiple ways in which women can be oppressed. The feminist therapist acknowledges that misogyny and violence exist in all women's lives and that it can be emotionally, physically, and spiritually damaging. In analyzing how these factors affect the client's life, the feminist therapist focuses on strengths rather than deficits. Women's behaviors are seen as understandable efforts to respond adaptively to oppressive occurrences.

Therapeutic outcomes are listed in Tenets 7 through 13. The feminist therapist works collaboratively with the client to establish the goals, direction, and pace of therapy. Girls and women are helped to understand how they have incorporated societal beliefs and values into their thinking and behavior. The therapist and client work together to challenge and transform those constructs that are destructive to the self and to create their own perspectives. Within this process is the expansion of the girl's and woman's alternatives, options, and choices across the life span. The feminist therapist strives to help clients recognize, claim, and embrace their individual and collective power as girls and women. These client–therapist interactions take place within an egalitarian, mutually respectful, and non-authoritarian relationship.

Feminist therapists adhere to certain attitudes and guidelines for their behavior (Tenet 14–16). The therapist acknowledges that feminist therapy is a demystification process that validates and affirms the shared and diverse experiences of girls' and women's lives. Feminist therapists are committed to monitoring continually their own biases, distortions, and limitations especially with respect to cultural, social, political, economic, and historical aspects of girls' and women's experiences. Feminist therapists understand that occasional self-disclosure must always be done in an appropriate manner and should be monitored for potential problems. One's therapeutic practice, including self-awareness, must constantly be evaluated and monitored.

CONCLUSION

This chapter presents a feminist examination of and reflection on feminist therapy. This process was the vehicle for examining the humanness and professionalism of feminist therapy and the interconnectedness with psychological theory, therapeutic practice, research, and training. We recognize the need to constantly reexamine our assumptions in a world in which clients experience changing stresses. The implications of our work for feminist training, practice, supervision, and research are numerous. These issues are addressed in other chapters in the book. Time limitations prevented the therapy working group from discussing issues of feminist techniques, men as providers or clients of feminist therapy, or the implications of managed care for feminist therapists.

Our process was a collaborative, feminist process that transcended our differences in theoretical orientation and enabled us to identify mutually agreed on tenets of feminist therapy. We hope that readers who are also therapists find this discussion helpful and useful in evaluating their own practice.

APPENDIX
CORE TENETS OF FEMINIST THERAPY

1. Feminist therapy recognizes that being female always occurs in a cultural, social, political, economic, and historical context and affects development across the life span.
2. Feminist therapy focuses on the cultural, social, political, economic, and historical factors of women's lives as well as intrapsychic factors across the life span.
3. Feminist therapy includes an analysis of power and its relationship to the multiple ways women are oppressed; factors such as gender, race, class, ethnicity, sexual orientation, age, and ablebodiness, singly or in combination, can be the basis for oppression.
4. Feminist therapy acknowledges that violence against women, overt and covert, is emotionally, physically, and spiritually damaging.
5. Feminist therapy acknowledges that misogyny exists in all women's lives and is emotionally, physically, and spiritually damaging.
6. Feminist therapy's primary focus is on strengths rather than deficits. Therefore, women's behaviors are seen as understandable efforts to respond adaptively to oppressive occurrences.
7. Feminist therapy is committed to social change that supports equality for everyone.
8. Feminist therapy is based on the constant and explicit monitoring of the power balance between therapist and client and pays attention to the potential abuse and misuse of power within the therapeutic relationship.
9. Feminist therapy strives toward an egalitarian and nonauthoritarian relationship based on mutual respect.
10. Feminist therapy is a collaborative process in which the therapist and client establish the goals, direction, and pace of therapy.
11. Feminist therapy helps girls and women understand how they have incorporated societal beliefs and values. The therapist works collaboratively with them to challenge and transform those constructs that are destructive to the self and helps them create their own perspectives.
12. Feminist therapy empowers girls and women to recognize, claim, and embrace their individual and collective power as girls and women.
13. Feminist therapy expands girls' and women's alternatives, options, and choices across the life span.
14. Feminist therapy is a demystification process that validates and affirms the shared and diverse experiences of girls' and women's lives.
15. Feminist therapy involves appropriate types of self-disclosure. However, because self-disclosure may be harmful, it must be both value and theory driven and always in the client's best interest. Therapists must develop methods of continually monitoring their level of self-awareness.
16. Feminist therapists are committed to continually monitoring their own biases, distortions, and limitations, especially with respect to cultural, social, political, economic, and historical aspects of girls' and women's experiences.

REFERENCES

Broverman, I. K., Broverman, D. M., Clarkson, F. L., Rosenkrantz, P., & Vogel, S. R. (1970). Sex role stereotypes and clinical judgments of mental health. *Journal of Consulting and Clinical Psychology, 34,* 1–7.

Brown, L. S. (1992). While waiting for the revolution: The case for a lesbian feminist psychotherapy. *Feminism and Psychology, 2,* 139–253.

Brown, L. S., & Brodsky, A. M. (1992). The future of feminist therapy. Special issue: The future of psychotherapy. *Psychotherapy, 29,* 51–57.

Cantor, D. W. (1990). *Women as therapists: A multitheoretical case-book.* New York: Springer.

Claster, B. L., & Towns, S. K. (1988). *Executive summary of the Pennsylvania Task Force for Mental Health: Women.* Harrisburg, PA: Office of Mental Health, Department of Public Welfare.

Comas-Díaz, L., & Greene, B. (1994). *Women of color: Integrating ethnic and gender identities in psychotherapy.* New York: Guilford Press.

Contratto, S., & Hassinger, J. (1995). Violence against women. In E. Rave & C. Larsen (Eds.), *Ethical decision making in therapy: Feminist perspectives* (pp. 124–152). New York: Guilford Press.

Enns, C. Z. (1993). Twenty years of feminist counseling and therapy: From naming biases to implementing multifaceted practice. *The Counseling Psychologist, 21,* 3–87.

Espin, O. (1994). Feminist approaches. In L. Comas-Díaz & B. Green (Eds.), *Women of color: Integrating ethnic and gender identities in psychotherapy* (pp. 265–286). New York: Guilford Press.

Fodor, I. (1993). A feminist framework for integrative psychotherapy. In G. Stricker & J. Gold (Eds.), *Comprehensive handbook of psychotherapy integration* (pp. 217–235). New York: Plenum Press.

Greenspan, M. (1983). *A new approach to women and therapy.* New York: McGraw-Hill.

Hare-Mustin, R., & Maracek, J. (Eds.). (1990). *Making a difference: Psychology and the construction of gender.* New Haven, CT: Yale University Press.

Hawes, S. E. (1993, October). *Reflexivity and collaboration in the supervisory process: A role for feminist poststructural theories in the training of professional psychologists.* Paper presented at the National Council of Schools in Professional Psychology Conference on Clinical Training in Professional Psychology, Las Vegas, NV.

Keita, G., & Sauter, E. (Eds.). (1992). *Work and well-being: An agenda for the 1990's.* Washington, DC: American Psychological Association.

Laidlaw, T. A., & Malmo, C. (1990). *Healing voices: Feminist approaches to therapy with women.* San Francisco: Jossey-Bass.

Lerman, H., & Porter, N. (1990). *Feminist ethics in psychotherapy.* New York: Springer.

Rawlings, E. E., & Carter, D. K. (Eds.). (1977). *Psychotherapy for women: Treatment toward equality.* Springfield, IL: Charles C Thomas.

Rice, J. D., & Rice, J. K. (1973). Implications of the Women's Liberation Movement for psychotherapy. *American Journal of Psychiatry, 130*(2), 191–196.

Rice, J. K. (1994). Reconsidering research on divorce, family life cycle, and the meaning of family. *Psychology of Women Quarterly, 18,* 549–574.

Rosewater, L. B. (1993). Counseling battered women. Special Issue: Psychotherapy with women from a feminist perspective. *Journal of Training and Practice in Professional Psychology, 7,* 67–80.

Silverstein, L. B. (1991), Transforming the debate about child care and maternal employment. *American Psychologist, 46,* 1025–1032.

Walker, L. (1989). Psychology and violence against women. *American Psychologist, 44,* 695–702.

Worell, J. (1993). Grader in close relationship: Public policy vs. personal prerogative. *Journal of Social Issues, 49,* 203–218.

Wyche, K. F. (1993). Psychology and African-American women: Findings from applied research. *Applied and Preventive Psychology, 2,* 135–141.

5

FEMINIST RESEARCH: PRACTICE AND PROBLEMS

FRANCES K. GROSSMAN, LUCIA A. GILBERT, NANCY P. GENERO,
SUSAN E. HAWES, JANET S. HYDE, AND JEANNE MARECEK

WITH LAURA JOHNSON

The nature of feminist research and the characteristics that make it distinctive are receiving considerable attention (e.g., Fonow & Cook, 1991; Stewart, 1994). Issues raised in discussions about feminist research typically center around the appropriate methods for research; new pragmatic, political, and ethical issues that are raised by these methods; the influence of patriarchal structure of the academic world and the research establishment on feminist research practices; and the uses to which feminists' rich experiences as women can be put to illuminate new understandings of psychology.

This literature is increasingly driven by the compelling questions raised daily in the lives of feminist scholars about how to proceed with research in a way that feels connected to their personal beliefs and understandings, viable for their professional lives, safe for their students, and valuable to the participants and their communities. It was within the framework of this literature and these questions that the research working group held its discussions.

We begin this chapter by discussing who we are and describing our process, and then we address at length the following four questions: What is feminist research? What are the ethics of feminist research? How is feminist research transformative of psychology, of women's lives, and of our conceptualizations of knowledge? What are some of the land mines and obstacles to doing feminist research? We conclude the chapter by examining the ways that we can work toward change in the field.

OUR SETTING, PROCESS, AND GOALS

The research working group consisted of seven women—six psychologists who had said our first interest at the conference was to discuss issues in feminist research and a graduate student (Laura Johnson) who had volunteered to be the group's recorder. We were, to differing degrees, intrigued, excited, and anxious about how our ideas would be received and in some cases anxious about how well we would meet our group responsibilities. Some of us knew well at least one or two others in the group; some of us knew others a little; some of us knew others only by name or not at all.

"Feminist research" is an immense topic. It was clear that the shape of our conversation over the next 4 days would be largely determined by who we were—our interests, our abilities, and our skills—as well as who we became in combination. In many ways, we were quite similar to one another. All of us were involved full-time with academic departments, either as faculty or as a graduate student; all of us were committed to research; and all of us considered ourselves feminists, however we understood that term. One of us identified herself as Latina; the rest were Caucasians. We were all born in this country. Except for our recorder who was in her early 30s, our range in age was limited: We were in our 40s and 50s. Several of us had been active and successful in the organization and political activities of the American Psychological Association (APA) and its Division 35 (Psychology of Women). Several of us were clinicians as well as researchers and teachers.

An interesting set of differences related to our stance toward the psychological establishment. We varied in how much we felt ourselves to be part of the mainstream of psychology; how much we continued to aspire to recognition by the field of psychology; and how much we had concluded that such recognition was limited or not possible because of our values, style, or type of research. These differences were important in the discussions; we often returned to this issue. It became clear that, although there are numerous individual factors that influence our particular paths and choices, we all struggle at times with the risks of being marginalized within our academic fields. We agreed that recognition in the field is to some degree tied to adhering to conventional practices. We agreed less regarding how much institutionalized psychology in the United States (as opposed to, for instance, women's studies, critical studies, critical theory, or the British school) commands our intellectual respect and serves as a valued reference group.

We spent the first several hours considering the assignment, which included constructing a list of questions we wanted to address during the 4 days. Our conversations on this topic, as well as throughout the meeting, tended to be lively, free flowing, sometimes seemingly wandering, and always interesting. As we got to know one another and felt safer in the group, the discussion became sometimes edgy and conflicted as we explored ideas far from accepted psychological practice. Virtually all of the discussions brought us to a new level of awareness or clarity. By the end of each day, many of us felt enriched, exhausted, overstimulated, and (despite the differences of opinion) acknowledged and supported.

We noted that during the 4 days we worked together as a group, we became less and less directed by the instructions of the Coordinating Committee. It was clear to us, and totally understandable, that they were making and revising decisions as they went along because the experience of the conference was new to everyone. Furthermore, the structure of the conference provided considerable potential independence for the working groups. That autonomy was helpful to us, and over time, we increasingly made our own choices about where and how to focus discussion, to a degree that seems to have distinguished us from other groups. A case in point pertains to how this chapter was constructed. On the last day, when asked to come up with universal themes from the summaries of each of the nine working groups, we quickly decided we had other conversations to hold that seemed more important to us. We went with our own agenda, which included how each of us could participate in the writing of this chapter and what form we would like the chapter to take. We decided that each of us would write a section so as to better reflect and preserve the language, accuracy, and nature of our discussions. Hence, readers will note differing styles and emphases, which together provide an increased clarity of our deliberations and conclusions.

On the first day, we settled on the following eight questions, understanding full well that these questions did not cover the possible range of topics about feminist research. We selected them because they seemed intrinsically important or were of significant interest to at least several of us. Some of them were questions about which we had something we wanted to say.

1. What is feminist research?
2. What are the ethics of feminist research?
3. How is feminist research transformative of psychology, of women's lives, and of our conceptualizations of knowledge?

4. What are some of the land mines and obstacles to conducting feminist research?
5. How do we legitimize feminist research in traditional research contexts, including the training of graduate and postdoctoral students?
6. What are important research topics that feminist mental health professionals believe would help their practice?
7. How do political commitments influence the feminist research agenda?
8. How do we incorporate different feminisms and different metatheories into feminist psychology?

Because of time constraints, we were able to discuss only the first four questions at length.

WHAT IS FEMINIST RESEARCH?

We agreed that we should not put ourselves in the position of defining what particular research project or researcher was or was not feminist; we were committed to an inclusive view. Thus, the group discussion focused on capturing and characterizing the diversity and breadth of feminist scholarship in psychology. We considered two issues: (a) the content of feminist research and its relation to feminist theory and to applied feminist practice and (b) methods and epistemological debates within feminist scholarship.

Content of Feminist Research and Its Relation to Feminist Theory and to Applied Feminist Practice

Although we recognized that there are certain areas of research in which feminist contributions have been central, we believe it would be a mistake to define feminist research scholarship in terms of content areas. To equate feminist scholarship with a specific set of topics would pose two difficulties. First, it would set limits on the range of concerns that feminist scholars might examine and thus might discourage creativity. Second, research on virtually any topic within psychology can be either feminist or nonfeminist; it is the approach rather than the topic that determines whether the work is feminist.

We agreed that feminist research is purposeful. Considering the corpus of work produced thus far, three central purposes can be identified. First, feminist inquiry has illuminated the lives of women and girls. That is, new knowledge has been generated about aspects of women's lives that were invisible, unaddressed, or deemed unimportant by mainstream psychology. Illustrations of this point are projects that study life experiences unique to women (e.g., pregnancy, breast-feeding, menopause) and experiences tied to women's position in the sex–gender system (e.g., violence against women by partners, sexual harassment, sexual discrimination).

Feminist psychologists more recently have focused attention on another purpose: to give "voice" to women who have been marginalized by their social, cultural, or class positions. We recognized the urgency of expanding the purview of feminist psychology to include such women. Furthermore, we noted that implicit in the phrase "give voice to" is a notion of the research participant as an active agent. This approach to participants is in contrast to traditional psychological research, which positions the researcher as the spokesperson for, and interpreter of, the experiences of the research "subjects." Thus, the purpose of giving voice to previously marginalized women invites departures from both conventional research methods and conventional APA-style research reports.

A third purpose of feminist inquiry in psychology has been the development of a critique of the discipline of psychology. In a sustained flow of scholarly work, researchers have identified and critiqued androcentric biases in psychological theory, concepts, methods, and clinical practices (e.g., Crawford & Marecek, 1989; Sherif, 1979). Other lines of endeavor have attempted to situate psychology as a cultural institution and to formulate a cultural and social history of the discipline (Morawski, 1994). Still others have studied the social practices and conditions of work for female working psychologists (e.g., Scarborough & Furomoto, 1987).

By asserting that feminist psychology is purposeful, we acknowledged that women and their lives are central to the construction, evaluation, and applications of knowledge that underlie feminist inquiry. We also acknowledged that such inquiry is necessarily influenced and informed by the political and social context in which it takes place.

As these comments imply, we understood feminist inquiry to be informed by, and to inform, feminist thought and practice. Over the past quarter of a century, feminist theory has developed and deepened, women with diverse social and cultural experiences have contributed their knowledge and energies to the feminist movement, and the cultural and political conditions that form a backdrop to feminism have shifted. Thus, many strains of feminist discourse and of feminist social and political philosophy have emerged.

Many of these diverse strains of thought are represented among feminist psychologists and inform their work (see, e.g., Marecek, 1995; Morawski, 1994; Nicholson, 1990). The journal *Feminism & Psychology: An International Journal*, now in its fifth year of publication, provides examples of "cutting edge" feminist research and reappraisals of feminist classics as well as a forum for feminist theoretical debates and debates within the field of women's psychology (Wilkinson, 1994). The fundamental function of *Psychology of Women Quarterly*, the journal of APA's Division 35, is advancing the development of feminist theory and research. In her editorial statement, Worell (1990) noted that "one of the important goals for [*Psychology of Women Quarterly*] is to maintain a continuing focus on the multiple ways in which feminist experience and thought can stimulate theory and empirical research in order to expand our images of reality and create new understandings" (p. 2). Criteria used by the journal in evaluating a manuscript for publication include the following: (a) It challenges traditional or devaluing views of women, (b) it uses methods of inquiry that provide alternative views of women's lives, (c) it looks at women within the meaningful contexts of their lives, (d) it engages in collaborative efforts with participants, (e) it solicits samples other than college groups, (f) it considers sex and gender contrasts in context and within explicit theoretical frameworks, (g) it explores alternatives that empower women and minorities, and (h) it contains implications for social change (Worell, 1990).

It is important that the field of feminist psychology accept and validate the diverse strains of thought and scholarship represented among feminist psychologists. It is also important to encourage reflexive consciousness so that those researching and writing in feminist psychology are aware of (and make their readers aware of) their political commitments (Hawes, 1992). Much of our attention in this discussion was focused on methods and epistemological debates within feminist scholarship.

Methods and Epistemological Debates Within Feminist Scholarship

Feminist research in psychology has involved the use of a broad variety of methods of inquiry (cf. Harding, 1987; Reinharz, 1992). We believe it is important to emphasize that all the methods of inquiry in psychology can be used to produce feminist knowledge. These methods include quantitative approaches, qualitative approaches, experimental approaches, survey approaches, clinical case studies, textual studies, naturalistic studies, and historical studies. Different methods are suited to different questions, but no method in and of itself is "nonfeminist" (Peplau & Conrad, 1989).

We were aware of the ongoing debates regarding the nature of science and the scientific method and the delimitation of objects of study from a positivistic perspective (Keller, 1985). In this context, some group members expressed concern that certain terms (e.g., *data, research, scientific*) have come to imply and give legitimacy to a narrow aspect of intellectual inquiry conducted using traditional experimental procedures. Developing and using a language for research that is not so tied to traditional methods appears important to enabling researchers to imagine and value a broader range of methods of inquiry. A case in point is the use of the term *participant* rather than *subject* when referring to individuals involved in a study. Participants participate and thus are active agents; subjects, in contrast, are objects studied by the researcher.

Feminist philosophy, feminist theory, and cultural history have been important resources in the debates about the positivist presuppositions of psychology (see the discussion in the section Transformations of Epistemologies or Conceptualizations of Knowledge). Moreover, some feminist psychologists have joined in the critique of conventional epistemologies and foundational assumptions of psychology and in the efforts to construct alternative epistemologies and research practices (e.g., Bohan, 1993; Riger, 1992). We acknowledged that some of these views are competing and mutually exclusive. We continue to seek inclusiveness, and we sought formulations that would not pit one feminist psychologist against another.

Another methodological question we considered is whether conventional methods of psychological inquiry are sufficient to produce knowledge about women and gender. Some group members emphasized the importance of positioning research participants as agents fully capable of construing their own experiences. Other group members asked how the methods of conventional psychological inquiry might be reformed to produce knowledge grounded in the actual experiences of participants. We struggled with what is often framed as a dichotomy (and disparity) between research knowledge and clinical knowledge. In our view, the therapeutic process has been a rich source of psychological knowledge. Examples include the development of theories based on women's experiences such as self-in-relation theory and the identification of factors influencing women's development such as sexual discrimination, incest, and other forms of abuse.

All methods of psychological inquiry—conducted in both research and clinical settings—are informed by ethics and, in turn, engender new ethical dilemmas. Feminist researchers should attend to these issues and strive toward responsible methodological approaches.

WHAT ARE THE ETHICS OF FEMINIST RESEARCH?

From the beginning of our conversation about feminist research, we recognized that questions of ethics, and of new ethical issues raised by such research, had to be considered. In fact, some feminist scholars have developed methods and questions in part to solve ethical problems. One example of an ethical problem is the damage caused by misinformation conveyed about people's psychologies and lives when they are described only by scientists from a different and socially more powerful group. A second example is the possible exploitation of the "subject" by the "experimenter" by using information gathered from participants, not to enhance the lives of participants, but to advance researchers' own professional agendas.

We also recognize that feminist research methods can create new ethical dilemmas as well as exacerbate existing ones (e.g., Acker, Barry, &

Esservel, 1991; Coterrill, 1992; Stacey, 1988). Although the group acknowledged that many of these issues are addressed by APA's (1992) Ethical Principles of Psychologists and Code of Conflict, we agreed that as feminist researchers we should explicitly attend to the thorny ethical dilemmas that can arise in field and laboratory settings. The following section summarizes some of the particular, and occasionally unique, issues raised by feminist research.

As feminist researchers, we seek responsible methodological approaches that can accurately capture a person's experience. However, it seems that the more we try to capture the "true" person and use methods that allow us to represent others' feelings and thoughts accurately, the more we risk misrepresenting or perhaps abandoning them. For example, one member of the group was conducting qualitative research on resiliency in adult survivors of childhood sexual abuse (Grossman & Moore, 1994). To obtain rich and open narratives, interviewers took great care in developing safe and relatively egalitarian relationships with the participants. The total length of the interviews ranged from 5 to 10 hours.

This kind of research, which is in many ways closer to the clinical endeavor but with a different purpose, raises several questions. In some instances, ending a study during which feelings of mutual connection have developed can trigger feelings of loss and may be interpreted as abandonment or exploitation. How do participants and researchers respond to these feelings? In cases where interviews or survey questionnaires raise, but do not address, difficult issues for participants, are we obligated to provide a safety net or some mechanism to protect study participants? Moreover, involvement in the pain and complexities of people's lives may heighten the researcher's own sense of powerlessness. When involved in community intervention studies, minority researchers—who are often viewed as "insiders" and are expected to know the answers—may feel especially vulnerable. (See Zinn, 1979, for a review of ethical and political issues of field research in minority communities.)

From a conventional scientific perspective, involvement in the details of respondents' lives and the potential need for supportive interventions challenges notions of objectivity. In fact, the feminist researcher is often confronted with the tension between the textbook approach to objective scientific analysis and the vicissitudes of "real world" studies. As we increasingly recognize that all science occurs in the context of particular perspectives and cultural values, questions about the misinterpretation and consequences of particular research findings become acute. We are mindful that we probably often do not know what causes harm in the long run or what complex mix of good and harm will emerge from what we do. What happens if we carry out a study in a particular community and believe that the results, as we interpret and understand them, might be harmful to the community? Do we always, or ever, know what is harmful to a community?

How do or should possible consequences influence the choices we make about what research to conduct and what research to publish? Is it possible, or even desirable, to reconcile these ways of thinking with the concept of impartiality that we were taught is the cornerstone of science?

Early in our discussion of ethics, we defined the task of feminist research ethics as developing a research process that does not create an exploitative or oppressive relationship between researchers and study participants, for the community in which the participants live, or for the group carrying out the research. The usual power–status differences, deriving from such dimensions as sex differences and racial–ethnic group backgrounds, continue to operate in research settings.

Several other contexts particular to the research endeavor in which there are power differentials across individuals include students and research assistants in relation to faculty and senior researchers, participants in relation to researchers, and the community represented by the participants in relation to the researchers. Because most of us have been socialized to be blind to the exploitation of the less powerful by the more powerful, developing workable feminist ethical standards requires a lifelong vigilance and sensitization to these issues and how they manifest themselves in our practice and research. Even as we raise these issues, we are aware that if ethical constraints make the research process too difficult, then ethically concerned feminist researchers simply are not able to conduct studies that might be of value to society. Indeed, these ethical questions require active and continuous dialogue.

HOW IS FEMINIST RESEARCH TRANSFORMATIVE?

The third question posed by our group was, "How is feminist research transformative?" Feminist research has the potential to create three kinds of transformations: (a) transformations of traditional psychology, (b) transformations of epistemologies or conceptualizations of knowledge, and (c) transformations of women's lives including the transformation of participants' and researchers' lives.

As we considered each of these kinds of transformations, we quickly developed a heightened consciousness of the diversity of viewpoints found in our group and in feminist psychology more broadly. Our viewpoints were diverse, yet we shared a set of beliefs that unites feminist psychologists. We experienced our own impassioned differences in the context of a warm, collaborative relationship and commitment to inclusiveness. This powerful combination allowed us to see how vital it is for feminism that our conceptions of research practices embrace and affirm the various differences and similarities in the ways feminism can be practiced. As we describe the three areas of transformations in greater detail, we also explore the diversity of feminist viewpoints on each.

Transformations of Traditional Psychology

The greatest divergence in our views was expressed over the question of feminism's prospects for transforming the field of psychology. On the one hand, feminists perform research that tackles questions of crucial value for women's lives, yet they do so within preexisting epistemological and methodological frameworks in dominant forms of psychological research (e.g., Genero, Miller, Surrey, & Baldwin, 1992; Gilbert, 1993; Hyde, 1994). The struggle to change psychology's understanding of women from within the discipline begins from such research. When such research is accepted by the field, it has great credibility. The field is stretched and its patriarchal assumptions challenged by greater numbers of women bringing women's issues to the forefront of psychological inquiry, even when they operate from traditional methodologies and epistemologies. Feminist researchers have already affected the field of psychology, and continue to do so, by demanding that women's lives be considered important.

On the other hand, less optimistic voices in our group were informed by postmodernist critiques of the contextual qualities of knowledge and knowledge construction. This view argues that traditional research practices in psychology are among the many ways that the dominant culture marginalizes women and other nondominant cultural groups. The conduct of research as usual is itself a gendered practice and distances itself from the very people it seeks to understand, while relegating human phenomena to supposedly universal laws and dualisms, such as that people are psychologically healthy or ill, masculine or feminine (e.g., Haraway, 1988; Keller, 1985; Morawski, 1990). Some feminist psychologists, then, argue for "further separation from the master discourse and the need to both identify desired values and engage in explicit deconstruction of that discourse" (Morawski, 1990, p. 171).

Psychologists who are engaged in critical studies of the master discourses of psychology (and of the culture) draw on interpretive and narrative methods of inquiry. Such a preference tends to marginalize the researcher further from traditional research communities and rewards, but the benefits can be great: the creation of insights obtainable only from an oppositional consciousness (Haraway, 1988). This view argues that (mis)information about women is created within a patriarchal culture and a patriarchal science and can be counteracted only by devising different methods for creating knowledge. From this theoretical stance, the view of transforming psychology from within is problematic, if not deluded and self-defeating (Fine, 1992; Marecek, 1995; Marecek & Hare-Mustin, 1991; Morawski, 1990, 1994; Morawski & Steele, 1991).

Transformations of Epistemologies or Conceptualizations of Knowledge

The question of transforming psychology leads to the more fundamental question of epistemology, or how we come to learn about the world. Modern scientific psychology is based on a tradition of logical positivism, the belief that there is an objective reality of human behavior, which scientists can directly discover through the application of the scientific method, which yields scientific "facts" (Wittig, 1985). Social constructionism and other postpositivist approaches, in contrast, posit that scientists' knowledge is powerfully shaped by the context in which the data are collected and the viewpoints of the researcher (Sherif, 1979; Wittig, 1985).

These different epistemologies lead to differing methodologies. Logical positivism favors the tightly controlled laboratory experiment, which has long been the tradition in psychology. Postpositivist approaches argue for the inclusion of methods that are interpretive, contextual, and person oriented, methods often considered unconventional and of questionable scientific value.

Logical positivism is central to the core of psychology in the 20th century; chipping away at its foundation may cause the whole edifice to crumble. Insofar as feminists are critical of logical positivism and advocate social constructionist and other postpositivist approaches, they challenge the most essential assumptions of traditional psychology. If the arguments of feminist psychology can persuade a majority of research psychologists, the epistemologies of psychology will have undergone a radical transformation.

Transformations of Women's (including Participants' and Researchers') Lives

Feminist research has transformed women's lives and has the potential for profound transformations in the future (cf. Worell & Etaugh, 1994). At the most basic level, feminist researchers have created new conceptualizations and terms to describe those concepts—that is, they have named the previously unnamed—in ways that have enabled women not only to understand their experiences better but also to be more effective in changing oppressive or harmful conditions.

Creating new concepts and words has important implications for how behavior is understood and whether it is accepted. One example is the coining of the concept and term *sexual harassment* (MacKinnon, 1979), a transformation that helped change societal and legal practices. Another example, the term *date or acquaintance rape* (Koss, 1985), illustrates well the complex and possible dual-edged nature of such transformations. People on both sides of the controversy about the nature and prevalence of date rape understand that it has important implications for who has power in the world and how that power is wielded.

Members of the group were in strong agreement that the acts of conceptualizing, teaching, and engaging in feminist research were important and sometimes transformative for those involved. For some, the commitment to feminist research has made it impossible to teach or perform research in traditional ways, despite pressures to do so. Feminism's challenge to patriarchal hierarchies and assumptions of objectivity lead some to become more personal and collaborative in their work and less willing to work in contexts where others do not make themselves equally open.

Thus, there can be costs to the feminist transformation of professional lives. The move toward the margins of the field produces both creative and threatening ripples in the academic community. Educators engaged in feminist research may become more sensitive to and protective of their students, especially students who themselves are committed to feminist research. These students may be taking a risk and need strong support and mentoring from feminist faculty.

On the other hand, some members of the group spoke of the liberation and exuberance they experienced as a result of doing research that mattered most to them; they noted that this was true even during the early years of their careers, when colleagues were most likely to be discouraging. Some told stories of being consistently encouraged by female colleagues, expressed the desire to do the same for their own students, and observed how these processes renew and revitalize our commitments.

Feminist research may also transform participants, a prospect that is both thrilling and sobering. For example, participants can become better informed as a result of their participation, and knowledge is a powerful force. In one case, women in a study of psychological aspects of maternity leave (Hyde, Klein, Essex, & Clark, 1995) became better informed of their legal rights to job-guaranteed parental leave; several discovered that they had been denied their rights by an employer's policy, and they pressed for appropriate remedies.

Although feminist psychology is potentially transformative on many levels, those practicing feminist psychology must always be cognizant of the land mines and obstacles that reside both in the traditions of psychology and within the very nature of emerging feminist research.

WHAT ARE SOME OF THE LAND MINES AND OBSTACLES FOR FEMINIST RESEARCH?

Land mines in, and obstacles to, feminist research surfaced within the first hour of our discussions and continued to resurface throughout. Such problems, which we all experienced in academic environments, informed our process and brought us to new questions and issues. Discussions often spontaneously brought us back to personal struggles, such as how to be true to our personal notions of feminist research and at the same time frame our research questions and methods in ways that make them competitive for external funding. When it came time to address this specific question, we found that we had a lot to say about what possible obstacles and land mines are but relatively little to say other than that they are there. After much discussion we crafted one summary paragraph: "As feminist psychologists become more established, new forms of opposition emerge. We also acknowledge that the traditional structural, economic, and systemic obstacles remain. We need to be alert to them and devise strategies for counteracting them."

The specific land mines and obstacles that emerged in our discussions took two forms. The first concerned resistance within the discipline and the field to conducting feminist research, particularly research that uses unconventional research methods, and to recognizing feminist research as valid. For example, the subject of gender and the study of women's lives, however studied, in some academic circles is considered nonacademic and atheoretical and as not contributing to psychological theory (Sommers, 1994).

The second set of obstacles concerned dilemmas intrinsic to the practice of feminist research itself. For example, is the research too far removed from mainstream psychology to be published or to be viewed as making a contribution? If students do feminist research for their dissertations, are they less attractive candidates for junior faculty positions in psychology departments? Can we engage in research that is not exploitative?

This last dilemma received a good deal of discussion. We all agreed that it is important to develop research processes that do not create an exploitative or oppressive context among members of the research group, between researchers and participants, or for the community in which the participants live. We also agreed that accomplishing these goals, although extremely important, is very difficult to do and that these are goals feminists work toward or strive to achieve. We recognized that we can exploit and oppress in ways we do not even always understand (e.g., by misinterpreting participants' experiences) and that to some extent these kinds of dynamics or processes are inevitable. Moreover, power is an issue in every type of practice, and as researchers we must accept this responsibility. Research is yet another context involving social relations in which explicit and implicit power differentials are unavoidable.

Further discussion made apparent the interactive nature of these two forms of land mines and obstacles. That is, some obstacles and land mines reside in traditions within psychology, such as assumptions that science is objective and patriarchal structures and values, whereas other obstacles reside in the very nature of the emerging feminist research in the ways described in this chapter. Furthermore, the two forms co-exist, with each form mutually influencing the other. Some examples from our dialogues during the conference illustrate the complexity of these issues and help clarify their interactive nature.

As one example, at various points in the discussion we considered this question: What is the relationship between the inquiring individual and the participant? Allowing for and recognizing diversity of experience requires that the researchers or inquirers make an effort to understand the experience of the participant, which in turn often requires a change in the researchers' attitudes and methods. Yet changing or shifting methods in order to be more genuinely responsive to diversity can be problematic in that it becomes more difficult for the work to be published.

In discussions describing our group's process during the days of the conference, we noted that it is often useful to bring strong feelings that emerge in the process of doing research into the research process itself. For example, in the qualitative study of resilient survivors of childhood sexual abuse (Grossman & Moore, 1994), members of the research group learned that voicing their feelings about the traumatic material they were coding reduced their inevitable reactivity to it and permitted a more thoughtful and considered response. Some scholars today argue that leaving out the researcher's feelings ignores one of the most important sources of data and even of validation (e.g., Kleinman & Copp, 1993). Research validity, however, is often questioned by traditional researchers if a researcher's emotional commitment becomes apparent. Thus, from this more traditional perspective, which is quite common in current psychological research, a feminist researcher would take a great risk in bringing her private feelings into her research and writing.

Still another example from our discussions illustrates the extent to which the two forms of land mines and obstacles are intertwined. In reflecting on our own experiences in creating feminist research groups and doing feminist research, we described how this process has changed our teaching and has brought personal experience, honesty, and feelings into our work. At the same time, for some of us it becomes increasingly less possible to teach required material conventionally. Not teaching in a manner acceptable to the academic worlds some of us inhabit also has serious consequences. As one member noted, "There are consequences; I can't be silent and that's not just in the research group, it also has consequences in relationships, marriages, careers." It has moved some psychologists to the margins of departments and to the margins of psychology. At the same time it has moved some psychologists to the center of scholarship on women.

One final example from our discussions concerned the politics of research and its publication. Several of us knew of projects that were stopped by department or university review committees; in one case, a study of childhood sexual abuse was stopped by a member of the committee who did not believe such abuse occurs. Objections grounded in the politics of a research project can be couched in terms of methodological objections. New methods can be deemed "nonrigorous" by those wedded to traditional approaches. Moreover, the content of feminist work can be disparaged by colleagues on review committees and panels (e.g., referring to it as "that stuff"). A good deal of feminist research occurs at research centers primarily supported by "soft" money; not being competitive for research grants for these kinds of reasons can be risky to an individual's career. Moreover, because feminist research practices often involve field projects and large research teams, it is often the type of research that yields multiple publications with multiple authors, which can cause problems in tenure evaluation. Finally, feminist research can be more costly not only in the time required to complete a study for publication but also in the money needed to conduct the research project. As soon as one goes beyond college student populations and "subject" pools, research becomes very expensive; at times it can be difficult to put a research topic in fundable form and maintain feminist goals. Despite all these land mines and obstacles, we all felt that we had been successful in finding ways to do the kind of research we cared about and to work with students and colleagues who shared our visions.

The conclusions reached by the research working group are summarized in the Appendix.

TOWARD THE FUTURE

We have all developed strategies for survival in traditional institutions. Whereas we disagreed to some degree about the extent to which a feminist researcher can comfortably and productively locate herself within the boundaries of psychology, we agreed on a number of ideas for ways we could work toward change in the field.

One set of ideas involved working within APA to create a more hospitable climate for feminist research and researchers. We decided to write a letter to the appropriate individuals involved in APA publications, emphasizing the importance of anonymous reviewing procedures for journals and openness to new methods for conducting research. We agreed to take actions to ensure feminist researchers were included on the committee to be appointed within the next year to revise the APA research guidelines.

Journals such as *Psychology of Women Quarterly* and *Feminism & Psychology* provide examples of feminist research. A second set of ideas included ways to provide examples of feminist research not only that would show its breadth and diversity but that would also illustrate aspects of the processes involved. We considered the possibility of writing a casebook on feminist research, describing in detail how these projects came about, what they accomplished, what problems they encountered, and what can be learned from those experiences by others interested in feminist research.

Perhaps the most important conclusion we reached was how immensely heartening and energizing it was to meet with a group of psychologists committed to the same goals. We were clear we wanted to meet again soon with one another and with groups at our home institutions and communities. We encourage this as a model for all feminist researchers.

APPENDIX
CONCLUSIONS ABOUT FEMINIST RESEARCH

1. Feminist research is purposeful. It
   (a) illuminates the lives of women and girls
   (b) gives voice to marginalized women
   (c) develops a critique of the discipline of psychology
   (d) reflects feminist values.
2. All methods of inquiry can be used to produce feminist knowledge.
3. The task of feminist research ethics is to develop a research process that does not create an exploitative or oppressive relationship for anyone involved in or affected by the research.
4. Feminist research has the potential to transform traditional psychology, epistemologies, women's lives, and participants' and researchers' lives.
5. Feminist research can generate new opposition and the traditional structural, economic, and systemic obstacles remain. Feminist researchers need to be alert to them and to devise strategies for counteracting them.

REFERENCES

Acker, J., Barry, K., & Esservel, J. (1991). Objectivity and truth: Problems in doing feminist research. In M. M. Fonow & J. Cook (Eds.), *Beyond methodology: Feminist scholarship as lived research* (pp. 133–153). Bloomington: Indiana University Press.

American Psychological Association. (1992). Ethical principles of psychologists and code of conduct. *American Psychologist, 47,* 1597–1611.

Bohan, J. S. (1993). Regarding gender: Essentialism, constructionism, and feminist psychology. *Psychology of Women Quarterly, 17,* 5–22.

Coterrill, P. (1992) Interviewing women: Issues of friendship, vulnerability, and power. *Women's Studies International Forum, 15,* 593–606.

Crawford, M., & Marecek, J. (1989). Psychology constructs the female: 1968–1988. *Psychology of Women Quarterly, 13,* 147–166.

Fine, M. (1992). *Disruptive voices: The possibilities of feminist research.* Ann Arbor: University of Michigan Press.

Fonow, M. M., & Cook, J. A. (1991). *Beyond methodology: Feminist scholarship as lived research.* Bloomington: Indiana University Press.

Genero, N. P., Miller, J. B., Surrey, J., & Baldwin, L. M. (1992). Measuring perceived mutuality in close relationships: Validation of the Mutual Psychological Development Questionnaire. *Journal of Family Psychology, 6,* 36–48.

Gilbert, L. A. (1993). *Two careers/one family: The promise of gender equality.* Beverly Hills, CA: Sage.

Grossman, F. K., & Moore, R. P. (1994). Against the odds: Resiliency in an adult survivor of childhood sexual abuse. In C. Franz & A. Stewart (Eds.), *Women creating lives: Identities, resilience, and resistance* (pp. 71–82). Boulder, CO: Westview Press.

Haraway, D. (1988). Situated knowledges: The science question in feminism and the privilege of partial perspective. *Feminist Studies, 14,* 579–599.

Harding, S. (Ed.). (1987). *Feminism and methodology. Social science issues.* Bloomington: Indiana University Press.

Hawes, S. E. (1992, September). *Reflexivity and collaboration in the supervisory process: A role for feminist poststructural theories in the training of professional psychologists.* Paper presented at the meeting of the National Council of Schools in Professional Psychology, Las Vegas, NV.

Hyde, J. S. (1994). Can meta-analysis make feminist transformations in psychology? *Psychology of Women Quarterly, 18,* 451–462.

Hyde, J. S., Klein, M. H., Essex, M. J., & Clark, R. (1995). Maternity leave and women's mental health. *Psychology of Women Quarterly, 19,* 257–285.

Keller, E. F. (1985). *Reflections on gender and science.* New Haven, CT: Yale University Press.

Kleinman, S., & Kopp, M. A. (1993). *Emotions and fieldwork.* London: Sage.

Koss, M. P. (1985). The hidden rape victim: Personality, attitudinal, and situational characteristics. *Psychology of Women Quarterly, 9,* 193–212.

MacKinnon, C. (1979). *Sexual harassment of working women.* New Haven, CT: Yale University Press.

Marecek, J. (1995). Psychology and feminism. In A. Stewart & D. Stanton (Eds.), *Feminisms in the academy.* Ann Arbor: University of Michigan Press.

Marecek, J., & Hare-Mustin, R. T. (1991). A short history of the future: Feminism and clinical psychology. *Psychology of Women Quarterly, 15,* 521–536.

Morawski, J. (1990). Toward the unimagined: Feminism and epistemology in psychology. In R. T. Hare-Mustin & J. Marecek (Eds.), *Making a difference: Psychology and the construction of gender* (pp. 150–183). New Haven, CT: Yale University Press.

Morawski, J. (1994). *Practicing feminisms, reconstructing psychology: Notes on a liminal science.* Ann Arbor: University of Michigan Press.

Morawski, J., & Steele, R. (1991). The one or the other? Textual analysis of masculine power and feminist empowerment. *Theory & Psychology, 1,* 107–131.

Nicholson, L. J. (Ed.). (1990). *Feminism/postmodernism.* New York: Routledge.

Peplau, L. A., & Conrad, E. (1989). Beyond nonsexist research: The perils of feminist methods in psychology. *Psychology of Women Quarterly, 13,* 381–402.

Reinharz, S. (1992). *Feminist methods in social research.* New York: Oxford University Press.

Riger, S. (1992). Epistemological debates, feminist voices: Sciences, social values, and the study of women. *American Psychologist, 47,* 730–740.

Scarborough, E., & Furumoto, L. (1987). *Untold lives: The first generation of American women psychologists.* New York: University of Columbia Press

Sherif, C. (1979). Bias in psychology. In J. A. Sherman & E. T. Beck (Eds.), *The prism of sex: Essays in the sociology of knowledge* (pp. 93–133). Madison: University of Wisconsin Press.

Sommers, C. H. (1994). *Who stole feminism: How women have betrayed women.* New York: Simon & Schuster.

Stacey, J. (1988). Can there be a feminist ethnography? *Women's Studies International Forum, 11*(1), 21–27.

Stewart, A. (1994). Towards a feminist strategy for studying women's lives. In C. E. Franz & A. J. Stewart (Eds.), *Women creating lives: Identifies, resilience, and resistance* (pp. 11–35). Boulder, CO: Westview Press.

Wilkinson, S. (1994). Editorial note. *Feminism and Psychology, 4*, 499–500.

Wittig, M. A. (1985). Metatheoretical dilemmas in the psychology of gender. *American Psychologist, 40*, 800–811.

Worell, J. (1990). Feminist frameworks: Retrospect and prospect. *Psychology of Women Quarterly, 14*, 1–5.

Worell, J., & Etaugh, C. (1994). Transformations: Reconceptualizing theory and research with women [Special Issue]. *Psychology of Women Quarterly, 18*(4).

Zinn, M. B. (1979). Field research in minority communities: Ethical, methodological, and political observations by an insider. *Social Problems, 27*, 209–219.

6

FEMINIST CURRICULUM DEVELOPMENT: PRINCIPLES AND RESOURCES

JEAN LAU CHIN AND NANCY FELIPE RUSSO

WITH JILL BLOOM, DIANE FELICIO, MARGARET MADDEN,
CAROLYN ZERBE ENNS, ELOISE STIGLITZ,
PATRICIA ROZÉE, AND NICOLE SIMI

How do we educate and train women and men in psychology so that they possess the knowledge, skills, and sensitivity to generate and apply feminist principles in their work? Members of the curriculum working group concurred that curriculum design should be based on feminist principles and values and should be responsive to women's diverse identities and sociocultural contexts. We deemed it more important to identify key principles for feminist curriculum development rather than attempt to define specific feminist content for the following reasons: (a) The lives and circumstances of women are ever changing, which means that the context of knowledge about women continues to change; (b) it is important to respect

We thank Ria Hermann-Currie, Stephanie Wall, and Linda Hines for their assistance in preparing the text. Allen Meyer provided helpful feedback.

diversity of perspectives and to recognize differential emphases among feminists about core knowledge areas; and (c) a focus on principles maintains a respect for academic freedom necessary to effect transformation toward a more inclusive curriculum.

This chapter delineates eight key principles for feminist curriculum development identified by the curriculum working group and discusses how they can be integrated into the curriculum at the high school, graduate, and postgraduate levels. We begin, however, by discussing the group itself—our perspectives and processes.

FEMINIST PROCESS AND GROUP OBJECTIVES

The multiple perspectives represented in the group were a great strength in the discussions. Our professional training encompassed subfields of clinical, counseling, experimental, developmental, school, and social psychology and psychoanalysis. Members of the group worked in a variety of settings, ranging from private practice and community mental health centers to colleges and universities. Group members had also worked as consultants, deans, faculty members policy advocates, administrators, program directors, researchers, and therapists. From the beginning we sought to model a feminist process. The group was small enough for all voices to be heard in discussion, and for most of the time the group functioned as a whole. We divided into smaller groups to discuss actions to be taken at different educational levels when time pressure on the last day required speeding up the process. These discussions were brought back to the larger group. Graduate student Nicole Simi took notes and provided daily summaries of the discussions.

The principles and issues identified in this chapter reflect the consensus of the full group. We find it interesting that differences in points of view were relatively easy to incorporate into the overarching feminist principles that emerged from the group's discussions. In writing this chapter, we elaborate on these principles by providing more specific examples and references to curriculum resources available in the field. We chose to define feminist scholarship and practice broadly and sketched out a feminist process for curriculum development important in the training of feminist professional psychologists. In keeping with a principle of inclusiveness, the goals of a feminist curriculum should promote applications of psychology in various professional roles, including administrator, educator, expert witness, forensics specialist, policy advocate, researcher, teacher, and therapist. Feminist process is inclusive of all voices, values diversity, and acknowledges power dynamics inherent in teacher–student relationships. It requires integrating research, teaching, and practice. Research is informed by the insights of practitioners and vice versa; theories and models from multiple disciplines and perspectives guide the understanding of specific individuals.

After defining feminist process and identifying the principles of feminist development outlined below, we addressed the following question: What are the essential components of an inclusive feminist curriculum at each level of education: high school, college, graduate, and postgraduate? The principles can be used to guide curriculum transformation at all levels of educational experience. Given our current state of the art, feminist curriculum development requires anticipating resistance to change and recognizing the need for political action to effect change. The process for developing a curriculum from a feminist perspective should be a dynamic one, that is, it should change in response to the context, not simply making "add-ons" to earlier developments.

The development of a feminist curriculum requires a comprehensive approach that involves all aspects of the educational experience, including training experiences, educational content, teaching processes, and classroom climate. Questions of content should be integrated with questions about pedagogy and supervision and should have a basis in feminist research and theory. A feminist curriculum establishes a basis for feminist action; it should raise consciousness and be transformative. Curriculum transformation is not complete until we incorporate issues of diversity (including racial and ethnic differences and the range of sexualities), the influence of male-dominant societies, and social class inequalities into definitions of feminist scholarship and competent practice. Curriculum transformation is also not complete until women are full participants in all aspects of the education and training process, including policy-making roles, administrative functions, training directors, accreditation, licensing, and regulatory bodies.

We illustrate below how these key principles can be applied to curriculum development at the high school, undergraduate, graduate, and postgraduate levels and during supervision. Because applications of feminist principles can be adapted to a wide variety of settings and content areas, we did not attempt to specify an ideal curriculum or particular program of courses. Instead, the discussion focused on resources and models for curriculum transformation at these different levels and recommendations for promoting such transformations in psychology.

In discussing the key principles, it became very difficult to avoid issues of pedagogy, especially when discussing relevant skills. Mindful of the boundaries of our task, however, we left discussions of pedagogy to the working group charged with these issues (see chapter 7, "Preaching What We Practice: Principles and Strategies of Feminist Pedagogy"; see also Enns, 1993a).

CORE FEMINIST PRINCIPLES

We identified eight principles that constitute a framework for developing and evaluating a feminist curriculum. These principles reflect a web of assumptions underlying values, which underlie the development of knowledge (i.e., what we know) and aid the acquisition of skills (i.e., how we practice). These principles inform curriculum development rather than define curriculum content. They elicit a feminist process of thoughtful examination rather than a blueprint of what people should teach. The eight principles are not exhaustive of those important to curriculum development; rather, they reflect a feminist perspective and commitment to a dynamic process of continuing self-examination. The principles are also not mutually exclusive; they interact and overlap. Although some skills may be more critical to certain principles over others, most cut across principles. That is, critical thinking skills, verbal and nonverbal communication, group process, active listening, and quantitative and qualitative research methods all contribute in multiple ways to effective feminist practice.

Principle 1. Diversity

Assumption

Each person is located within a sociocultural context. Differences among individuals' realities, perspectives, and worldviews are based on cultural, ethnic, racial, and other dimensions of individuality. Diversity is broadly defined to encompass a great variety of social categories beyond race and ethnicity (Comas-Díaz, 1991; Reid & Comas-Díaz, 1990), such as ablebodiedness (Fine & Asch, 1988), age (Cavallaro, 1991; Datan, 1989; Rodeheaver & Datan, 1988), class (Belle, 1990; Bramel & Friend, 1981), and sexual orientation (Boston Lesbian Psychologies Collective, 1987; L. S. Brown, 1989, 1992; Wilkinson & Kitzinger, 1993).

Value

Given the great variety of individuals and cultures, the recognition and value of diversity are key to a feminist curriculum. We value multiple perspectives of reality over dichotomous ones. The interacting influences of gender, ethnicity, race, class, sexuality, and ablebodiedness affect the way we view the world.

Curriculum Content

Theories chosen for a feminist curriculum must come from a standpoint of equality and be multicultural. They should enable us to conceptualize human behavior and psychology not only through our own eyes but also through the eyes of those who differ from ourselves in many ways.

These theories should link psychology with the historical, sociocultural, and political contexts of which our discipline is a part and reflect how we think and see the world. Although many values are commonly held across cultures, communities, and individuals, the priority level attributed to these values may differ; our theories should not automatically privilege one set of values over another.

Many existing theories express one view of the world, which is often presented as "correct" and universal. The quest for a monolithic theory of human behavior, however, can result in marginalizing and devaluing those theories that encompass diverse and multiple perspectives. A broad range of theories as well as theories of diversity are essential to the development of a feminist curriculum if we are to incorporate frameworks in which all voices are heard (e.g., Landrine, 1995). Theories of acculturation, cross-cultural communication, and stress and coping within a feminist curriculum also provide models for conceptualizing differences in experience, worldviews, and group perspectives (see Enns, 1994, for a discussion of teaching about the cultural relativism of psychological constructs).

Several theories exemplify such models. Comas-Díaz and Greene (1994) claimed that the diversity among women of color creates a tension between what connects them and what separates them. Chin, De La Cancela, and Jenkins (1994) defined *diversity* as an openness to new experiences and ideas and argued that understanding it requires an authentic exploration of personal and reference group histories. Gender, race, ethnicity, and social class are thus embedded in society in general and psychotherapy in particular. This dialectic between personal and reference group histories should influence the inclusion of diversity issues throughout clinical practice and the development of feminist curricula. Tyler, Sussewell, and Williams-McCoy (1985) used an ethnic validity model that emphasizes a variety of ways of living, each of which offers strengths and limitations; some are convergent (i.e., valid across cultural contexts), some are divergent (i.e., different), and some are in conflict. These different ethnic worldviews significantly influence cross-ethnic patterns of interaction and should receive particular attention in formulation of theoretical and practical approaches.

Skills Required for Feminist Practice

Development of multicultural competence involves acquisition of a variety of skills (e.g., LaFromboise & Rowe, 1983). Activities that emphasize role taking, cross-cultural differences, and multiple perspectives can help individuals appreciate differences between groups and cultures in their rules and meanings. Challenging students to ask the unanswered questions and to hear all voices promotes a feminist perspective. We should develop critical thinking and empathic skills that enable individuals to take multiple perspectives and appreciate the realities of their students, clients, research participants, and colleagues who differ in culture, ethnicity, race, social class, gender, sexual orientation, age, and physical abilities. Learning more than one language can play an important role in comprehending how different people may hold different concepts about similar phenomena. We should also teach how to be positive and express support to other women in multiple contexts. If we recognize that there are men who hate women and who trivialize women's experiences because those experiences are different from their own, we should make explicit valuing women's perspectives as a feminist assumption. Narratives that affirm women's roles and identities in various contexts and teach behaviors that affirm women-centered values and experiences can play an important role in developing the interpersonal and cross-cultural sensitivity needed for practitioners to value diversity.

Principle 2. Egalitarianism and Empowerment

Assumption

One's perspective is a function of her or his position in the sociocultural structure from which one's degree and type of power (or oppression) emanates.

Value

Given the historical oppression and disempowerment of women, we strive for egalitarianism and empowerment of women.

Curriculum Content

We need new ways to think about power and to disentangle the concepts of mastery, masculinity, and domination. We should recognize boundaries for power. If we recognize and are conscious of differentials of power, privilege, and position, we can make explicit the impact of such differentials within faculty–student relationships, classroom settings and policies, selection of academic content, and the ways in which values and goals are defined and communicated. Concepts of power, privilege, and entitlement, as well as stereotyping, prejudice, discrimination, tokenism, and oppression, must be articulated and their dynamics and applications in various contexts understood. In heterosexual relationships, the new scholarship on male violence against women, including physical and sexual abuse, rape, battering, and sexual harassment, is particularly important here because such behavior plays a central role in maintaining power differentials between women and men (for a summary of this literature, see Koss et al., 1994).

Powerlessness and devaluation are linked. Traditionally feminine values, roles, and personal attributes have been devalued; an affirmative use of women-oriented perspectives can be used to challenge myths about differences that have been construed as negative (e.g., Hyde, 1994). Exposure to positive female role models and supportive mentoring relationships are key to educating and training for empowerment (see Gilbert & Rossman, 1992, for a discussion of these issues). Groups designed to build self-esteem through raising consciousness and fostering assertiveness skills can also be used to counter effects of devaluation (Enns, 1992). The use of life story narratives or myths can take advantage of styles of communication that are congruent with women-centered values and concerns. In particular, the use of life story narratives to teach complex or technological skills may empower students to overcome the legacy of stereotyping and devaluation that persists in fields traditionally closed to women and ethnic minorities.

Although egalitarianism and empowerment are key concepts in any feminist curriculum, we recognize the inherent hierarchy of faculty and supervisors vis-à-vis students within the educational context. The assumption of unequal power in the faculty–student and supervisor–supervisee relationship is reflected in the American Psychological Association's (1992) ethical guidelines; all parties, students and faculty, should know these guidelines and their underlying rationale. Furthermore, it should be recognized that self-disclosure with supervisees, patients, and students by supervisors, therapists, and faculty, even when well-intentioned, can be inappropriate and disempowering. For example, for students or clients who value respect for elders and expect dignified or professional behavior from them, culturally inappropriate personal disclosures from people in authority (teachers, therapists) can be upsetting and disruptive to learning and therapeutic processes. If such self-disclosure occurs in a large classroom setting where there is no opportunity to discuss the student's emotional response to the personal information, the learning process may be undermined.

Skills Required for Feminist Practice

Women need empowering skills because they have been oppressed for centuries. Antidomination training, which helps women identify oppressive tactics and respond effectively to them, should be explicit (L. S. Brown, 1993). All psychologists should learn to apply their skills without mystifying them so that students, clients, and research participants can become active collaborators in the processes of education, therapy, and inquiry. Thus, arcane jargon should be avoided or explained. Rationales and reasoning processes should be presented along with conclusions. Labeling a source as "expert" is not a substitute for laying out the evidence for an argument. Critical skills for promoting women's empowerment include (a) oral and written communication skills, which enable women to articulate their concerns and help others understand and empathize with their points of view; (b) leadership, group process, and organizational skills, including skills that enable women and men to identify and intervene in chilly or hostile climates and resolve disputes; and (c) the ability to use information technology to access Internet resources, which is an increasingly important source of information and influence to promote collective action. Classroom discussions about rape, violence, and other aspects of discrimination and oppression can produce intense personal reactions ranging from "paralyzing fury" (Westkott, 1983) to tears and depression (Register, 1979, cited in Adler, 1984); thus, teachers should be equipped to establish supportive learning environments and mechanisms for referring students who need more than the level of support and counseling appropriate to the teaching role (Adler, 1984). Finally, skills to promote empowerment are important, but teachers should not lose sight of cultural differences that may differentially define skills such as assertiveness training (Wood & Mallinckrodt, 1990).

Principle 3. Self-determination

Assumption

Women are active agents, not passive victims. We both shape and reflect our social context in an interactive process as we try to select the best of choices open to us.

Value

We recognize the value of self-determination, and we respect diversity in the behaviors and coping strategies that women use to adapt to and deal with their environments. Women may behave differently in coping with life experiences depending on such factors as their beliefs, values, and options. A focus of feminist practice thus becomes one of enhancing women's ability for self-determination. Although this principle is closely related to that of empowerment, the emphasis of self-determination is on changes within the person rather than on the environmental context. It also recognizes that women may have their own ideas about what is empowering and what is not.

Curriculum Content

Feminist practitioners should have the knowledge and skills to help each woman clarify her own notions of empowerment, consistent with the value of self-determination. Instead of viewing women as passive victims of their environments, this principle acknowledges women's behavior as interactive and recognizes women's capacity as an active agent. Consequently, the lens for change is on both the person and the situation, with efforts directed toward teaching women how to modify or ameliorate the effects of unhealthy settings. However, women may develop maladaptive coping strategies as a result of the dynamics of their powerlessness. This knowledge is needed to avoid blaming or pathologizing women and other groups for how they have learned to survive in environments with limited options and discriminatory practices. Lectures, textbooks, and other pedagogical materials should challenge stereotyped thinking of women as passive and pathology-ridden; they should be refocused to identify sources of strength and effectiveness amid disempowering situations. Educational knowledge should include helping women students and clients to identify and create multiple options. Curriculum content that provides opportunities for students to set their own learning goals and direct their learning activities and experiences promotes this principle.

Skills Required for Feminist Practice

Experiences that enhance decision-making skills can help women optimize their choices. Leadership and organizational skills to enable organizing people for collective action are particularly critical for equipping women to take action and create new options in their environments. Role-playing, communication, and intercultural skills can facilitate interaction between individuals from differing contexts so that their options can be understood. Feminist practitioners need therapeutic techniques to promote insight and coping with relationships and environments conducive to powerlessness and stress. Such techniques must be combined with teaching women the skills that enable them to change or leave unhealthy environments.

Principle 4. Complexity

Assumption

Reality is complex. Dichotomous thinking is both ineffective and unrealistic. Providing effective representations of human behavior in context requires conceptions that are multidimensional, interactive, and inclusive of differences.

Value

We value understanding complexity and seek to develop representations of human behavior that reflect it. Valuing complexity means that differences across individuals are not automatically equated with deviance. Individual, cultural, and other variations are framed from a positive view.

Curriculum Content

Models and methods must be inclusive, encompassing complexity and difference among and within individuals (e.g., L. S. Brown & Root, 1990). Understanding the complexity of human behavior has affective as well as cognitive implications. We understand the emotional attraction of a focus on our commonalities with others. After all, it creates soothing bonds between us. In contrast, dealing with the complexity of human behavior and the differences it creates can invoke anxiety, threat, resistance, and rejection. The use of normative models often seeks to ignore or minimize differences. For example, culture- and gender-related behaviors are often viewed as deviant or pathological when compared against majority group- or male-dominant norms. Trait theories exemplify such models; women or members of ethnic groups are defined as deficient or deviant because they possess more or less of a trait defined as normal relative to the dominant group.

New models of human behavior in context are needed that help to reframe the interpretation of differences and commonalities from the perspectives of our students, clients, and research participants (i.e., nondominant groups). Models that recognize the complexity of reality, including cultural differences, promote change and innovation. The positive benefits of this approach are many, as suggested by L. S. Brown (1994), Comas-Díaz and Greene (1994), and Worell and Remer (1992). Chin's (1994) framework for psychology is based on difference and posits that our underlying assumptive frameworks influence the ways in which we view human behavior and practice psychotherapy. These assumptions result in "troublesome concepts" that bias our thinking and practice toward a "mainstream" and limited perspective as opposed to ones that promote competence in working with diverse populations.

Skills Required for Feminist Practice

Teaching complex models that encompass difference requires skills for dealing with the anxiety and resistance that such models elicit. Practitioners and teachers must be able to go beyond simply naming biases and know how to establish a positive context for analyzing how gender shapes human experience and how the concept of gender varies across social categories of ethnicity, sexuality, and class (e.g., Enns, 1993b). Skills in promoting cooperative learning, safety, respectful debate, and conflict resolution are needed to effectively apply this principle (e.g., Cannon, 1990; Tatum, 1992; also see chapter 7 in this volume). Developing and testing complex models of knowledge also require complex methods. Quantitative versus qualitative research methods and deductive versus inductive reasoning skills exemplify methods valuing different points of view, which have become coupled with gender and characterized as masculine versus feminine thinking. A dichotomous social construction of gender that equates masculinity with rationality and femininity with emotionality is destructive to both men and women because it stifles growth, complexity, and diversity in human development.

Principle 5. Connection

Assumption

Connection is the basis for human interaction. It is important to humans, particularly those who are oppressed, as a survival mechanism.

Value

Collaboration and connection are important to feminist thinking and to a feminist curriculum; they should be the basis for feminist action. We value a collaborative, affirming, and positive approach that reclaims women's history (i.e., connects us with the past) and reflects feminist values.

Curriculum Content

Research and theory that examine women and the relationships they form have a central place in a feminist curriculum. Particular attention must be paid to the contexts that support or undermine these relationships, that is, issues of power, competency criteria, and status within cross-gender relationships.

Skills Required for Feminist Practice

Methods that encourage students to collaborate with and respect their fellow students promote this principle (see chapter 7). Interpersonal skills such as listening, communicating, and empathizing also promote this principle. The learning process can be a collaborative one through an emphasis on experiential learning activities. Explicit training in how to prevent or interrupt sexual, racial, or any other forms of harassment is also essential for feminist practitioners (see Van Nostrand, 1993, on training for gender-responsible leadership).

Principle 6. Social Action

Assumption

Given current power inequalities and the social structures that reinforce them, women's status will not improve without intervention.

Value

Social action and change are essential if we are to evolve into an egalitarian society. Feminist psychologists are proactive and visionary in challenging the existing status quo.

Curriculum Content

Students and faculty should be able to view themselves as change agents in a larger social system that has historically disempowered women, made them unequal, and distorted their realities. A mandate to challenge the status quo must persist until all voices are heard and inequities addressed. In addition to acquiring knowledge about power dynamics and notions of equality (Principle 2), learning effective strategies for promoting social change is important to a feminist curriculum. This includes using women as role models and as agents of social change to promote a positive reframing of women as competent and empowered.

Skills Required for Feminist Practice

Leadership and community-organizing skills are more effective than individual solutions to address problems that stem from structural and social inequalities. Internship and field experiences that expose students to communities, social issues, and public policy are important to train practitioners and researchers to observe and appropriately diagnose need. Strategies for community empowerment are important to learn how to promote social change with an eye toward egalitarianism.

Principle 7. Self-reflection

Assumption

The process of self-reflection occurs at multiple levels: within a personal domain, within psychology, and within the feminist movement. This process is continuous and is informed by feminist principles. Self-reflection enables us to evaluate our values, ethics, and biases.

Value

An active and self-reflective process is basic to feminist principles. This includes the ability to suspend and critique our own point of view and to consider other points of view.

Curriculum Content

Self-reflection is a process that enables us to value humility, to be aware of our fallibility, and to avoid arrogance or dogmatism about our own biases. As new theories emerge and develop, we need to be aware of how our previous conceptions may limit our understanding of new circumstances. Although our discipline teaches us to critique and evaluate others, we are sometimes more protective and less critical of ourselves. A constant process of self-reflection is essential to a dynamic process of feminist thinking.

When we accept that all human behavior is rooted within historical, sociocultural, and personal contexts, we recognize that all theories similarly are rooted in such contexts and that *objective* does not mean *value-free*. Therefore, when designing and conducting research, developing lesson plans for our courses, or carrying out other professional activities, we must reflect on how our values and perspectives influence our understanding and thinking and how our views may differ from those of others. Knowledge of feminist ethics is particularly important for individuals who are confronted with conflicts of interest—for example, when in positions of power, when self-interests can dominate, or when viewed as an expert (Hall & Greene, 1994; Lerman, 1994; Porter & Yahne, 1994). The ability to make self-referrals, apply diagnostic labels, or influence research funds are some examples. Ethics should prevail when funding sources such as pharmaceutical or tobacco companies that use funds to maintain power inequities or distort unwanted research results.

Skills Required for Feminist Practice

Critical thinking, decision-making, and role-taking skills are important for identifying our personal biases, predicting the consequences of our actions, and evaluating the impact of our decisions. Activities that enable students to model appropriate self-disclosure about personal biases can also promote self-reflection and clarification of values.

Principle 8. Integrative Perspectives

Assumption

Human behavior, including actions, emotions, and cognitions, is a function of multiple factors in interaction—physiological, biological, psychological, sociocultural, spiritual, and situational.

Value

We value approaches that integrate perspectives from many fields of knowledge (including psychology's subfields) over those that isolate or emphasize any one of them. Integrating interdisciplinary ways of thinking about human behavior is crucial.

Curriculum Content

Any single disciplinary perspective considers and measures limited dimensions of human behavior. Principle 8 recognizes the interrelatedness of multiple perspectives about human behavior and the dangers of conceptualizations that rely on any single perspective. For example, a theory that views causation from a biological perspective may view field-based, community research as irrelevant for understanding why humans act, feel, or think as they do; this conceptualization can diminish the importance of social issues, such as violence, racism, and sexism. As a result, interventions for social problems may be viewed as futile, and programs aimed at changing unhealthy environments may be undermined.

Skills Required for Feminist Practice

Skills in both quantitative and qualitative methods are essential for developing a multimodal approach to understanding human behavior. The development of more sophisticated instruments for measuring human experience should not be bounded by our limited conceptualizations of that experience. Disciplinary bias, cultural values, personal histories, and environmental context influence our ability to conceptualize human experience. Thus, the development of collaborative research across disciplines, and academic-community partnerships between academe and the people living these experiences, can help to promote breadth, diversity, and complexity in our perspectives. The use of interactive models and methods over those that focus on factors in isolation promotes this feminist principle. For example, the common polarization of rationality versus emotions is often used to characterize the differences between male and female; yet, it is simplistic and ignores the interrelationship between cognition and emotion for all human beings (stress and coping models provide one example of approaches that focus on this interrelationship; Lazarus & Folkman, 1984).

APPLICATIONS: CURRICULUM DEVELOPMENT

Developing a comprehensive curriculum on the basis of the eight feminist principles requires a developmental perspective that considers values, knowledge, and skills to be developed at the high school, college, graduate, and postgraduate levels within and across disciplines. What happens at each level of academic training should build on the previous one. At each level, we should ask how a feminist perspective changes both the goals and the strategies of education and what forms of knowledge should be acquired and created. To be effective, the process for curriculum development itself must reflect these principles. The process should be self-critical, that is, it should continuously reflect on how biases influence thoughts and actions. By applying these principles, a feminist knowledge base can be identified and a curriculum can be designed to include as inherent features such as diversity, empowerment, self-determination, complexity, connection, social action, self-reflection, and integration of multiple perspectives.

The specific components of an inclusive feminist curriculum (i.e., the mix of courses and field experiences) will differ depending on local, state, and regional factors, including funding resources available in specific institutional contexts. Making academic institutions effective requires understanding how students from diverse social, economic, and cultural backgrounds actually experience their educational context. With this understanding, we can develop a repertoire of innovative teaching methods and materials responsive to variations in student values, norms, and learning styles (see Adams, 1992). General curriculum considerations for different academic levels are identified below, followed by an example of application of the principles across disciplines.

High School

In general, requirements for training feminist practitioners at this level do not differ greatly from those of other levels; rather, the emphasis is on promoting equity within the institution. Some researchers (Klein, 1985; Sadker, Sadker, & Klein, 1991) discussed strategies for achieving equity within elementary and secondary school education. At this level, basic feminist principles and the vocabulary needed to express them from a variety of disciplines (e.g., biology, English, mathematics, and social sciences) are particularly important because they form the foundation for later learning. The increasing importance of a global economy, modern technology, and women in various roles suggests that foreign language and computer courses also are important for building an early foundation for later learning. Emotional and interpersonal issues should be addressed, emphasizing confidence building and assertiveness training for female adolescents. Data suggest that they experience "silencing" during this developmental period, which may undermine their ability to protect themselves at a time when they are at risk for date rape and other forms of dating violence (L. M. Brown & Gilligan, 1992; Fine & Gordon, 1991; Koss, Heise, & Russo, 1994).

At the high school level, it is important to integrate new scholarship on women into psychology courses and to increase the number of those courses. In particular, students should be exposed to feminist perspectives and feminist role models. There should be an emphasis on piquing interest in gender issues and avoiding stereotypic thinking or prejudicial behaviors that preclude future receptiveness to learning diverse and multiple perspectives.

Undergraduate

At the undergraduate level, a broad-based exposure to existing theories on feminism would be important while enabling students to maintain a critical posture in evaluating gender and other biases within theories. We can expose students to methods of critique and intervention derived from feminist theories. Diversity issues should be integrated into all courses. There should be a minimum of two separate courses on the psychology of women. One course would be at the lower division level for 2- or 4-year colleges or institutions. Such a course would have no prerequisites, and it would be open to students majoring in any discipline. This course would be designed to introduce students to the psychology of women, stimulate their interest in feminism, and equip them with critical feminist skills necessary to evaluate information for various forms of bias that they encounter in college, the media, and elsewhere. The second course would be an upper division senior seminar for feminist or psychology majors, and it would focus on the development and application of feminist theory and research in psychology. Both courses would include discussions of feminist theory and content and would integrate feminist epistemologies in the exploration of research methods (e.g., Ewick, 1994).

In keeping with the principle of self-determination, students at the undergraduate level would also be encouraged to use feminist principles to design independent study projects. The undergraduate experience would also include internships and field experiences whose purpose is to expose students to women's issues within life settings, such as battered women's shelters, homeless shelters, and rape crisis hotlines. Honors psychology students could design projects to test aspects of feminist theory. Students could obtain a minor in women's studies, which should be inclusive of diverse populations (e.g., women of color) and diverse theories. To promote the integration of perspectives, psychology programs should encourage electives in anthropology, biology, sociology, history, and ethnic studies.

Graduate

At the graduate level, preparation toward professional careers becomes a specific educational goal. Students should master methods of intervention, diagnosis, and scientific inquiry congruent with feminist principles and begin their own original contributions to knowledge. Critical analysis of biases within existing theory and practice that undermine inclusivity and empowerment of any one segment of the population is a key element of graduate education in psychology. Emphasis on developing research interests and areas of expertise while remaining open to a variety of paradigms is also critical. Hoshmand (1989) provided such a model; it is applicable to counseling psychology and has insights applicable to other subfields. Awareness of feminist practice outside one's institution and local area should be encouraged through mentoring experiences and activities that promote participation in state, regional, and national organizations involving women and feminist thinking.

Postgraduate

At the postgraduate level, the student is assumed to have learned feminist principles and to have acquired the basic knowledge, concepts, and methods to act on those values. Training at this level should emphasize specialization, retraining, or advanced training. Scholarship and research should be more intensive and address current feminist concerns. Retraining may be synonymous with relearning those frameworks inconsistent with feminist principles. Experiential learning continues to be important and should emphasize issues that bias or impair the ability of the feminist practitioner to achieve scholarship and practice consistent with feminist principles (see chapter 10).

Supervision

Supervision is viewed as an essential part of a feminist curriculum at all academic levels. Feminist principles emphasize egalitarianism, but the supervisor–supervisee relationship is inherently unequal. Consequently, although the supervision process is important in offering potential feminist role models, it can also be abused because of inherent power dynamics. Whereas supervision often results in revealing one's own personal experience vis-à-vis a client, one should distinguish between appropriate and inappropriate self-disclosure on the part of both supervisor and supervisee.

Because supervision is also a critical process of examination, it often evokes issues of self-worth. Open, honest, and direct communication is important to validate all voices; both supervisor and supervisee should respect different styles of self-disclosure and communication across different racial–ethnic, gender, and other groups. From a feminist perspective, *supervising* means reinforcing appropriate boundaries while promoting self-examination, avoiding dogmatic thinking or dualistic positions, and recognizing inherent biases within a power relationship (see chapter 8).

CURRICULUM DEVELOPMENT ACROSS DISCIPLINES

The usefulness and flexibility of the eight basic principles for guiding curriculum development across disciplines was demonstrated by the Education and Training Working Group[1] in developing its final research agenda for the conference Psychosocial and Behavioral Factors in Women's Health: An Agenda for the 21st Century. The goal of the conference report, *Research Agenda for Psychosocial and Behavioral Factors in Women's Health* (American Psychological Association, 1996), was to guide researchers, practitioners, and policy makers into the 21st century by setting out a women's agenda for research, health services, education and training, and public policy. Sandra Tangri adapted these principles for the report of the Education and Training Working Group, which developed the education and training agenda section of the conference report. The Appendix summarizes how the eight values represented in the feminist principles were applied to the training of health professionals at all levels, from undergraduate to postdoctoral. Space limitations preclude discussion of the assumptions, values, knowledge, and skills involved in applying this knowledge across the health professions, however. This application of the eight feminist principles to articulate values for curriculum development within the health professions is one example of how the principles can be applied across disciplines.

RESOURCES

Efforts to transform the curriculum in psychology to include feminist thinking reflect the impact of the second wave of the women's movement that emerged in the 1970s. Because existing curricula had not adequately captured the knowledge, values, and experiences of all segments of the population (including the experiences of women), concerted efforts were made to critique omissions and distortions of theories and methods across the disciplines (McMillen, 1987). Curriculum transformation was given a substantial boost during the 1980s when the federal government and private foundations funded innovative curriculum projects at a variety of academic institutions across the United States.

Women of color became an active part of the feminist movement through curriculum development within both women's studies and ethnic studies programs during this period. Women of color strongly criticized feminism as a White, middle-class endeavor that excluded segments of women and was, therefore, inconsistent with its own principles (e.g., Dill, 1983; Hull, Scott, & Smith, 1982). This movement dovetailed with the growing numbers of minorities both within the profession and within U. S. society; society became more concerned with issues of diversity. Funding sources began to emphasize diversity as an objective for curriculum

---

[1]The working group was led by Nancy Felipe Russo and included Leona Aiken, Joan C. Chrisler, Alice Dan, Karen Ericksen, Rosalie Sagraves, Sandra S. Tangri, Donna M. Waechter, and Nancy Fugates Woods.

projects. Consequently, numerous projects emphasized diversity, provided models, and identified specific "dos and don'ts" for transforming the curriculum and the disciplines to be more inclusive (Bauer & Arenas, 1995; Dinnerstein, O'Donnell, & MacCorquodale, n.d.; Fowlkes & McClure, 1984; Franzosa & Mazza, 1984; Fritsche, 1984; McIntosh, 1990; Paludi & Steuernagel, 1990; Schmitz, 1985; Schuster & Van Dyne, 1985; Spanier, Bloom, & Boroviak, 1984; Spender, 1981). Some of this work specifically focuses on the sciences (Barr & Birke, 1994; Bleier, 1988; Rosser, 1986, 1990) and goes beyond defining diversity solely in terms of ancestry (e.g., Cruikshank, 1982; Crumpacker & Vander Haegen, 1984; Friedenfels, 1992).

Current discussions continue to focus on development of an inclusive curriculum that can conceptualize differences among women (Bauer & Arenas, 1995; Border & Chism, 1992; Butler & Walter, 1991; Higgenbotham, 1990; Timberlake, Cannon, Guy, & Higginbotham, 1988, 1990). Although feminist activity in psychology began almost as long ago as the field itself (O'Connell & Russo, 1991), the nature and form of that feminist activity have reflected the larger social context of which psychology is a part (Russo, 1988; Russo & Dabul, 1994). Consequently, the issues and thinking have shifted in consonance with current concerns of the field and of society (e.g., women's roles, violence). The chapters in this volume represent the cumulative efforts of nearly three decades of concerted thought, discussion, and debate that have generated a new body of feminist scholarship on women in psychology (see also Denmark & Paludi, 1993). Although we have yet fully to implement feminist ideals (Fine & Gordon, 1991; Reid, 1991; Reid & Kelly, 1994), there is clearly a consensus on the value of diversity as a standard for education, theory, research, and practice in feminist psychology.

Curriculum transformation to implement feminist principles and achieve feminist ideals requires revision of old courses and the development of new ones. Toward this end, curriculum projects have focused on developing materials to evaluate psychology courses (Kimmel, 1991, 1992; Russo & Malovich, 1982) and textbooks (Birk et al., 1974; A. Brown, Goodwin, Hall, & Jackson-Lowman, 1985; Campbell & Schram, 1995; Chun, 1975; Gray, 1977; Harris & Lightner, 1980; Percival, 1984; Pollis, 1986). Collections of course syllabi, bibliographies, and summaries of resources provide a wealth of ideas and examples that can be adapted in designing a feminist curriculum (e.g., Bronstein & Quina, 1988; Chrisler, Levin, & Koster-Lossack, 1992; Committee on Women in Psychology, n.d.; Crawford & Marecek, 1989; Denmark, 1982, 1986; Furumoto, 1984; Golub & Freedman, 1987; Hoffnung, 1984; Paludi, 1990; Sanchez, 1994; Task Force on Representation in the Curriculum, 1995; Walsh, 1986). However, the rapidly advancing nature of our society and technology quickly makes obsolete those areas we now consider to be so current. Therefore, curriculum projects devoted to putting course syllabi electronically on-line will contribute to ready accessibility and rapid update. The Internet provides a wide medium of information exchange; it makes available interdisciplinary discussion lists related to teaching, research, and action issues involving women (Glazier, 1994), and many on-line databases may be helpful to curriculum transformation efforts (Atkinson & Hudson, 1990).

The National Center for Curriculum Transformation Resources on Women, part of the Institute for Teaching and Research on Women of Towson State University, is a centralized source of curriculum transformation across the disciplines, including that of psychology (e.g., Madden & Russo, 1997). Resources collected at the center and catalogued for paper and computer access include analyses of central issues in curriculum transformation work; bibliographies; model projects; lists of prior projects and consultants; revised syllabi; disciplinary critiques and contributions; and manuals on how to start projects, locate funding, evaluate projects, and deal with resistance.

CONCLUSIONS

In conclusion, curriculum transformation is an ongoing, dynamic process. The curriculum working group identified eight feminist principles core to informing a process of change to be applied over a wide variety of settings and educational levels. The group offered five recommendations for curriculum transformation:

1. Raise consciousness among faculty and students to feminist issues.
2. Redesign curricula to incorporate knowledge of feminist scholarship for faculty, students, and supervisors at the high school, undergraduate, graduate, and postgraduate levels.
3. Change accreditation standards to include feminist principles (accreditation standards for psychology doctoral training programs are only a small part of accreditation activity of the nation's colleges and universities).
4. Provide incentives, awards, and rewards for feminist scholarship at local, regional, and national levels.
5. Form a Curriculum Transformation Task Force through the American Psychological Association's Division of the Psychology of Women (Division 35) to organize a clearinghouse for the dissemination of feminist curriculum materials within psychology and across disciplines.
6. Create instruments to evaluate outcomes of feminist curricula.

Division 35's Task Force on Representation in the Curriculum[2] was subsequently established, and it continues to work on these issues. One of its first projects was development of a pamphlet, *Including Diverse Women in the Undergraduate Curriculum: Reasons and Resources* (Task Force, 1995).

This work is part of an ongoing process. If curricula are to be transformed to include a feminist perspective, we should expect resistance to change and recognize that vigilance is the price of success. Implementation plans should include strategies for dealing with resistance (particularly on the part of individuals with decision-making power in educational institutions) and measuring competence. New curriculum materials reflecting a feminist perspective are needed, from traditional forms of lectures, textbooks, and lab manuals, to hi-tech forms of videos, films, computer-assisted instruction, and electronic-classroom bulletin boards. With a clear understanding of our assumptions and values and a commitment to feminist principles and to each other, we can progress toward our goal of a vibrant psychology that is inclusive of all women, whatever their dimensions of difference.

---

[2]The Division 35 Task Force on Representation in the Curriculum is co-chaired by Margaret Madden and Hazel Spears and includes Joan Chrisler, Diane Felicio, Ellen Kimmel, Agnes O'Connell, and Karen Wyche.

APPENDIX
GUIDING PRINCIPLES FOR THE EDUCATION AND TRAINING
OF HEALTH CARE PROFESSIONALS: AN APPLICATION OF
FEMINIST PRINCIPLES OF CURRICULUM DEVELOPMENT

1. Training health professionals to recognize and value diversity is of paramount importance to ensure the quality of health care.
    Institutions that offer health education should actively strengthen the diversity of their curriculum, student bodies, faculty, administration, and governing bodies.
2. Health professionals should be taught to value egalitarianism and collaboration with their clients, patients, and research participants.
    The goal is to enable patients to become active collaborators in the health-promoting process and to make the most informed judgments about participating in the health enterprise.
3. A model of human behavior that assumes individuals are active and adaptive (rather than passive victims) leads to more effective health interventions.
    Blaming or pathologizing women and other subordinate groups for the manner in which they cope with the challenge of surviving in a sexist, racist, classist, homophobic, "ablist," and violent environment is a poor intervention strategy. Health professionals need to be taught to recognize the dynamics and sequelae of the many coping strategies developed by relatively powerless individuals, their cultural components and validity.
4. Lectures, textbooks, and other pedagogical materials should challenge negative stereotyped thinking and assumptions regarding individual, cultural, and other differences in the framing of research and other questions, interpretations of research findings, characterizations of peoples and illnesses, and therapeutic possibilities.
5. Educators of health professionals need to create or adapt mechanisms that encourage students/trainees to collaborate; to respect and value themselves and their fellow students/trainees; to be intolerant of sexual, racial, or any other harassment; and to interrupt such behavior should it occur.
6. Health professionals should be encouraged to see themselves as part of a larger social system which creates, exacerbates, or ignores health problems as well as diminishes or eliminates them.
    Training in awareness, analysis, and amelioration of these problems should be intrinsic to the education of all health professionals.
7. There should be continuous evaluation of and reflection on values, ethics, and practices.
    In particular, health professionals need to examine accepted practices that benefit or accommodate themselves more than those they serve (e.g., self-referrals, unnecessary surgeries, skimming the cream of a pool of research participants to maximize favorable outcomes for therapeutic evaluations). Supercilious attitudes toward nontraditional and indigenous therapies need re-examination.
8. Health is a complex function of the interaction of economic, political, cultural, biological, psychological, physiological, spiritual, and familial factors.
    Health prevention and intervention efforts that do not take into account this complexity will be less effective than they could be.

Reprinted from *Research Agenda for Psychological and Behavioral Factors in Women's Health* (pp. 21–22) by American Psychological Association, 1996, Washington, DC: Author. Copyright 1996 by the American Psychological Association.

REFERENCES

Adams, M. (Ed.). (1992). *Promoting diversity in college classrooms: Innovative re-sponses for the curriculum, faculty, and institutions.* San Francisco: Jossey-Bass.

Adler, E. S. (1984). *"It happened to me": How faculty handle student reactions to class material* (Working Paper No. 132). Wellesley, MA: Wellesley College Center for Research on Women.

American Psychological Association. (1992). Ethical principles of psychologists and code of conduct. *American Psychologist, 47,* 1597–1611.

American Psychological Association. (1996). *Research agenda for psychosocial and behavioral factors in women's health.* Washington, DC: Author.

Atkinson, S. D., & Hudson, J. (Eds.). (1990). *Women online: Research in women's studies using online databases.* New York: Haworth Press.

Barr, J., & Birke, L. (1994). Women, science, and adult education. Toward a feminist curriculum? *Women's Studies International Forum, 17,* 473–483.

Bauer, D. M., & Arenas, A. (Eds.). (1995). *Full circle: The women of color in the curriculum project* (Working Paper Series No. 16). Madison: University of Wisconsin Women's Studies Research Center.

Belle, D. (1990). Poverty and women's mental health. *American Psychologist, 45,* 385–389.

Birk, J. M., Barbanel, L., Rooks, L., Herman, M. H., Juhasz, J. B., Seltzer, R. A., & Tangri, S. S. (1974). A content analysis of sexual bias in commonly used psychology textbooks. *Catalog of Selected Documents in Psychology, 44,* 1–33.

Bleier, R. (1988). *Feminist approaches to science.* New York: Pergamon Press.

Border, L. L. B., & Chism, N. V. N. (Eds.). (1992). *Teaching for diversity.* San Francisco: Jossey-Bass.

Boston Lesbian Psychologies Collective. (Eds.). (1987). *Lesbian psychologies: Explorations & challenges.* Urbana: University of Illinois Press.

Bramel, D., & Friend, R. (1981). Hawthorne, the myth of the docile worker, and class bias in psychology. *American Psychologist, 36,* 867–878.

Bronstein, P. A., & Quina, K. (Eds.). (1988). *Teaching a psychology of people: Resources for gender and sociocultural awareness.* Washington, DC: American Psychological Association.

Brown, A., Goodwin, B. J., Hall, B. A., & Jackson-Lowman, H. (1985). A review of psychology of women textbooks: Focus on the Afro-American woman. *Psychology of Women Quarterly, 9,* 29–38.

Brown, L. M., & Gilligan, C. (1992). *Meeting at the crossroads: Women's psychology and women's development.* Cambridge, MA: Harvard University Press.

Brown, L. S. (1989). New voices, new visions: Toward a lesbian/gay paradigm for psychology. *Psychology of Women Quarterly, 13,* 445–458.

Brown, L. S. (1992). While waiting for the revolution: The case for a lesbian feminist psychotherapy. *Feminism & Psychology, 2,* 239–253.

Brown, L. S. (1993). Antidomination training as a central component of diversity in a clinical psychology education. *The Clinical Psychologist, 46*, 83–87.

Brown, L. S. (1994). *Subversive dialogues: Theory in feminist therapy.* New York: Basic Books.

Brown, L. S., & Root, M. P. P. (Eds.). (1990). *Diversity and complexity in feminist therapy.* New York: Haworth Press.

Butler, J. E., & Walter, J. C. (Eds.). (1991). *Transforming the curriculum: Ethnic studies and women's studies.* Albany: State University of New York Press.

Campbell, R., & Schram, P. J. (1995). Feminist research methods: A content analysis of psychology and social science textbooks. *Psychology of Women Quarterly, 19*, 85–107.

Cannon, L. W. (1990). Fostering positive race, class, and gender dynamics in the classroom. *Women's Studies Quarterly, 18*(1/2), 126–134.

Cavallaro, M. (1991). Curriculum guidelines and strategies on counseling older women for incorporation into gerontology and counseling coursework. *Educational Gerontology, 17*, 157–166.

Chin, J. L. (1994). Toward a psychology of difference: Psychotherapy for a culturally diverse population. In J. L. Chin, V. De La Cancela, & Y. M. Jenkins (Eds.), *Diversity in psychotherapy: The politics of race, ethnicity, and gender* (pp. 69–91). Westport, CT: Praeger.

Chin, J. L., De La Cancela, V., & Jenkins, Y. M. (Eds.). (1994). *Diversity in psychotherapy: The politics of race, ethnicity, and gender.* Westport, CT: Praeger.

Chrisler, J. C., Levin, T., & Koster-Lossack, A. (1992). Feminist psychology: Curriculum and pedagogy [Special issue]. *Women's Studies Quarterly, 20*(Whole No. 1/2).

Chun, H. (1975). Teaching the Asian–American experience: Alternatives to the neglect and racism in textbooks. *Amerasian Journal, 3*, 40–58.

Comas-Díaz, L. (1991). Feminism and diversity in psychology. *Psychology of Women Quarterly, 15*, 597–609.

Comas-Díaz, L., & Greene, B. (Eds.). (1994). *Women of color and mental health.* New York: Guilford Press.

Committee on Women in Psychology (n.d.). *Changing herstory: Integrating diversity into the teaching of psychology: A collection of syllabi, reading lists, and other resources for curriculum development.* Washington, DC: American Psychological Association.

Crawford, M., & Marecek, J. (1989). Feminist theory, feminist psychology: A bibliography of epistemology, critical analysis, and applications. *Psychology of Women Quarterly, 13*, 477–491.

Cruikshank, M. (Ed.). (1982). *Lesbian studies: Present and future.* Old Westbury, NY: The Feminist Press.

Crumpacker, L., & Vander Haegen, E. M. (1984). *Integrating the curriculum: Teaching about lesbians and homophobia* (Working Paper No. 138). Wellesley, MA: Wellesley College Center for Research on Women.

Datan, N. (1989). Aging women: The silent majority. *Women's Studies Quarterly*, *17*, 12–19.

Denmark, F. L. (1982). Integrating the psychology of women into introductory psychology. *The G. Stanley Hall Lecture Series*, *3*, 33–71.

Denmark, F. L. (Ed.). (1986). *Social/ecological psychology and the psychology of women*. Amsterdam: Elsevier Science.

Denmark, F. L., & Paludi, M. (1993). *Psychology of women: A handbook of issues and theories*. Westport, CT: Greenwood Press.

Dill, B. (1983). Race, class, and gender: Prospects for an all-inclusive sisterhood. *Feminist Studies*, *9*(1), 131–150.

Dinnerstein, M., O'Donnell, S. R., & MacCorquodale, P. (n.d.). *How to integrate women's studies into the traditional curriculum* (Working Paper No. 9). Tucson, AZ: Southwest Institute for Research on Women.

Enns, C. Z. (1992). Self-esteem groups: A synthesis of consciousness-raising and assertiveness training. *Journal of Counseling and Development*, *71*, 7–16.

Enns, C. Z. (1993a). Integrating separate and connected knowing: The experiential learning model. *Teaching of Psychology*, *20*, 7–13.

Enns, C. Z. (1993b). Twenty years of feminist counseling and therapy: From naming biases to implementing multifaceted practice. *The Counseling Psychologist*, *21*, 1–16.

Enns, C. Z. (1994). On teaching about the cultural relativism of psychological constructs. *Teaching of Psychology*, *21*, 205–219.

Ewick, P. (1994). Integrating feminist epistemologies in undergraduate research methods. *Gender & Society*, *8*, 92–108.

Fine, M., & Asch, A. (Eds.). (1988). *Women with disabilities: Essays in psychology, culture, and politics*. Philadelphia: Temple University Press.

Fine, M., & Gordon, S. M. (1991). Effecting the center at the margins: Life at the intersection of psychology and feminism. *Feminism and Psychology*, *1*, 19–28.

Fowlkes, D. L., & McClure, C. S. (Eds.). (1984). *Feminist visions: Toward a transformation of the liberal arts curriculum*. University: University of Alabama Press.

Franzosa, S. D., & Mazza, K. A. (1984). *Integrating women's studies into the curriculum: An annotated bibliography*. Westport, CT: Greenwood Press.

Friedenfels, R. (1992). Long-lived and invisible: Old women and gender integration into the curriculum. *Transformations*, *2*, 73–80.

Fritsche, J. M. (1984). *Toward excellence and equity: The scholarship on women as a catalyst for change in the university*. Orono: University of Maine Press.

Furumoto, L. (1984). *Placing women in the history of psychology course* (Working Paper No. 139). Wellesley, MA: Wellesley College Center for Research on Women.

Gilbert, L. A., & Rossman, K. M. (1992). Gender and the mentoring process for women: Implications for professional development. *Professional Psychology*, *23*, 233–238.

Glazier, M. (1994). Internet resources for women's studies. *C&RL News*, March, 139–143.

Golub, S., & Freedman, R. J. (1987). *Psychology of women: Resources for a core curriculum*. New York: Garland.

Gray, V. A. (1977). The image of women in psychology textbooks. *Canadian Psychological Review, 18*, 46–55.

Hall, R. L., & Greene, B. (1994). Cultural competence in feminist family therapy: An ethical mandate. *Journal of Feminist Family Therapy, 6*, 5–11.

Harris, B., & Lightner, J. (1980). The image of women in abnormal psychology: Professionalism versus psychopathology. *Psychology of Women Quarterly, 4*, 396–411.

Higgenbotham, E. (1990). Designing an inclusive curriculum: Bringing all women into the core. *Women's Studies Quarterly, 18*, 7–23.

Hoffnung, M. (1984). *Feminist transformation: Teaching experimental psychology* (Working Paper No. 140). Wellesley, MA: Wellesley College Center for Research on Women.

Hoshmand, L. L. S. T. (1989). Alternate research paradigms: A review and teaching proposal. *The Counseling Psychologist, 17*, 3–79.

Hull, G. T., Scott, P. B., & Smith, B. (1982). *All the women are White, all the Blacks are men, but some of us are brave: Black women's studies*. Old Westbury, NY: The Feminist Press.

Hyde, J. S. (1994). Can meta-analysis make feminist transformations in psychology? *Psychology of Women Quarterly, 18*, 451–462.

Kimmel, E. (1991). Treatment of gender and diversity in psychology textbooks: Report from the Task Force. *Psychology of Women Newsletter, 18*(4), 5.

Kimmel, E. (1992). Consumer alert! How you can expedite mainstreaming gender and diversity in psychology texts. *Psychology of Women Newsletter, 19*(4), 4.

Klein, S. (Ed). (1985). *Handbook for achieving sex equity through education*. Baltimore: The Johns Hopkins University Press.

Koss, M. P., Goodman, L. A., Browne, A., Fitzgerald, L., Keita, G. P., & Russo, N. F. (1994). *No safe haven: Male violence against women at home, at work, and in the community*. Washington, DC: American Psychological Association.

Koss, M. P., Heise, L., & Russo, N. F. (1994). The global health burden of rape. *Psychology of Women Quarterly, 18*, 509–530.

LaFromboise, T., & Rowe, W. (1983). Skills training for bicultural competence: Rationale and application. *Journal of Counseling Psychology, 30*, 589–595.

Landrine, H. (Ed.). (1995). *Bringing cultural diversity to feminist psychology*. Washington, DC: American Psychological Association.

Lazarus, R. S., & Folkman, S. (1984). *Stress, appraisal, and coping*. New York: Springer.

Lerman, H. (1994). The practice of ethics within feminist therapy. *Women & Therapy, 15*, 85–93.

Madden, M., & Russo, N. F. (1997). *Women in the curriculum: Psychology.* Towsen, MD: National Center for Curriculum Transformation Resources on Women.

McIntosh, P. (1990). *Interactive phases of personal and curricula re-vision: A feminist perspective* (Working Paper No. 124). Wellesley, MA: Wellesley College Center for Research on Women.

McMillen, L. (1987). More colleges and more disciplines incorporating scholarship on women into the classroom. *Chronicle of Higher Education, 34,* A15–A17.

O'Connell, A. N., & Russo, N. F. (Eds.). (1991) Women's heritage in psychology: Origins, development, and future directions. *Psychology of Women Quarterly, 15*(Whole No. 4).

Paludi, M. (1990). *Exploring/teaching the psychology of women: A manual of resources.* New York: State University of New York Press.

Paludi, M. A., & Steuernagel, G. A. (Eds.). (1990). *Foundations for a feminist restructuring of the academic disciplines.* Binghamton, NY: Harrington Park Press.

Percival, E. (1984). Sex bias in introductory psychology textbooks: Five years later. *Canadian Psychology, 25,* 35–42.

Pollis, C. A. (1986). Sensitive drawings of sexual activity in human sexuality textbooks: An analysis of communication and bias. *Journal of Homosexuality, 13,* 59–73.

Porter, N., & Yahne, C. (1994). Feminist ethics and advocacy in the training of family therapists. *Journal of Feminist Family Therapy, 6*(3), 29–37.

Register, C. (1979). Brief, amazing moments: Dealing with despair in the women's studies classroom. *Women's Studies Newsletter, 7*(Winter), 7–10.

Reid, P. (1991). Preface. *Psychology of Women Quarterly, 15,* 493–494.

Reid, P., & Comas-Díaz, L. (1990). Gender and ethnicity: Perspectives on dual status. *Sex Roles, 22,* 397–407.

Reid, P. T., & Kelly, E. (1994). Research on women of color: From ignorance to awareness. *Psychology of Women Quarterly, 18,* 477–486.

Rodeheaver, D., & Datan, N. (1988). The challenge of double jeopardy: Toward a mental health agenda for aging women. *American Psychologist, 43,* 648–654.

Rosser, S. V. (1986). *Teaching science and health from a feminist perspective: A practical guide.* New York: Pergamon Press.

Rosser, S. V. (1990). *Female-friendly science.* New York: Pergamon Press.

Russo, N. F. (1988). Women in psychology: Reflecting and shaping the social context. In A. N. O'Connell & N. F. Russo (Eds.), *Models of achievement: Reflections of eminent women in psychology* (Vol. 2, pp. 9–27). Hillsdale, NJ: Erlbaum.

Russo, N. F., & Dabul, A. (1994). Feminism, diversity, and psychology. In E. J. Trickett, R. Watts, & D. Birman (Eds.), *Human diversity: Perspectives on people in context* (pp. 81–100). San Francisco: Jossey-Bass.

Russo, N. F., & Malovich, N. (1982). *Assessing the introductory psychology course.*

In J. Gappa & J. Pearce (Eds.), *Sex and gender in the social sciences: Reassessing the introductory course*. Washington, DC: American Psychological Association.

Sadker, M., Sadker, D., & Klein, S. (1991). The issue of gender in elementary and secondary education. *Review of Research in Education, 17,* 269–334.

Sanchez, J. (1994). *Bibliography on the mental health of ethnic minority women.* Computer disk available from J. Sanchez-Hucles, Psychology Department, Old Dominion University, Norfolk, Virginia 23529.

Schmitz, B. (1985). *Integrating women's studies into the curriculum: A guide and bibliography.* Old Westbury, NY: The Feminist Press.

Schuster, M., & Van Dyne, S. (1985). *Women's place in the academy: Transforming the liberal arts curriculum.* Totowa, NJ: Rowman & Allanheld.

Spanier, B., Bloom, A., & Boroviak, D. (1984). *Toward a balanced curriculum: A sourcebook for initiating gender integration projects.* Cambridge, MA: Schenkman.

Spender, D. (Ed.). (1981). *Men's studies modified: The impact of feminism on the academic disciplines.* New York: Pergamon Press.

Task Force on Representation in the Curriculum, APA Division 35. (1995). *Including diverse women in the undergraduate curriculum: Reasons and resources.* Washington, DC: Author.

Tatum, B. D. (1992). Talking about race, learning about racism: The application of racial identity development in the classroom. *Harvard Educational Review, 62*(1), 1–24.

Timberlake, A., Cannon, L. W., Guy, R. F., & Higginbotham, E. (1988). *Women of color and Southern women: A bibliography of social science research, 1975–1988.* Memphis, TN: Memphis State University, Center for Research on Women.

Timberlake, A., Cannon, L. W., Guy, R. F., & Higginbotham, E. (1990). *Women of color and Southern women: A bibliography of social science research (Supplement).* Memphis, TN: Memphis State University, Center for Research on Women.

Tyler, F. B., Sussewell, D. R., & Williams-McCoy, J. (1985). Ethnic validity in psychotherapy. *Psychotherapy, 22,* 311–323.

Van Nostrand, C. H. (1993). *Gender responsible leadership: Detecting bias, implementing interventions.* Newbury Park, CA: Sage.

Walsh, M. R. (1986). The psychology of women course: A continuing catalyst for change. *Teaching of Psychology, 12,* 198–203.

Westkott, M. (1983). Women's studies as a strategy for change: Between criticism and vision. In G. Bowles & R. D. Klein (Eds.), *Theories of women's studies* (pp. 210–218). London: Routledge & Kegan Paul.

Wilkinson, S., & Kitzinger, C. (1993). *Heterosexuality: A feminism and psychology reader.* London: Sage.

Wood, P. S., & Mallinckrodt, B. (1990). Culturally sensitive assertiveness training for ethnic minority clients. *Professional Psychology: Research and Practice, 21,* 5–21.

Worell, J., & Remer, P. (1992). *Feminist perspectives in therapy: An empowerment model for women.* Chichester, England: Wiley & Sons.

7

PREACHING WHAT WE PRACTICE: PRINCIPLES AND STRATEGIES OF FEMINIST PEDAGOGY

ELLEN KIMMEL AND JUDITH WORELL

WITH JUDITH DANILUK, MARY ANN GAWALEK, KATHY LERNER, GERALDINE STAHLEY, AND SUSAN KAHOE

This book and this chapter owe a large debt to Naomi Weisstein (1968), who was among the first to critique the discipline of psychology. In *Kinder, Kuche, Kirche as Scientific Law: Psychology Constructs the Female*, she wrote, "Psychology has nothing to say about what women are really like" (p. 135). Men described women from their perspective and for their benefit "while the powerless (women) had little choice but to accept not just the content, but the criteria of credibility" (Spender, 1982, p. 6). As women began to construct their female (e.g., Unger & Denmark, 1975), it became clear that more was required than just adding content. We would have to change the way knowledge was both created and disseminated in the classroom.

Feminists moved from a room of our own to a knowledge of our own

We wish to acknowledge Elizabeth Cardenas and Elysse Dressman, both of whom are graduate students in school psychology at the University of South Florida, for their diligent assistance in developing the bibliography to support the principles and strategies.

(Raymond, 1985). We soon realized that this knowledge also required a process of its own, and feminist pedagogy emerged as a current within the stream of the new feminist movement. Beginning with descriptions of what transpired in feminists' classrooms, we have moved to more theoretical analyses of the fundamental restructuring of education necessary to impart the new scholarship. Even the word *impart* is problematic because feminist studies classrooms are also the site of the production of knowledge. As students and faculty co-construct and de-construct research and theory on women's experience, the classroom becomes a collaborative laboratory where the outcomes are not always predetermined in the syllabus.

This chapter on feminist pedagogy is divided into a recounting of how our working group arrived at its conclusions—the process section—and what we concluded—the outcomes section—acknowledging up front the falseness of the dichotomy. In a similar vein, the group explicitly tried to separate the process of feminist teaching from its content, in deference to the work of the group mapping feminist curriculum. This division was and is difficult. The literature and our understanding clearly demonstrate that feminist pedagogy is driven by content that cannot be handled by doing business as usual.

In lieu of a separate section reviewing the literature, we opted to weave references into the narrative and provide a representative bibliography tied to each of our principles, strategies, and risk-benefit analysis of feminist teaching. Particularly useful bibliographies, journals, and other resources are also listed as aids to those wishing to learn more about feminist pedagogy. It should become apparent that a substantial body of publications has accrued on this topic, representing many disciplines of which only a sample can be provided here. We apologize to the many contributors whose works we could not include.

GROUP PROCESS: CHALLENGE AND CONSENSUS

What better medium to consider feminist process than within a group that explores the dimensions of feminist pedagogy? A fundamental starting principle required that final decisions were to be determined by group consensus rather than by majority vote. Challenged to articulate and to create new ways of viewing feminist pedagogy, we found the process of arriving at a consensus to be truly an exercise in reality testing. Could we enact what we professed to believe? The task was not as simple as we had anticipated. In the feminist classroom, power and authority are shared but remain essentially within the assigned domain of the teacher (Morgan, 1987; Schniedewind, 1983; Shrewsbury, 1987b). How do we manage this power sharing among professionals when we agree that all group participants are equally knowledgeable and equally responsible for the outcomes of the discussion?

Although small in number, we were quite diverse in age, experience, type of institutional affiliation, and specialty in psychology. We all taught, but several held or had held administrative positions, and we were housed in different departments and with different academic climates. All were academics, but some of us primarily trained practitioners and others worked only with undergraduates. We were diverse in our experiences and personalities but quite limited by our racial and ethnic homogeneity.

Because feminist process had not yet been defined within the group, the struggle to articulate our individual understandings with a group consensus was evident. The dialectic within a group having high levels of expertise was both to advance and to promote our individual views and yet to retreat and to conciliate with the views of others. Was the final outcome to be arbitration among diverse views, negotiation of disparate meanings, or a zero sum result in which one view prevailed over another? As it turned out, all three outcomes were evident in the process of arriving at consensus. From our perspective, the saving factor overall was the common core of understanding that we each carried, both implicitly and explicitly, about the tenets of feminist pedagogy and the goals we aimed to achieve. The exciting and transformative experience for all participants emerged from the challenge to integrate our individual views into a cohesive and affirmative statement of principles and strategies of feminist pedagogy.

From a small group of six feminist college and university teachers, most of whom were previously unacquainted, a set of principles and strategies emerged that represented the collective thinking of all. At the close of the working agenda, the group expressed appreciation for our process and for the fact that none of us had acted in a pre-emptive or self-centered way. We noted that our ideas often contradicted one another, yet we merged ideas, collaborated on the work, were open to feedback, and were genuinely respectful in our approach to one another and to the work. We were also able to laugh at ourselves and to view playfulness as essential to the process. We acknowledged and appreciated the contributions of the student recorder, without whom most of this information might have evaporated into the recesses of our fragile memories and have been lost forever. That we can document the process and product is an important testament to her participation as an active and valued member of the group. Not only did she chronicle the events of the group, but she also contributed with ideas and feedback that expanded our vision.

WHAT ARE THE QUESTIONS IN FEMINIST PEDAGOGY?

In this section, we discuss some of the dynamics of feminist process as revealed through the deliberations and discussions that moved the group toward consensus on each question. We focus here specifically on issues of power and authority as representative of feminist concerns that assume a central focus in all student–faculty interactions. In carving out the essential dimensions of feminist pedagogy, we discovered first that we needed to keep feminist process in the foreground as we considered the questions to be asked and then answered them.

The pedagogy working group started from a pool of 10 questions that might be relevant to understanding process and procedures in feminist pedagogy. From them, we forged five broad questions that constructed the baseline for subsequent work:

1. Is there a feminist process of pedagogy?
2. What is the personal experience of the feminist teacher?
3. What are the special dynamics between feminist faculty and students?
4. What responsibility do we have for the impact of feminism on the personal lives of the students?
5. How do we measure the effects of feminist pedagogy?

In our attempt to grapple with these broad questions, subsidiary issues arose. Examples of additional questions we wanted to address included the following:

1. Who determines the significant content, standards, and process in any course and how are these decisions balanced with beliefs about power, authority, and equality?
2. How does good teaching coincide with feminist teaching practices? Is feminist teaching "just good teaching"?
3. How can we be inclusionary, integrating the needs of women of diverse groups as well as other issues of diversity?

In a final decision, we reduced the critical questions to three. These three questions then served as the foundation for framing the work to be accomplished:

1. What are the principles of feminist instruction?
2. What are the major strategies of feminist pedagogy?
3. What are the personal experiences of being a feminist teacher?

How were we able to address these critical questions within the time span allowed us? Each question demanded its place and each was given its share of deliberation. From the many topics that stimulated our reflection and debate, we chose those of power and authority as central both to the process at hand and to the task to be accomplished.

ISSUES OF POWER AND AUTHORITY

Throughout the 4 days of discussion and dissent regarding feminist pedagogy, issues of power and authority were central to our struggle for understanding and consensus. We focus on this discussion as a model for how the group process moved from raising questions, to discussing, to dissenting, and finally to reaching a consensus, although not necessarily in that order. What remains less articulated here are the additional processes that emerged as members of our working group met in "triads" with members of all other groups. As a result of these triads, certain conclusions reached in our working group became modified, and principles and strategies were added to acknowledge the perspectives of other working groups. The process was thus recursive and inclusive. We concluded with a set of principles and strategies that reflected the views of all who had the opportunity to participate.

We divide this section according to focal questions related to the dimensions of power that were raised in the work group:

What do we mean by equality in the classroom?

How can we effectively use the power of language to articulate our goals?

How shall we acknowledge our own power and authority?

Establishing Equality in the Classroom

If each person has a voice that is valued, then are all voices equally welcome? Two passionate positions were articulated—one position would challenge or negatively evaluate the bigot, the sexist, the homophobic, or the racist voice by restricting its opportunity to be heard. An opposing view would encourage all voices and ideas but would refrain from honoring ideas that were demeaning to others. One rationale here was the idea that unspoken values and attitudes may be more damaging than those that are articulated and therefore open to challenge.

In affirming the principle that the right to be heard and to have a voice is an essential feminist value, the corollary of this position states that some messages may not be equally valued or supported. Furthermore, there may be value in the expression of differing views, even if these views run counter to one's beliefs. An essential component of feminism is to avoid silencing the dissenter. Instead, we encourage free expression of ideas, but we also confront racist or homophobic messages. One way for feminist teachers to respond to bigoted ideas is to process openly the group's reaction to these ideas and include their own response, thereby providing feedback to the student. In this manner, all student views are welcomed, but a feminist position is also clearly articulated. The outcome of this heated discussion was the first principle to be written: All voices are encouraged, valued, and heard.

In confronting bias, it is incumbent on feminists to make their own biases known. We do not hide our values behind a curtain of assumed objective knowledge. From a discussion of openly acknowledging our feminist values to students, a second principle was articulated: Fundamental to feminist pedagogy is a consciousness of differential power, privilege, and oppression, and that is made explicit.

Recognizing the Power of Language

The implicit power of language became explicit when one of us objected to use of the word *oppression* in the phrasing of the second principle. Instead, the word *status* was suggested as an alternative concept. One person asserted that *oppression* is overused, and its use may lead to our feminist positions being discounted as extreme. Who wants to be labeled as the oppressor? Should a more neutral term be used that does not imply intentional harm but that acknowledges differential privilege? Are not many "oppressors" themselves caught in the system that denies equal opportunity to all? The resolution of this discussion was to retain the concept of oppression because historically it has a common meaning. Here, it was clear that consensus was not reached but that one voice conceded to another so that a consensus could be reached.

Particular attention was paid to choice of wording throughout the development of principles and strategies. We recognized the need to consider ways to assist the larger community in being open to our ideas, to listen to what we have to say, and to accept what we produce. To disseminate ideas and products effectively, it is vital that we use clear and concrete language that communicates without professional jargon. We do not wish to create a situation in which other people are unwilling to listen. Above all, we want our ideas to be accessible as well as transformative.

Acknowledging Our Power and Authority

The third tough power issue arose over the paradox of power and authority (see especially Morgan, 1987) confronting the principle of egalitarianism. How do we balance the goal of equality in the classroom and beyond with the assigned role power of the teacher? Do we do a disservice to students by presenting ideas of equality but then denying the real power that we as teachers have over them? Our power as teachers is experienced in the classroom by students in many ways: through seating arrangements, course structure, and reading and activity assignments and in evaluation and grading procedures. Outside the classroom, we provide opportunities for access to resources, financial support, and letters of recommendation.

Can the practice of evaluation of faculty by students equalize this power differential? Not really, because giving voice to students implies that we have the power to give it.

The dialectic surrounding the concepts of power and authority suggested that even as we give power over to others, we assert our ability to do so. Do we really want to be equal? At one level, we move toward student empowerment, while at the same time we recognize and value our expertise. We should acknowledge that we have power and authority in the classroom and beyond and strive to use it well. Some members felt that this position is paradoxical, and some did not. If our struggle is with how power operates in the world, the classroom is a laboratory. Faculty may "own" the power, but they share it rather than give it away.

We operate with a set of principles that are in conflict with the institutions within which we function (Heald, 1989). Can we acknowledge hierarchical relationships without making them oppressive? Some members objected to use of the word *hierarchy* with respect to faculty-student relationships. This issue seemed to generate tension among feminists, on the one hand valuing voice and on the other claiming our expertise. We determined that power sharing is important in teaching because it enhances growth and learning. The intent of sharing power is to increase the students' sense of control in their lives. At the end of this heated discussion, another principle was articulated: Feminists acknowledge the power in their teaching role and seek ways to empower students in the learning process.

DEVELOPING PRINCIPLES AND STRATEGIES

Before presenting the answers to the three questions our group addressed, a few comments are in order. First, we dealt with the issue of whether feminist pedagogy exists distinct from other teaching models or from just "good teaching." We asserted that feminist pedagogy exists if we can articulate a group of principles and strategies that characterize it. We then set about to do just that. Many of the ideas we brainstormed were not original to us but reflect those of the larger community of scholars who have grappled with defining feminist teaching. Similar to them, we could not separate the process from the person who used it. Hence, our treatment of the experience of feminist teachers became part of the definitional work.

Is feminist pedagogy more than just good teaching, or is it simply a reflection of current educational reform movements? Although there are elements of these movements in feminist pedagogy—the activism of Paulo Freire (1971), active learning of David Kolb (1984) and others, or the analysis of power that marks critical pedagogy (e.g., Giroux, 1988)—feminist pedagogy emanates from a different place.

EXHIBIT 1
Dimensions of the Personal Experience of Being a Feminist Teacher

Risks

Backlash from negative reactions to feminism
Unrealistic student expectations for unconditional support
Institutional sanctions in tenure and promotion decisions
Sexual harassment as a visible and vulnerable target
Stigmatization and devaluing of feminist scholarship
Professional liabilities in feminist publishing
Marginalization of career and scholarship efforts
Overextension from too many demands on time and energy

Challenges

Struggling with appropriate use of power with peers and students
Negotiating the special dynamics of faculty–student interactions and relationships: Ethics and boundaries
Becoming a realistic and useful role model for students
Attending to the impact of feminist teaching on students' academic and personal lives
Assessing the effects of feminist pedagogy on the individual, the institution, and the larger social system
Developing resources and methods to meet the goals of feminist pedagogy

Rewards

Affirmation of self in the pursuit of important goals
Congruence between personal values and professional life
Visibility and voice within the institution and community
A sense of meaning and purpose associated with membership in a revolutionary social movement
Connection to the feminist community
Being a midwife to the emergence of feminist consciousness in students
Participating in students' personal growth and empowerment
Learning from students
Collaborating with students and colleagues

Needed supports

Institutional resources for research, library, assistance
More feminist faculty
Strong women's studies program
More feminists in leadership roles
Modifications in evaluation forms to reflect feminist pedagogy
Strategies for thriving in hostile environments

Certainly, none of these analyses had women in mind (see Ellsworth, 1989, for a particularly acute analysis of critical pedagogy as sexist, racist, etc.). Feminist teachers search for new ways to promote the tenets of a social movement and the corpus of new scholarship. Three assumptions drive this search: (a) Women are worth it; (b) public examination of women's lives has been all but nonexistent so that we must invent methods to discover and teach about women that are free of biases inherent in traditional methods of examination; and (c) if we are successful in this endeavor for women of all groups, these strategies also can be applied to groups of oppressed men (Maher, 1985).

The Matrix of Principles and Strategies listed in the Appendix and the experiences of the feminist teacher summarized in Exhibit 1 constitute the major outcomes of the pedagogy working group. We made an overall assumption that the principles and strategies apply equally across all teaching and training settings as well as to all content areas in the curriculum. Furthermore, we stated that each principle must be accompanied by at least one strategy (the shaded areas in the matrix). Although a strategy could serve more than one principle, no strategy could be included that violated any principle.

The 14 principles were clustered into four areas: power and authority, process, content, and outcomes or goals. They appear in that order in the matrix, although they were not necessarily generated in that order in our free-flowing discussion. It is interesting that we spontaneously paralleled the sequence in which they have been discussed in the literature. The numbers in each cell are keyed to the References and Bibliography to provide a sample of related literature for each principle (lower left) and strategy (upper right).

Focusing on Power and Authority

Analysis of differential power was uppermost on our minds, as noted in the section Group Process: Challenge and Consensus (see Principles 1 and 2). The strategies were organized into eight clusters: language (Strategies 1 and 2), social change (Strategies 3–5), woman centered (Strategies 6–8), life experiences (Strategies 9–11), class participation (Strategies 12–16), group process (Strategies 17–20), active learning (Strategies 21–25), and evaluation (Strategies 26–28). A number of strategies deal with issues of power, capitalizing on the fact that the dynamics of power in the classroom mirror those in society at large (e.g., Bezucha, 1985; Ellsworth, 1989; Hoffman, 1985). These issues must be addressed early and throughout the term to create a place where all voices can be heard. To this end, Strategies 17, 19, and 20 are commonly used: engaging students in group work, demystifying group process, and using this process as a tool to illuminate how power shapes behavior in and out of class.

Feminists agree with Zen masters who say that to become accustomed to anything is a terrible thing. Transformation requires vigilance against the status quo—always, everywhere. Likewise, attention to language (Strategies 1 and 2) and specific ways to induce participation and equalize it for students (Strategies 12–18) also address power and privilege as they are recapitulated in the classroom. Almost every writer on feminist pedagogy deals with power and authority in some way, and a sample of their work is noted in the matrix by the numbers keyed to the numbers in the References and Bibliography.

Using Process to Confront Diversity

We discussed empowerment through process (Principles 3–9) that recognizes differences (Strategies 8, 10, and 23) in such characteristics as race or ethnicity, class, age, gender, sexual orientation, ablebodiedness, learning styles (Strategies 21 and 25), family backgrounds (Strategy 11), stages of development (Strategy 5), and the myriad sources of human diversity. Feminist pedagogy "embodies a concept of power as energy, capacity and potential . . . as the glue holding the community together" (Shrewsbury, 1987b, p. 8). This perspective is realized by teachers through the processes of (a) connecting learning to personal experience, including feelings and nonlinear analytic thought as valid structures for knowing; (b) encouraging holistic learning (e.g., Poplin, 1988; 1991; Shrewsbury, 1987b); and (c) engaging in a mutual learning process and sharing power with students.

Underpinning the group's discussion and the literature is the thesis that the differences among women (i.e., cultural identity, race, social class, and age) are integral to understanding the concepts of privilege. The classroom is the laboratory for confronting any and all sources of difference and its consequences, including the greater power ascribed to the instructor in our institutions of higher learning. As Nancy Jo Hoffman (1985) stated, "There *is* a feminist way of being in the world" (p. 154). It involves breaking silences and taking a stance that automatic power should be challenged and that knowledge or expertise should be used in the service of learning and teaching on the part of both teachers and students.

When teachers visibly strive to increase their knowledge of diverse cultural realities or when they model an acceptance of their own authority based on expertise (Principles 8 and 9), they empower students to do the same. Nancy Miller (1985) went further by asserting that our presence in the classroom demonstrates that one can survive as a feminist inside the private bailiwick of the patriarchs after all. Without giving students hope, all strategies to empower them are doomed.

Using Process to Empower Students

Many strategies are directed at students' empowerment, including active learning activities (Strategies 18, 21–25), women-centered assignments and women role models (Strategies 6–8), incorporation and journaling of life experiences (Strategies 10 and 11), contextualizing everything (Strategy 9), and engaging students in activist projects for social change (Strategies 3–5).

Activism was seen by our group and in the literature as a cornerstone of feminist pedagogy. Ultimately, one is empowered only by exerting power successfully (e.g., May, 1970). Awareness is foundational to consciousness raising. Viewed developmentally (Strategy 5), however, awareness must lead to concrete action to improve group life before real change is effected. That is, if the personal is political, action should follow reflection as a means of moving beyond victimization. Researchers (Stake, Roades, Rose, Ellis, & West, 1994) documented that students who took feminist studies courses engaged in increased activism compared with students taking non-women's studies courses with either women's studies or non-women's studies faculty. All three groups of faculty were women. As an interesting aside, it appears that feminist and nonfeminist teachers in non-gender-centered courses behaved differently, perhaps further evidence that what one teaches changes how one teaches.

Strategies that involve students in their evaluation (Strategies 26–28), one of the stickiest issues for many feminist teachers, also enhance opportunities for student empowerment. We can encourage students to participate not only in decisions about what to learn (Strategy 23) but also in how that learning is evaluated, a basic tenet in adult education generally (see, e.g., Knowles, 1986, on learning contracts).

Dealing With Content

We made valiant efforts not to invade the curriculum working group's territory. However, Principle 10 relates to content; it states that we are committed to the inclusion of multiple sources of knowledge. Strategies 7 to 11, 21, 22, and 25 speak to this principle; personal and public, empirical data and narrative accounts are all viewed as legitimate for consideration in analyzing gender and constructing our version of woman.

Reaching Goals

We dealt with the outcomes or goals of feminist pedagogy. Principles 11 to 14 speak to the beliefs that learning serves both social change (Strategies 3–5) and personal development (Strategies 5, 6, 12, 16, 18, 22, and 23). Its purpose includes reclaiming women's histories and contributions (Strategies 7–10). Its ultimate aim is to transform the discipline of psychology to include the breadth of human experience. In one sense, all the strategies work toward this last principle.

EXPERIENCE OF FEMINIST TEACHERS

When male dominance in the academy was questioned, defenses were ready and strong. Men hid under the banner of science, objectivity, and truth, pronounced to be universal and eternal. From their privileged place, those in power reviled women challengers as emotional, political, neurotic, or just "inappropriate." Thus, in most institutions the risks were high for women who participated in generating the new scholarship and practicing the new pedagogy in the early years of this wave of the women's movement. These risks included exclusion from hiring; favorable work assignments; adequate resources; facilitative climate (e.g., Grauerholz, 1989); and from consideration for raises, tenure, and promotion.

Many early feminist academics risked virtually everything to pursue the analysis of gender roles (see Grument, 1988). Why was this so? Once a feminist consciousness develops, there is no turning back. The discovery (or re-discovery) of one's self in the universe is too powerful to reject. Women in psychology needed to know about the double shift as much as any woman attempting to have family and a career; they needed to understand why marriage could be lethal to them (Bernard, 1972) or why only men might be considered healthy (Chesler, 1974). They were driven to comprehend why their words were ignored and their contributions to the field invisible. The professional was personal (Kimmel, 1985; McIntosh, 1984).

Today, discussion of the joys and pains of life as a "woman who works on women" (N. Miller, 1985, p. 196) may not be about such dramatic circumstances, although there are still many inhospitable institutions or departments of psychology. Most campuses have women's studies programs and psychology of women courses, though the backlash (a sign of progress) is ever present and evolving. In addition to the outward resistance to feminists' presence in academe, "inside" forces both challenge and reward feminist teachers (Cocks, 1985). Exhibit 1 presents a synopsis of the risks and rewards experienced by feminist teachers today.

For an in-depth description of the experience of feminist academicians, readers should consult Worell and Crosby (1992), who studied 77 psychologists whose names were taken from the roster of Division 35 membership. Lynn Reinardy's (1992) guide for feminist teaching provides an excellent summary of these experiences. Baxter Magolda's (1992) introductory chapter about the research project that led to the book *Knowing and Reasoning in College* affords an insightful account of how our content shapes the process and action. She was profoundly changed by her data and the ways she evolved to analyze and interpret them, a common experience of feminist teachers in their classrooms. The group did not elaborate further on the general experience; because of time limits, we proceeded to enumerate the risks, challenges, rewards, and special needs listed in Exhibit 1.

Risks

The more blatant institutional hostility has abated for most feminist psychology teachers, but we continue to be devalued in subtle and not-so-subtle ways. When examining the "departmental lives" of feminist academics in psychology, one must pause and heed Michelle Fine and Susan Merle Gordon's (1989) assessment of our place in the scheme of things. Often our feminist work is covert, and the savvy mainly keep their mouths shut. We have created a small space with our students and networks that nurture us, but we have not transformed most of our colleagues or the major content of our discipline. In the shadows, on the periphery, we are necessarily colored by location in the margin (see also Heald, 1989). We shy from really screaming out every day that the personal is political, and, when we let out our exasperation at unguarded moments, we are viewed askance, if not labeled *fanatic*. When we touch terms such as *oppression*, *dominance*, or *resistance*, even many women instantly recoil; they fear (rightly so) that these topics will only anger those on whose good humor we depend for some level of comfort in our everyday work worlds. Thus, an overarching outside risk is having to behave like an "ostrich" (Crosby, Pufall, Snyder, O'Connell, & Whalen, 1989). We lay low most of the time except when in the sanctuaries of our classrooms and gatherings with one another.

Not all risks are from the outside, however, and those from the inside may be most painful if our group's discussion is indicative of others' experience. We suffer from the unrealistic expectations and demands of students whose lives we are changing. As Margo Culley and her colleagues wrote in an article, "The Politics of Nurturance" (Culley, Diamond, Edwards, Lennox, & Portuges, 1985), feminist teachers are "both our fathers' daughters and our daughters' mothers" (p. 12). We are our students' compatriots and mentors, co-conspirators and representatives of the professorate. We are not clearly "us" or "them." When we combine the roles of nurturer and intellectual, confusion results. "Neither one's mother nor one's therapist had to grade one's dreams . . ." (p. 12).

Because we are the midwives of feminist consciousness of our students (a particular joy, we all agreed), we feel responsible to nurture and protect this fragile moment of development. At the same time, we are invested in the intellectual life in a way that students cannot be and are torn by our devastation of the very structures that house us. Furthermore, we are invested in producing the new scholarship, and that is its own taskmistress, incompatible with an open door policy for students. A final consideration is this: How can we nurture and then judge them? We both love and evaluate the students, bearing the difficult task of creating safe environments for enormous growth with realistic assessments. For some students, the confusion leads to hurt, hostility, or rejection, and the competing demands on faculty time and energy lead to exhaustion.

These demands result in overextension of our time and energies. Both students and administrators may believe they need "one of them" on every committee. The majority of psychology students are women, but the minority of faculty are women. There are too few of us to spread around. We often find it difficult to set boundaries, hoisted by our own petards as it were, by our principles and commitments to social action as well as to teaching, mentoring, and research.

The challenges should be familiar to the reader. Handling the risks of feminist teaching presents daily challenges as we struggle to invent new models of teaching and research. While mindful of the immediate and larger contexts of our work, we must find ways of relating to students and colleagues that eschew whatever privileges our particular attributes afford (race or ethnicity, rank, affectional preference, ablebodiedness, etc.).

Rewards

Although life at times can be overwhelming, contradictory, or infuriating, the rewards are unbeatable, so we hold our course. These rewards are personal, connecting our lives to our work, making powerful and lasting bonds with feminist friends, and finding voice in our community, to name a few. However, there are more. We identified our altruistic purposes in connection to a revolutionary movement and to the community of other feminists both compelling and challenging. While we struggled as role innovators to find ways to model for and mentor students and foster their development, we ourselves were pushed in our own development. We learned from our students if we could muster the courage to open ourselves and our privilege for scrutiny.

Finally, we quickly enumerated some desired supports (see also Chamberlain, 1988) for feminist teaching. More feminists in academic institutions would help to alleviate token status (Kanter, 1977) and our marginalization and to reduce the workload.

Meanwhile, we need immediate strategies to survive, including such things as revisions in student teaching evaluations to mirror changes in pedagogy and techniques to deal with hostile men (and sometime women) students (see De Danaan, 1990, especially), to handle sensitive subjects such as religions beliefs, or to defuse religious or political ultraconservatives. More resources to accommodate the labor-intensive methods feminists use, such as essay exams, journals, political activities, and group activities, also would be welcomed.

Final Note on Outcomes

Given the short time available and our small number in the pedagogy working group, a few ideas are missing in Exhibit 1 and the Appendix, as might be expected. For example, nowhere do we explicitly state that feminist pedagogy is gender-centered, although we all meant that. Surprisingly, we never used the term *gender*.

We also did not emphasize consciousness raising as a major activity, although that too was implied, especially in the rewards discussion. Perhaps the most problematic omission was the importance of interdisciplinary approaches. Although we draw on the work of other social sciences and even the humanities to inform our own thinking and writing, we did not speak about how, if at all, we integrate these perspectives in the classroom. Psychology and psychologists increasingly are crossing disciplinary borders on such fields as health, education, sports, and law, but are feminist psychologist teachers also interdisciplinary? Perhaps we are, but less so than our women's studies colleagues, who are more explicit in their commitment to interdisciplinary work (e.g., Reinardy, 1992). In Principle 10, we talked about multiple sources of knowledge, but we referred to data sources and methods rather than disciplines.

SUMMARY AND CONCLUSIONS

As Berenice Fisher (1981) said so well, "Feminist pedagogy is not merely the 'women's department' of educational reform" (p. 20). Our matrix demonstrates that feminist pedagogy is unique and represents the intentional incorporation of key features of the women's movement into teaching. Fisher pointed out that this pedagogy, like the movement itself, embodies two conflicting views of education. The liberal view, supported by the equal rights faction in the movement, holds education as an instrument for gaining social power. We teach and learn to change the hierarchy and eliminate sexism, racism, classism, and so on. Two hundred years ago, Rousseau (1762, cited in Fisher, 1981) exhorted individuals (men) to oppose their social roles; thus, this aspect alone is not unique except that feminists specifically target gender roles. Even the more radical feminists agree that education must be possessed to gain access to the "socialist public sphere" or to seize and overthrow the patriarchal order.

Education is seen by the activist view of radical feminists as taking place in the process of action (Fisher, 1981). At the turn of the century, John Dewey (1902) stressed the importance of action in education, and the last decade has been marked by a broad movement in education to use "active" versus "passive" teaching techniques (e.g., Kolb, 1984; Johnson & Johnson, 1997; Slavin, 1993). The difference is that feminist pedagogues, unlike Rousseau or Dewey and his modern-day cohorts, use specific methods to encourage new feminists, a process that might generally be described as consciousness raising (CR).

We focus on two main features of CR, derived from Rosa Luxemburg's (Waters, 1970) argument that the working class learns its basic political lesson while striking or Myles Horton's (1973) insistence that real education takes place through participation in an ongoing social movement: that self-education is the means for self-definition and that an awareness of feelings is central.

What differentiates feminists' emphasis on experience from that of Dewey is the recognition that the process of having an experience is problematic. As women, our experiences have been systematically discounted and recast. Thus, we cannot turn directly to them anymore than we can to prior theory. We must find another way by using a highly developed capacity for "feeling thought" that has been nurtured and strengthened by oppression (see Poplin, 1988, 1991). To radical feminists, this capacity for intuitive thought is a sensitive instrument for perceiving the world and understanding how to change it. Here, such things as felt thought, aesthetic knowledge, and "truth, not thought out" (Belenky, Clinchy, Goldberger, & Tarule, 1986, p. 69) are not seen as emotional outlets or beacons to light the way to psychodynamic insight but as perceptual tools (Sarachild in Tanner, 1970). These tools help us to sort out authentic from imposed understanding from our experience. This definitional work then leads to finding tools to change what is oppressive, namely, to create theory to be tested in behalf of action for change.

Feminists who wound up in the academy attempted to apply CR techniques to highly heterogeneous groups of participants who were (and are) frequently hostile or passive. The tensions we described in our section on the costs and benefits of feminist teaching often stemmed from the struggle to "reconcile the CR vision with the realities of higher education" (Fisher, 1981, p. 22). Feminists must overcome the inherently individualistic and competitive environment of college classrooms and university bureaucracies and develop trust and a communal view of learning through passionate thought and action specifically related to the women's movement. Resistance to this comes not only from students but also from the entire academic culture, where knowledge is seen as deriving from dispassionate discourse.

Following the principles and using the strategies of feminist pedagogy lead to several special difficulties. First, even when CR is successful in liberating parts of students' selves that were suppressed and unacknowledged, teachers must then help students find environments where newly freed parts can be nurtured and strengthened or they will wither. Most likely the traditional parts will "work better" in mainstream conditions, and the efforts to sustain new values and ideas can be overwhelming. Second, there is now a body of fact, theory, and analysis about which the feminist teacher is an expert and most students are novices. Yet, the belief that knowledge should be mutually generated may often feel at odds with the role of teacher as expert and judge. Using one's expertise only to facilitate others requires walking a difficult tightrope. Third, the relation between the teacher and her students to today's women's movement has been reversed since its inception, when students were the vanguards challenging and sensitizing their teachers and institutions. Now, faculty are at the forefront of feminist thought and action at the same time that feminist pedagogy rejects vanguardism. All women, not just some intellectuals, should be involved in the women's movement. In fact, the movement is foreign to most students of the 1990s, who see it as something their mothers fretted about but is no longer relevant or needed.

Fisher (1981) posited CR as the viable method to address the deep philosophical and political divisions that have characterized feminists (e.g., maximalists vs. minimalists, liberal vs. radical, etc.). The exploration of feelings about our experiences can enable us to discover whether or not we have enough in common to act together. There are no vanguards when it comes to transcending the differences among women. The serious attention to these differences is the most notable characteristic of the current women's movement. It is interesting that this was the first issue to be discussed by the Boston Conference group (see Principle 3) and may imply a reemergence of CR strategies to examine and resolve how feminists can forge new understandings of education and its purposes.

We are challenged to learn to embrace diversity in the classroom. "Differences cannot be used to gauge deficiency" (Spender, 1982, p. 146). Thus, in undermining the hierarchical foundations of education, feminists must build a model of pedagogy that overcomes a legacy of differences as the basis for creating a social order. To this end, we celebrate the focus of this book on process as a means of creating consensus among diverse views and divergent experiences. As we move forward, we are committed to this process in our continuing search to discover how feminist principles and strategies can enrich and expand the teaching and learning environment.

REFERENCES AND BIBLIOGRAPHY

1. Allen, Carolyn. (1981). *Feminist teachers: The power of the personal* (Working Paper Series 3). Madison: Women's Studies Research Center, University of Wisconsin.

2. Alumnae and friends of women's studies newsletter. (1990, March 3). *Women's Studies Newsletter, 1*(1).

3. An interview with Estelle Freedman: Fear of feminism? C-R in the classroom (1990). *The Women's Review of Books, 7*(5), 25–26.

4. Bannerji, Himani, Carty, Linda, Dehli, Kari, Heald, Susan, & McKenna, Kate. (1992). *Unsettling relations: The university as a site of feminist struggles.* Boston: South End Press.

5. Bargad, Adena, & Hyde, Janet S. (1991). Women's studies: A study of feminist identity development in women. *Psychology of Women Quarterly, 15,* 181–201.

6. Baxter Magolda, Marcia B. (1990). Gender differences in epistemological development. *Journal of College Student Development, 31,* 555–561.

7. Baxter Magdola, Marcia B. (1992). *Knowing and reasoning in college.* San Francisco: Jossey-Bass.

8. Belenky, Mary F., Clinchy, Blythe M., Goldberger, Nancy R., & Tarule, Jill M. (1986). *Women's ways of knowing: The development of self, voice and mind.* New York: Basic Books.

9. Bernard, Jessie. (1972). *The future of marriage.* New York: World Publishers.

10. Bernard, Jessie. (1988). The inferiority curriculum. *Psychology of Women Quarterly, 12,* 261–268.

11. Berry, Ellen, & Black, Elizabeth. (1987). The integrative learning journal (or, getting beyond "true confessions" and "cold knowledge"). *Women's Studies Quarterly, 15*(3/4), 59–80.

12. Bezucha, Robert J. (1985). Feminist pedagogy as a subversive activity. In Margo Culley & Catherine Portuges (Eds.), *Gendered subjects: The dynamics of feminist teaching* (pp. 81–95). New York: Routledge & Kegan Paul.

13. Bogat, G. Anne, & Redner, Robin L. (1985). How mentoring affects the professional development of women in psychology. *Professional Psychology: Research and Practice, 16,* 851–859.

14. Brockett, Ralph G., & Hiemstra, Roger. (1991). *Self-direction in adult learning: Perspectives on theory, research, and practice.* New York: Routledge.

15. Bryant, Lizbeth A. (1993). Marginalized curriculums: Transforming one's place in the margins. *Transformations, 4*(2), 58–72.

16. Bunch, Charlotte. (1983). Not by degrees: Feminist theory and education. In Charlotte Bunch & Sandra Pollack (Eds.), *Learning our way: Essays in feminist education* (pp. 248–260). Trumansburg, NY: Crossing Press.

17. Bunch, Charlotte, & Pollack, Sandra. (Eds.). (1983). *Learning our way: Essays in feminist education.* Trumansburg, NY: Crossing Press.

18. Butler, Johnnella E. (1985). Toward a pedagogy of every women's studies. In Margo Culley & Catherine Portuges (Eds.), *Gendered subjects: The dynamics of feminist teaching* (pp. 203–239). New York: Routledge & Kegan Paul.

19. Butler, Johnnella E. (1991). Transforming the curriculum: Teaching about women of color. In J. E. Butler & J. C. Walter (Eds.), *Ethnic studies and women's studies* (pp. 67–87). New York: State University of New York Press.

20. Cannon, Lynn W. (1990). Fostering positive race, class, and gender dynamics in the classroom. *Women's Studies Quarterly, 18*(1/2), 126–134.

21. Casy, Kathleen. (1993). *I answer with my life: Life histories of women teachers working for social change.* New York: Routledge.

22. Chamberlain, Mariam K. (Ed.). (1988). *Women in academe: Progress and prospects.* New York: Russell Sage Foundation.

23. Chesler, Barbara M. (1974). Who wants to wash dishes? *Exceptional Parent, 4*(4), 12–5.

24. Clinchy, Blythe M. (1991). Issues of gender in teaching and learning. *Journal of Excellence in College Teaching, 1,* 52–67.

25. Cocks, Joan. (1985). Suspicious pleasures: On teaching feminist theory. In Margo Culley & Catherine Portuges (Eds.), *Gendered subjects: The dynamics of feminist teaching* (pp. 171–182). New York: Routledge & Kegan Paul.

26. Collins, Patricia H. (1989). The social construction of Black feminist thought. *Signs, 14,* 745–773.

27. Conway, Jill K. (1974). Coeducation and women's studies: Two approaches to the question of women's place in the contemporary university. *Daedalus, 103*(4), 239–249.

28. Crawford, Mary. (1989). Agreeing to differ: Feminist epistemologies and women's ways of knowing. In Mary Crawford & Margaret Gentry (Eds.), *Gender and thought: Psychological perspectives* (pp. 128–145). New York: Springer-Verlag.

29. Crawford, Mary, & Marecek, Jeanne. (1989). Feminist theory, feminist psychology: A bibliography of epistemology, critical analysis, and applications. *Psychology of Women Quarterly, 13,* 479–494.

30. Crawley, Donna, & Ecker, Martha. (1990). Integrating issues of gender, race, and ethnicity into experimental psychology and other social-science methodology courses. *Women's Studies Quarterly, 18*(1/2), 105–116.

31. Crosby, Faye J. (1992, March). *Feminist teaching in an undergraduate classroom.* Paper presented to the 17th annual meeting of the Association of Women in Psychology, Long Beach, CA.

32. Crosby, Faye J., Pufall, Ann, Snyder, Rebecca, O'Connell, Marion, & Whalen, Peg. (1989). The denial of personal disadvantage among you, me and all other ostriches. In Mary Crawford & Margaret Gentry (Eds), *Gender and thought: Psychological perspectives* (pp. 79–99). New York: Springer-Verlag.

33. Crosby, Faye, Todd, Janet, & Worell, Judith. (1994, March). *Feminism, activism, and pedagogy: A structured discussion.* Paper presented at the 19th annual meeting of the Association for Women in Psychology, Oakland, CA.

34. Crumpacker, Laurie, & VanderHaegen, Eleanor M. (1987). Pedagogy and prejudice: Strategies for confronting homophobia in the classroom. *Women Studies Quarterly, 15*(3/4), 65–73.

35. Culley, Margo, Diamond, Marilyn, Edwards, Lee, Lennox, Sara, & Portuges, Catherine. (1985). The politics of nurturance. In Margo Culley & Catherine Portuges (Eds.), *Gendered subjects: The dynamics of feminist teaching* (pp. 11–20). New York: Routledge & Kegan Paul.

36. Darder, Antonia. (1991). *Pedagogy and the struggle for voice.* Westport, CT: Bergin & Garvey.

37. Davis, Barbara H. (1985). Teaching the feminist minority. In Margo Culley & Catherine Portuges (Eds.), *Gendered subjects: The dynamics of feminist teaching* (pp. 245–252). New York: Routledge & Kegan Paul.

38. De Danaan, Lyn. (1990). Center to margin: Dynamics in a global classroom. *Women's Studies Quarterly, 18*(1/2), 135–144.

39. Deem, Rosemary. (Ed.). (1980). *Schooling for women's work*. Boston: Routledge & Kegan Paul.

40. Dewey, John. (1902). *The child and the curriculum*. Chicago: University of Chicago Press.

41. Elliot, Lisa B. (1993). Using debates to teach the psychology of women. *Teaching of Psychology, 20*(1), 35–38.

42. Ellsworth, Elizabeth. (1989). Why doesn't this feel empowering? Working through the repressive myths of critical pedagogy. *Harvard Educational Review, 59*(3), 297–324.

43. Enns, Carolyn. (1983). Integrating separate and connected knowing: The experiential learning model. *Teaching of Psychology, 20*(1), 7–13.

44. Evans, Sara M. (1979). *Personal politics: The roots of women's liberation in the civil rights movement and the new left* (1st ed.). New York: Knopf.

45. Fine, Michelle, & Gordon, Susan M. (1989). Feminist transformations of/ despite psychology. In Mary Crawford & Margaret Gentry (Eds.), *Gender and thought: Psychological perspectives* (pp. 146–174). New York: Springer-Verlag.

46. Fisher, Berenice. (1981). What is feminist pedagogy? *Radical Teacher, 18*, 20–24.

47. Fisher, Berenice. (1982). Professing feminism: Feminist academics and the women's movement. *Psychology of Women's Quarterly, 7*, 55–69.

48. Francis, Patricia L., & Russell, Kathryn. (1993). Transforming the core curriculum: A requirement in prejudice and discrimination. *Transformations, 4*(2), 46–57.

49. Frankenberg, Ruth. (1990). White women, racism, and anti-racism: A women's studies course exploring racism and privilege. *Women's Studies Quarterly, 18*(1/2), 145–154.

50. Frankenberg, Ruth. (1993). *White women, race matters: The social construction of whiteness*. Minneapolis: University of Minnesota Press.

51. Freire, Paulo. (1971). *Pedagogy of the oppressed*. New York: Continuum.

52. Friedman, Susan S. (1985). Authority in the feminist classroom: A contradiction in terms? In Margo Culley & Catherine Portuges (Eds.), *Gendered subjects: The dynamics of feminist teaching* (pp. 203–208). New York: Routledge & Kegan Paul.

53. Gabriel, Susan L., & Smithson, Isaiah. (Eds.). (1990). *Gender in the classroom: Power and pedagogy*. Chicago: University of Illinois Press.

54. Gentry, Margaret. (1989). Feminist perspectives on gender and thought. In Mary Crawford & Margaret Gentry (Eds.), *Gender and thought: Psychological perspectives* (pp. 1–16). New York: Springer-Verlag.

55. Giroux, Henry A. (1983). *Theory and resistance in education*. New York: Bergin & Garvey.

56. Giroux, Henry A. (1988). Literacy and the pedagogy of voice and political empowerment. *Educational Theory, 38*(1), 61–75.

57. Giroux, Henry A., & Freire, Paulo. (Eds.). (1989). *Critical studies in education and culture series*. New York: Bergin & Garvey.

58. Goetsch, Lori A. (1991). Feminist pedagogy: A selective annotated bibliography. *National Women's Studies Association Journal, 5*, 422–429.

59. Grauerholz, Elizabeth. (1989). Sexual harassment of women professors by students: Exploring the dynamics of power, authority, and gender in a university setting. *Sex Roles, 21*, 789–801.

60. Grument, Madeline. (1988). *Bitter milk: Women and teaching*. Amherst: The University of Massachusetts Press.

61. Haddock, Geoffrey, & Zanna, Mark P. (1994). Preferring "housewives" to "feminists": Categorization and the favorability of attitudes toward women. *Psychology of Women Quarterly, 18*(1), 25–52.

62. Harding, Sandra. (1990). Women's studies: The permanent revolution. *The Women's Review of Books, 7*(5), 17.

63. Heald, Susan. (1989). The madwomen in the attic: Feminist teaching in the margins. *Resources for Feminist Research, 18*, 22–26.

64. Henley, Nancy M. (1989). Molehill or mountain? What we know and don't know about sex bias in language. In Mary Crawford & Margaret Gentry (Eds.), *Gender and thought: Psychological perspectives* (pp. 59–78). New York: Springer-Verlag.

65. Hettich, Paul. (1990). Journal writing: Old fare or nouvelle cuisine? *Teaching of Psychology, 17*, 36–39.

66. Hoffman, Nancy J. (1985). Breaking silences: Life in the feminist classroom. In Margo Culley & Catherine Portuges (Eds.), *Gendered subjects: The dynamics of feminist teaching* (pp. 147–154). New York: Routledge & Kegan Paul.

67. Horton, Myles. (1973). Decision-making process. In Nobue Shimahara (Ed.), *Educational reconstruction* (pp. 323–341). Columbus, OH: Charles E. Merrill.

68. Howe, Florence. (1984). *Myths of co-education*. Bloomington: Indiana University Press.

69. Irigaray, Luce. (1985). *This sex which is not one*. Ithaca: Cornell University Press.

70. James, Joy. (1991). Reflections on teaching: Gender, race, and class. *Feminist Teaching, 5*(3), 9–15.

71. Jhirad, Susan. (1990). Gender gaps. *The Woman's Review of Books, 7*(5), 27.

72. Johnson, David, & Johnson, Frank P. (1997). *Joining together: Group therapy and group skills* (6th ed.). Boston: Allyn & Bacon.

73. Johnson, David, & Johnson, Roger T. (1983). Gifted students illustrate what isn't cooperative learning. *Educational Leadership, 50*(6), 60–61.

74. Jolley, J. M., & Mitchell, M. L. (1990). Two psychologists' experiences with journals. *Teaching of Psychology, 17*, 40–41.

75. Junn, Ellen N. (1989). "Dear Mom and Dad": Using personal letters to enhance students' understanding of developmental issues. *Teaching of Psychology, 16*, 135–139.

76. Kanter, Rosabeth M. (1977). *Men and women in the organization*. New York: Basic Books.

77. Kimmel, Ellen B. (1985, March). *Eminent women psychologists in the southeastern region: Perspectives*. Paper presented at the meeting of the Southeastern Psychological Association, Orlando, FL.

78. Knowles, Malcolm. (1980). *The modern practice of adult education: From pedagogy to andragogy* (2nd ed.). Chicago: Associated Press.

79. Knowles, Malcolm. (1986). The contract learning process: A hands-on experience. In Malcolm Knowles (Ed.), *Using learning contracts* (pp. 1–38). San Francisco: Jossey-Bass.

80. Kolb, David A. (1984). *Experiential learning: Experience as the source of learning and development*. Englewood Cliffs, NJ: Prentice-Hall.

81. Lewis, Magda, & Simon, Roger I. (1986). A discourse not intended for her: Learning and teaching within patriarchy. *Harvard Educational Review, 56*, 456–472.

82. Lipton, Jack P. (1986). A successful undergraduate psychology conference: Organized through a special course. *Teaching of Psychology, 13*, 111–115.

83. Luke, Carmen, & Gore, Jennifer. (1992). *Feminism and critical pedagogy*. New York: Routledge.

84. Lyons, Gracie. (1976). *Constructive criticism*. Oakland, CA: IRT Press.

85. Maher, F. (1985). Classroom pedagogy and the new scholarship on women. In M. Culley & C. Portuges (Eds.), *Gendered subjects: The dynamics of feminist teaching* (pp. 29–48). New York: Routledge & Kegan Paul.

86. Maher, F. (1987). My introduction to "Introduction to women's studies": The role of the teacher's authority in the feminist classroom. *Feminist Teacher, 3*(1), 9–11.

87. Maher, Frances A., & Dunn, Kathleen. (1984). *The practice of feminist teaching: A case study of interactions among curriculum, pedagogy, and female cognitive development* (Working Paper No. 144). Wellesley, MA: Wellesley College, Center for Research on Women.

88. Makosky, Vivian P., & Paludi, Michele A. (1990). Feminism and women's studies in the academy. In Michele Paludi & Gertrude Steuernagel (Eds.), *Foundations for a feminist restructuring of the academic disciplines* (pp. 1–37). Binghamton, NY: Harrington Park Press.

89. Markus, Hazel, & Oyserman, Daphna. (1989). Gender and thought: The role of the self concept. In Mary Crawford & Margaret Gentry (Eds.), *Gender and thought: Psychological perspectives* (pp. 100–127). New York: Springer-Verlag.

90. May, Rollo. (1970). *Power and innocence: A search for the sources of violence* (1st ed.). New York: Norton.

91. McIntosh, Peggy. (Ed.). (1984). The study of women: Processes of personal and curricular re-vision. *The Forum for Liberal Education, 6*(5), 2–4.

92. McLaren, P., & Lankshear, C. (1994). *Politics of liberation: Paths from Freire*. New York: Routledge.

93. McLaren, Peter, & Leonard, Peter. (1993). *Paulo Freire: A critical encounter.* New York: Routledge.

94. McVicker, Blythe, Belenky, Mary, Goldberger, Nancy, & Tarule, Jill. (1985). Connected education for women. *Journal of Education, 167,* 28–45.

95. Miller, Janet L. (1982). The sound of silence breaking: Feminist pedagogy and curriculum theory. *Journal of Curriculum Theorizing, 4*(1), 4–11.

96. Miller, Nancy K. (1985). Mastery, identity and the politics of work: A feminist teacher in the graduate classroom. In Margo Culley & Catherine Portuges (Eds.), *Gendered subjects: The dynamics of feminist teaching* (pp. 195–199). New York: Routledge & Kegan Paul.

97. Morgan, Kathryn P. (1987). The perils and paradoxes of feminist pedagogy. *Resources of Feminist Research, 16,* 49–52.

98. Moses, Yolanda. (1990). " . . . but some of us are (still) brave:" From a report on Black women in academe. *The Women's Review of Books, 7*(5), 31.

99. O'Malley, Susan G., Rosen, Robert C., & Vogt, Leonard (Eds.). (1990). *Politics of education: Essays from the radical teacher.* Albany: State University of New York Press.

100. Omolade, Barbara. (1987). A Black feminist pedagogy. *Women's Studies Quarterly, 15*(3/4), 32–39.

101. Palinscar, Annemarie, David, Yvonne, Winn, Deanna, & Brown, Arthur. (1990, March). *Examining the differential effects of teacher versus student controlled activity in comprehension instruction.* Paper presented at the meeting of the American Educational Research Association, Boston.

102. Paludi, Michele A. (1986). Teaching the psychology of gender roles: Some life-stage considerations. *Teaching of Psychology, 13,* 133–138.

103. Paludi, Michele A. (1990a). *Exploring teaching the psychology of women: A manual of resources.* Albany: State University of New York Press.

104. Paludi, Michele A. (Ed.). (1990b). *Ivory power: Sexual harassment on campus.* Albany: State University of New York Press.

105. Paludi, Michele A., & Barickman, R. B. (1991). *Academic and workplace sexual harassment: A resource manual.* Albany: State University of New York Press.

106. Perkins, David V. (1991). A case-study assignment to teach theoretical perspectives in abnormal psychology. *Teaching of Psychology, 18,* 97–99.

107. Perry, William G. (1970). *Forms of intellectual and ethical development in the college years.* New York: Holt, Rinehart & Winston.

108. Poplin, Mary S. (1988). Holistic/constructivist principles of the teaching/learning process: Implications for the field of learning disabilities. *Journal of Learning Disabilities, 21,* 401–416.

109. Poplin, Mary S. (1991, October). *Feminist theory and the non-cognitive in the classroom.* Paper presented to the first Culverhouse Conference on The New Paradigm and Education, Sarasota, FL.

110. Raymond, Janice G. (1985). Women's studies: A knowledge of one's own.

In M. Culley & C. Portuges (Eds.), *Gendered subjects: The dynamics of feminist teaching* (pp. 49–63). New York: Routledge & Kegan Paul.

111. Regan, Helen B. (1990, Summer). Not for women only: School administration as a feminist activity. *Teachers College, 91,* 565–577.

112. Reinardy, Lynn M. (1992, October). *Feminist teaching: An outline and resource guide.* Paper presented at the American Association of University Women/Mills College Conference, Oakland, CA.

113. Rich, Adrienne. (1979). Taking women students seriously. *Radical Teacher, 11,* 40–43.

114. Rich, Adrienne. (1985). Taking women students seriously. In Margo Culley & Catherine Portuges (Eds.), *Gendered subjects: The dynamics of feminist teaching* (pp. 21–28). New York: Routledge & Kegan Paul.

115. Richardson, Mary. (1982). Sources of tension in teaching the psychology of women. *Psychology of Women Quarterly, 7,* 45–54.

116. Ricketts, Mary. (1989). Epistemological values of feminists in psychology. *Psychology of Women Quarterly, 13,* 401–415.

117. Rose, Suzanna. (1989). The protest as a teaching technique for promoting feminist activism. *National Women's Studies Association Journal, 1,* 486–490.

118. Rosenberg, Jerome, & Blount, Ronald L. (1988). Poster sessions revisited: A student research convocation. *Teaching of Psychology, 15,* 38–39.

119. Rosnow, Ralph L. (1990). Teaching research ethics through role-play and discussion. *Teaching of Psychology, 17,* 179–181.

120. Russell, Michele G. (1983). Black-eyed blues connections: From the inside out. In Charlotte Bunch & Sandra Pollack (Eds.), *Learning our way: Essays in feminist education* (pp. 272–283). Trumansburg, NY: Crossing Press.

121. Russell, Michele. (1985). Black-eyed blues connections: Teaching black women. In Margo Culley & Catherine Portuges (Eds.), *Gendered subjects: The dynamics of feminist teaching* (pp. 155–168). New York: Routledge & Kegan Paul.

122. Ryan, M. (1989). Classroom and contexts: The challenge of feminist pedagogy. *Feminist Teacher, 4*(2/3), 39–42.

123. Sadker, Myra P., & Sadker, David M. (1982). *Sex equity handbook for schools.* New York: Longman.

124. Sandler, Bernice R. (1991). Women faculty at work in the classroom, or, why it still hurts to be a woman in labor. *Communication Education, 40,* 6–15.

125. Sarachild, Kathie. (Ed). (1975). *Feminist revolution.* New York: Random House.

126. Sargent, Alice. (1985). *Beyond sex roles.* New York: West Publishing.

127. Scanion, Jennifer. (1993). Feminist pedagogy and everyday teaching: Results of a women's studies program self study. *Transformation, 4*(1), 70–76.

128. Schlib, John. (1985). Pedagogy of the oppressors? In Margo Culley & Catherine Portuges (Eds.), *Gendered subjects: The dynamics of feminist teaching* (pp. 253–264). New York: Routledge & Kegan Paul.

129. Schniedewind, Nancy. (1983). Feminist values: Guidelines for teaching methodology in women's studies. In Charlotte Bunch & Sandra Pollack (Eds.), *Learning our way: Essays in feminist education* (pp. 261–271). Trumansburg, NY: Crossing Press.

130. Schulman, Barbara. (1990). Harassing the harassers: Women make campus policy. *The Woman's Review of Books, 7*(5), 27.

131. Schuster, Marilyn, & Van Dyne, Susan. (1984). Placing women in the liberal arts: Stages of curriculum transformation. *Harvard Educational Review, 54,* 413–428.

132. Shor, Ira. (1980). *Critical teaching and everyday life* (1st ed.). Boston: South End Press.

133. Shor, Ira. (1987a). *Freire for the classroom: A sourcebook for liberatory teaching.* Portsmouth, NH: Boynton.

134. Shor, Ira. (1987b). What is the "dialogical method" of teaching? *Journal of Education, 169*(3), 11–31.

135. Shrewsbury, Carolyn M. (1987a). Feminist pedagogy: A bibliography. *Women's Studies Quarterly, 15*(3/4), 116–124.

136. Shrewsbury, Carolyn M. (1987b). What is feminist pedagogy? *Women Studies Quarterly, 15*(3/4), 6–13.

137. Slavin, Robert E. (1993). *Educational psychology: Theory and practice* (4th ed.). Boston: Allyn & Bacon.

138. Smith, Page. (1990). *Killing the spirit: Higher education in America.* New York: Viking.

139. Snoek, Diedrick. (1985). A male feminist in a women's college classroom. In Margo Culley & Catherine Portuges (Eds.), *Gendered subjects: The dynamics of feminist teaching* (pp. 136–144). New York: Routledge & Kegan Paul.

140. Spelman, Elizabeth V. (1985). Combating the marginalization of Black women in the classroom. In Margo Culley & Catherine Portuges (Eds.), *Gendered subjects: The dynamics of feminist teaching* (pp. 240–244). New York: Routledge & Kegan Paul.

141. Spender, Dale (1982). *Invisible women: The schooling scandal.* London: Writers and Readers.

142. Stake, Jayne E., & Gerner, Margaret A. (1987). The women's studies experience: Personal and professional gains for women and men. *Psychology of Women Quarterly, 11,* 277–283.

143. Stake, Jayne E., Roades, Laurie, Rose, Suzanna, Ellis, Lisa, & West, Carolyn. (1994). The women's studies experience: Impetus for feminist activism. *Psychology of Women Quarterly, 18*(1), 17–24.

144. Stake, Jayne E., & Rose, Suzanna. (1994). The long-term impact of women's studies on students' personal lives and political activism. *Psychology of Women Quarterly, 18,* 403–412.

145. Stone, Lynda. (1994). Teaching and pedagogy: Toward a transformational theory of teaching. In Lynda Stone (Ed.), *The education feminism reader* (pp. 221–228). New York: Routledge.

146. Sugar, Judith, & Livosky, Marilyn. (1988). Enriching child psychology courses with a preschool journal option. *Teaching of Psychology, 15,* 93–95.

147. Svinicki, Marilla, & Dixon, Nancy M. (1987). The Kolb model modified for classroom activities. *College Teaching, 35,* 141–146.

148. Tanner, Leslie B. (Ed.). (1970). *Voices from women's liberation.* New York: New American Library.

149. Tarule, Jill M. (1992). Dialogue and adult learning. *Liberal Education, 78*(4), 12–19.

150. Thomas, N. S., & Eison, James. (1987). Using Kolb's learning style to teach experiential learning theory. In Vivian P. Makosky, Linda G. Whittemore, & Anne M. Rogers (Eds.), *Activities handbook for the teaching of psychology* (Vol. 2, pp. 69–71). Washington, DC: American Psychological Association.

151. Treed, David. (1992). *Cultural pedagogy.* Wesport, NY: Bergin & Garvey.

152. Treichler, Paula A. (1986). Teaching feminist theory. In C. Nelson (Ed.), *Theory in the classroom* (pp. 57–128). Urbana: University of Illinois Press.

153. Unger, Rhoda K. (1982). Advocacy versus scholarship revisited: Issues in the psychology of women. *Psychology of Women Quarterly, 7,* 5–17.

154. Unger, Rhoda K. (1989). Sex, gender, and epistemology. In Mary Crawford & Margaret Gentry (Eds.), *Gender and thought: Psychological perspectives* (pp. 17–35). New York: Springer-Verlag.

155. Unger, Rhoda K., & Denmark, F. L. (1975). *Woman: Dependent or independent variable.* New York: Psychological Dimensions.

156. Walsh, Catherine E. (1991). *Pedagogy and the struggle for voice.* Westport, CT: Bergin & Garvey.

157. Walton, Marsha D. (1988). Interviewing across the life span: A project for an adult development course. *Teaching of Psychology, 15,* 198–200.

158. Washington, Mary H. (1985). How racial differences helped us discover our common ground. In Margo Culley & Catherine Portuges (Eds.), *Gendered subjects: The dynamics of feminist teaching* (pp. 221–229). New York: Routledge & Kegan Paul.

159. Waters, Mary Alice. (1970). The mass strike, the political party, and the trade unions. In Mary Alice Waters (Ed.), *Rosa Luxemburg speaks.* New York: Pathfinder.

160. Weiler, Katherine. (1988). *Women teaching for change: Gender, class, and power.* Westport, CT: Bergin & Garvey.

161. Weisstein, Naomi. (1968). *Kinder, kuche, kirche as scientific law: Psychology constructs the female.* Boston: New England Free Press.

162. Weisstein, Naomi. (1971). Psychology constructs the female; or the fantasy life of the male psychologist. *Social Education, 35,* 362–373.

163. Whitten, Lisa. (1993). Managing student reactions to controversial issues in the college classroom. *Transformation, 4*(1), 30–44.

164. Worell, Judith. (1989). Feminist visions in a gendered society [Review of the

book, *Seeing female: Social role and personal lives*]. *Contemporary Psychology,* 34, 769.

165. Worell, Judith. (1990). Images of women in psychology. In Michele Paludi & Gertrude Steuernagel (Eds.), *Foundations for a feminist restructuring of the academic disciplines.* Binghamton, NY: Harrington Park Press.

166. Worell, Judith. (1992, March). *Feminist frameworks in graduate education.* Paper presented to the 17th annual meeting of the Association of Women in Psychology, Long Beach, CA.

167. Worell, Judith, & Crosby, Faye. (1992). *The feminist teaching project* (final report to the Women's College Coalition). Unpublished manuscript.

168. Zigmund, B. B. (1988, September). The well-being of academic women is still begin sabotaged by colleagues, by students, and by themselves. *Chronicle of Higher Education,* p. A44.

JOURNAL RESOURCES

Chronicle of Higher Education
Communication Education
Contemporary Psychology
Daedalus
Educational Review
Educational Theory
Ethnic Studies and Women's Studies
Feminism and Psychology
Feminist Teacher
The Forum for Liberal Education
Harvard Educational Review
Journal of College Student Development
Journal of Curriculum Theorizing
Journal of Education
Journal of Excellence in College Teaching

Journal of Learning Disabilities
Journal of Thought
Liberal Education
NWSA Journal
On Campus with Women
Professional Psychology: Research and Practice
Psychology of Women Quarterly
Radical Teacher
Resources for Feminist Research
Sex Roles
Teachers College Record
Teaching of Psychology
Transformations
The Women's Review of Books
Women's Studies Quarterly
Women's Studies Newsletter

Appendix
Feminist Pedagogy Working Group Matrix of Principles and Strategies

Principles	Strategies								
	1. Sensitizes students to the oppressive and transformative power of language.	2. Requires non-sexist, inclusionary language in all communications.	3. Helps students develop a sense that they can be social change agents.	4. Uses assignments that engage students in social-change efforts.	5. Makes use of a developmental view of the consciousness raising process.	6. Encourages affirmative attitudes and views of women.	7. Enhances and makes accessible resources relevant to the lives of women.	8. Brings in a variety of women to serve as role models.	9. Contextualizes learning materials and activities.
1. Fundamental to feminist pedagogy is a consciousness of differential power, privilege, and oppression that is made explicit through the instructor's planning, articulation of values and goals and through classroom policies.	20 37 45 / 10 18 19	20 37 45 54 / 20 35 38	4 5 12 21 / 49 51 52	16 31 42 / 53 66 70	5 56 / 81 86 94	15 24 / 99 102	21 70 / 114 115	3 13 / 129 139	78 / 141 142
2. Feminists acknowledge the power inherent in their teaching role and seek ways to empower students in the learning process.	54 56 61 / 10 35	55 61 64 70 / 41 43	31 42 44 46 / 56 86	50 79 82 / 101	66 85 / 103	31 52 / 112	81 / 136	69 94 / 139	79 / 144

Note. The numbers in each cell are keyed to the references to provide a sample of related literature for each principle (lower left) and strategy (upper right).

148   KIMMEL AND WORELL

3. All voices are encouraged, valued and heard, and a climate of respect for difference is fostered.	20 30 36	64 70 12	37 38 41	94 104 105 112	43 56 66	47 62 99 117	79 81 83	103 117 143	102	94 102	94	124 129	94	140 141	94	156 157	131 165	159 163	106
4. Feminist teachers are committed to recognizing and accommodating to multiple learning styles and respecting the different contexts of students' lives.	4 6	113 115 131	18 20	113 115 131	28 35	143 144 148 160 33	43 56	144 33	157	79 80	168	87 107	131	103	135	168			147

Appendix (Continued)

Strategies

Principles	10. Highlights the experiences of marginalized people.	11. Uses narratives, journals, and other activities to explicate life stories.	12. Facilitates the creation of a safe learning environment.	13. Models appropriate self disclosure to encourage students to make the learning process personally relevant.	14. Asks unasked questions and listens for silences.	15. Develops activities to assist students who find it difficult to participate in class.	16. Shares their learning process, incomplete thoughts, errors, ideas in progress, and personal reactions and invites students to do the same.	17. Makes use of group activities.	18. Uses cooperative learning activities.
5. Learning should be holistic, integrating cognition, feelings, and experience.	15 18 19 / 26 45	11 12 24 65 / 70 79	20 30 / 89 102	20 31 / 108 109	24 81 / 110 115	5 41 66 70 / 129 131	1 / 135	41 50 / 157	41 43 79 / 164
6. Feminist pedagogy makes the connections between personal experiences and social–political reality.	34 37 45 / 20 42	70 74 75 / 47 52	32 68 / 56 81	50 / 87 94	85 94 / 102 116	79 81 94 / 129	20 / 154	70 79 / 164	85 94 103 / 168

7. Feminist pedagogy assumes both teachers and students are engaged in a mutual learning process.	42 43	56 63 70	56 70	79 102 103	79 81	94 104	85	70	97	113 115	109	103 104 114	115	94	129	102 103	136	106 112
8. Feminist teachers continually strive to increase their knowledge of and sensitivity to diverse cultural realities.	20 28	98 100 103	30 38	106 111 114	50 56	105 135	89	85	100	119 131	115	115 118 140	131	116	140	146	141	129 137
9. Feminist teachers model an acceptance of their own authority and expertise.	1 13	112 121 131	52 87	146 147 157	86 88	163	94 96	94	97	140 153	115	141 146 157	129	142	136	147	168	141 157

Strategies

Principles	19. Uses the class process to illustrate feminist principles.	20. Illuminates group process as a teaching tool.	21. Employs experiential learning activities.	22. Has students function as experts in the learning process.	23. Provides opportunities for students to direct aspects of their learning experience.	24. Makes use of respectful debate.	25. Includes course assignments that teach students they can contribute to the knowledge base.	26. Makes evaluation a dialogic process.	27. Invites student feedback and provides opportunities for anonymous evaluation.	28. Provides opportunities for students to review and evaluate constructively the work of their peers.
10. Knowledge is contextual and emergent, and therefore feminist teachers are committed to including multiple sources of knowledge.	38 50 / 7 8 10	73 / 20 38 41	26 70 79 80 / 43 45	12 79 / 56 70	13 14 71 / 85 89	41 / 102 106	14 30 / 110 115	14 26 / 116 129	24 41 / 136 138	20 41 / 141 147
11. Learning is in the service of social change.	5	45	85 94 102 / 129	94 / 136	79 101 / 153	79	66 79 / 102	41 56	66	79

Principle																		
12. Learning is in the service of increasing self awareness and personal growth.	5 18	115 120	41 43	79	106 109 112	101	85	89	102 106	91	94	106	70 79	116	102	142	164	102
13. Feminist teachers help to reclaim women's histories and cultures.	13 18	121	19	20	120 121 123	112	35	56	119 146	60	112	101	131	85 106	141	118	164	106
14. Feminist pedagogy is aimed at transforming the discipline by critically examining existing constructs and working to develop theory that reflects the breadth of human experience.	12 15 18	126	19 20 45	48 50 56	126 147 150	136	60 87 85	91 95 119	147 157	131 136 144	145 147	106	149 152	147	141	153 157	160 166	157

8

COVISION: FEMINIST SUPERVISION, PROCESS, AND COLLABORATION

NATALIE PORTER AND MELBA VASQUEZ
WITH LEAH FYGETAKIS, LORRAINE MANGIONE,
EILEEN T. NICKERSON, JEAN PIENIADZ, MARCY PLUNKETT,
MARYHELEN SNYDER, AND BETH SIMPSON

Individual supervision constitutes the primary method of teaching the practice of psychotherapy (Newman, 1981; Pope, Schover, & Levenson, 1980); it is also the most memorable part of learning about psychotherapy. Years after graduation, therapists can vividly recount supervisory relationships and experiences that produced insight, understanding, and even transformation, as well as those that yielded disappointment, tedium, self-doubt, or pain.

Much has been written about psychotherapy supervision, but little has been written about it from a feminist perspective. Feminist therapists can easily detail what was not feminist about their own supervisory history, but they have not delineated what was or is feminist about their supervisory content, practices, standards, or processes. The literature is sketchy and fragmented. This chapter represents an attempt to define a comprehensive feminist approach to supervision, develop a coherent philosophy, and de-

This chapter is dedicated to the memory of Eileen T. Nickerson.

lineate its guiding principles. We also illustrate the process of our working group and the themes that guided our group's discussions.

CONFERENCE PROCESS

Prospective supervision working group members framed questions for the group to consider prior to the conference. The participants possessed diverse theoretical perspectives and experiences, which led to a broad and rich range of ideas. Each group member contributed unique topics and perspectives. Nonetheless, the questions also reflected a surprising level of commonality among the participants about the nature of the issues.

Supervision Themes

The themes, which were embodied in the questions, became the focus of much of the subsequent work. They fell roughly into three topical areas; readings that correspond to these topics were suggested prior to the conference.

1. The process of supervision, including an examination of the ideal use of power, a questioning of the hierarchical models traditionally used, and a search for more collaborative models: What is the role of power in a supervisory relationship? How can we create more collaborative models of supervision while not denying actual power differences or ignoring our responsibility as supervisors for quality control and evaluations? What would more collaborative models look like that demystify the role of supervisor and foster supervisee growth and self-examination? How does the concept of reflexivity contribute to a collaborative model of supervision? How do we work collaboratively with less experienced or less capable students? How do we balance or integrate the practices of empathy, dialogue, mutuality, empowerment, authenticity, and respect with the natural authority that may emerge from our experience and training and the conferred authority of institutional or organizational standards?
2. The content of supervision, including the integration of feminist and antiracist models: How do the current feminist discourses regarding dual relationships; therapeutic neutrality; transference and countertransference; diagnosis; and issues of race, class, gender, ethnicity, sexual orientation, age, and disability affect our supervisory practices? How do we assist our supervisees in reconceptualizing cases in less women-blaming

ways? Where does supervision fit in the larger pedagogical picture of teaching feminist theory, ethics, social activism, research, and scholarship? Do prevailing models of supervision promote or detract from feminist aims? What are feminist and cross-cultural models of supervision?

3. Ethical issues and problem areas for feminist therapists and supervisors: What are the key ethical issues pertaining to supervision? What are appropriate boundary issues in supervision, and what are the supervisor's responsibilities toward the supervisee? How do we deal with problems such as sexist practices or sexual harassment by supervisors?

In the first supervision working group meeting, each of us listed the topics we considered important to the subject of feminist supervision. This task consisted of stating the topics and questions detailed above. It also underscored the immensity of the job of developing a model of feminist supervision in a few days! We decided we needed to develop priorities because we would be unable to cover all the areas suggested through our questions or brainstorming.

Characteristics of Positive and Negative Supervision

Overwhelmed by the task ahead of us, we elected to revert to the tried and true feminist principle, "the personal is political." We discussed our own positive and negative experiences as both supervisors and supervisees.

Most participants mentioned that their best supervisors combined unconditional positive regard with intellectual and personal challenge. Group members mentioned feeling safe, respected, and even loved, yet challenged to explore new intellectual depths, to generate their own analyses, to look honestly at themselves, and to push for new understandings and meanings. All group members considered it essential to feel both cared for and challenged. Unconditional positive regard without challenge seemed patronizing, and challenge without relationship seemed unsafe or disrespectful. Positive supervisors were also described in the following ways: They respected the experience and knowledge of their supervisees; their supervisory style promoted mutual understanding and reciprocal dialogue; they helped supervisees find their voices for ideas they had been unable to articulate; they emphasized imparting knowledge rather than expecting obedience; and they addressed social–contextual issues.

Working group members defined poor supervisory experiences as those in which supervisors were overly directive or expected the supervisee to carry out the supervisor's directives, regardless of fit or comfort level for the supervisee; supervisors pathologized all of the supervisee's conflicts, fears, mistakes, or problems; supervisors did not encourage the supervisee to discuss or disagree with the supervisor's interpretations, usually pathology oriented, of the supervisee's behavior; laissez-faire supervisors provided little direction or structure; supervisors appeared to be meeting their own needs by spending too much time discussing their own issues or cases; supervisors promoted sexist, classist, or racist interpretations of behavior or ignored sociocultural factors in understanding psychopathology; and supervisors denigrated the supervisee for considering alternative models or explanations.

We asked: "How does good feminist supervision differ from good supervision in general? What is feminist about the list we generated?" This question led the group to generate a list of defining principles for feminist supervision and a definition of a feminist supervisor and to identify areas central to feminist theory and good supervisory practices.

The remaining meeting time was used to flesh out each of these topics. We worked until we developed consensus on each area; the final theoretical perspective was agreed on by all group members. Representatives of our working group met with representatives of each of the other groups, who provided feedback about our ideas. We incorporated their feedback into our process, adding or altering our ideas when appropriate to do so.

This reciprocal process was outstanding. We were living the ideal we were writing about. We elected to call this process *covision* instead of supervision. Covision included collaboration, mutuality, disagreement without disapproval, safety, regard for each person and her ideas, the ability to integrate many different perspectives, as well as the ability to encompass both relationship and challenge. This process will influence our own work and our own supervisory relationships in the future.

FEMINIST APPROACHES TO SUPERVISION: A REVIEW OF THE LITERATURE

To date, feminist authors have been concerned primarily with the process of supervision and the relationship between supervisor and supervisee. Topics pertinent to feminist therapy theory (outlined in other chapters), such as power and boundary issues and ethics, have been central to the feminist supervision literature.

Feminist Process in Supervision

The literature describing the feminist process in supervision is derived from the literature on feminist therapy theory. Hawes (1992) envisioned a collaborative supervisory process that involved genuine and reciprocal dialogue and recognition of the overlap of the roles of teacher and learner.

Porter (1985) described the feminist supervisory process as analogic to the feminist therapy process. In principle, the feminist supervisor respects the supervisee's autonomy, models the constructive use of power, and provides a safe environment that facilitates self-disclosure and self-examination.

The exploration of sociocultural and historical factors has been considered a key component of the feminist supervision process. Understanding the context of both the client's and the supervisee's behaviors, assumptions, expectations, and worldviews has been viewed as essential to feminist supervision. Hawes (1992) described the process of reflexivity in supervision. Supervisor and supervisee participate in a dialogue that includes examining their own assumptions and providing a social context for their beliefs; examining the social impact of their beliefs, including gender and culture; opening themselves up to multiple perspectives and to each other's differences; and dissecting the power relationships between them. Hawes considered both the supervisor and the supervisee responsible for including multiple discourses such as the personal, interpersonal, political, social, and historical. The supervisor holds the responsibility for modeling openness to the process, a view of individuals that is less "patronizing, patriarchal, and pathologizing" (p. 9), and a view of supervision that is less hierarchical than traditional supervision.

Supervisory processes aimed at increasing the supervisee's sensitivity and competence in treating women and ethnic minorities have been presented in the literature. Porter (1995) has proposed a four-stage process of supervision that promotes increasing awareness and competence in understanding the impact of gender, race, class, and ethnicity on one's work as a therapist. This approach (a) begins with a didactic exploration of how social constructs, such as gender, ethnicity, and class, influence the therapist's clinical understanding of the client; (b) progresses to an exploration of the roots of racism, ethnocentrism, sexism, classism, homophobia, and ageism in society and in one's clinical work; (c) examines the supervisee's own internalized racism, sexism, and other biases and their "transferential" consequences; and (d) encourages the development of a collective and active approach to combat these internalized oppressions and to promote social change.

Lopez et al. (1989) also outlined a stage model to describe the process experienced by supervisees who attempt to become more sensitive to culture and gender issues. They described supervisees as initially ignoring gender or cultural factors when diagnosing or treating clients, perhaps viewing psychological theories as universal (Stage 1). With time, the supervisees may become aware that gender and cultural factors are important, but they do not have the expertise to understand how they actually modify treatment or therapeutic formulations (Stage 2). Their therapeutic errors may change from initially excluding culture or gender in their formulations to overincluding or inaccurately interpreting gender and cultural information. As the supervisees gain experience and knowledge, they become more aware of the complexity of integrating contextual and cultural information into psychological formulations (Stage 3). The supervisees may become overwhelmed with the task of developing accurate interpretations of behavior and effective interventions. In the last stage (Stage 4), the supervisees become more culturally competent, better able to understand how culture and gender influence behavior, development, and the expression of mental health functioning and symptoms.

Ethical Issues

Newman (1981) described ethical issues pertaining to psychotherapy supervision, many of which overlap with feminist therapy theory. They included whether the supervisor possessed sensitivity toward issues of cultural diversity, whether the supervisee was able to collaborate on selecting supervisors and developing supervision goals, and whether supervisees were placed in inappropriate roles such as dual relationships.

Dutton Douglas and Rave (1990) enumerated several ethical guidelines for feminist supervisors. Feminist supervisors should (a) recognize, and integrate into their work with trainees, issues of cultural diversity and oppression; (b) be aware of power differences in the supervisor–supervisee relationship and use power responsibly; (c) monitor the "various responsibilities associated with multiple role relationships, including the overlap between professional and personal roles" (p. 143); (d) monitor their own personal and professional needs and use their resources to maintain responsible professional behavior and personal well-being; and (e) actively pursue social as well as individual change.

Another ethical concern involves the extent to which supervisors should explore the supervisee's personal emotional conflicts and relationship problems. The supervisor who focuses on the supervisee's personal characteristics and problems may be creating a dual relationship, by acting in both supervisory and therapeutic roles. Doing so without the supervisee's explicit consent may be destructive as well as unethical. On the other hand, ignoring personal qualities that interfere with the supervisee's ability to treat clients effectively may jeopardize the client's well-being and the supervisee's progress as a therapist. Sarnat (1992) advocated placing supervision in an interpersonal context, in which both supervisor and supervisee are seen as shaping the supervisory relationship. She proposed that when each is responsible for her respective role, feelings, strengths, and limitations, there is less pathologizing of the supervisee and less need for defensive reactions by the supervisee. The role of the supervisee's personal qualities can then be examined in a collaborative, empowering way.

Sterling and Bugental (1993) have developed an interesting method for intensifying the supervisee's awareness of countertransference phenomena and breaking through barriers to understand the client. This method, which they call the "meld experience," is also described and expanded on by Snyder (1995). The method extends empathic attunement in the parallel process of the therapist–client and supervisor–supervisee.

NEW APPROACHES TO FEMINIST SUPERVISION

Elements of Feminist Supervision

Definition of Feminist Supervision

The supervision working group defined *feminist supervision* on the basis of the literature and the conference process. *Feminist supervision* encompasses a collaborative relationship that is mutual and reflexive in nature. It is not egalitarian; rather, it is predicated on the principle of mutual respect characterized by clear, direct, and honest dialogic communication and responsible action. It encompasses awareness of and attention to the social, contextual nature of both the supervisory and the therapeutic processes. A feminist supervisory context embodies the feminist principles of therapy, including the analyses of power, boundaries, and hierarchy; an emphasis on social context and diversity; an examination of the relationship of language to the social construction of gender; and the promotion of social activism, ethics, and lifelong self-examination and professional development.

Characteristics of Feminist Supervisors

The group also defined the characteristics of feminist supervisors.

First, feminist supervisors adhere to the principles of feminist theory and therapy outlined above and in other chapters. They are proactive in their commitment to a feminist supervisory process. They attempt not only to teach feminist therapy content but also to model feminist process. They believe that the supervision process parallels the therapeutic process. Feminist supervisors model mutual respect, collaboration, and empowerment in the supervisory relationship, which they believe facilitates these processes in the supervisee–client relationship.

Second, feminist supervisors foster the discussion of issues central to the intimate nature of the therapeutic relationship and to the maintenance of good boundaries, such as sexual attraction, touching, outside contact, or breaking of the therapeutic frame. They empower the supervisee to address these issues with the client in ways that make it safe for the client to address them.

Third, feminist supervisors engage in ongoing self-examination and reflexivity in their relationships with supervisees. They realize that openness to the supervision process requires continuous self-examination and self-care and lifelong learning, education, and dialogue. They discourage rigid, dogmatic, dualistic, or dichotomized thinking, which inhibits dialogue. Instead, they honor an inclusive approach to dialogue, encouraging the multiplicity and integration of ideas. Feminist supervisors recognize the power abuses inherent in demanding adherence to one set of absolute truths.

Principles Guiding Feminist Supervision

Feminist principles are essential to feminist supervision. The key theoretical underpinnings of feminist therapy that differentiate feminist supervision from nonsexist, "good" supervision include understanding women's experience in society, greater equality in relationships, social change and advocacy, and working toward the empowerment of women.

Principle 1: Feminist supervisors are proactive in analyzing power dynamics and differentials between the supervisor and the supervisee, model the use of power in the service of the supervisee, and vigilantly avoid abuses of power.

The analysis of power is as central to the process of feminist supervision as it is to feminist theory and therapy. Feminist supervisors explicitly attend to power differences in their relationships with supervisees, clarifying roles, relationships, and boundaries. They link explicitly their modeling of power in the supervisory relationship with the supervisee's use of power in the therapeutic relationship. This analysis of power fosters safety and trust within the supervisory relationship. It models the paradigm on which feminist therapy is based: the use of power in the interest of client empowerment rather than as a way to exert control over an individual. The dynamics of power in supervision parallel those of the therapeutic relationship. The analysis of power in the supervisory context makes explicit for the supervisee a process that also should occur in the feminist therapeutic relationship.

The supervisor assists the supervisee in identifying the many factors contributing to power differentials, such as differences caused by ascribed roles and privilege embedded in the broader social structure. Ascribed role differences include the formal power possessed by supervisors to provide rewards and sanctions and to affect the supervisees' path in their chosen profession. More informally, the supervisor has the power to impart or withhold knowledge and information. Supervisees are vulnerable not only because of formal power relationships but also because they are the ones who must risk more interpersonally and personally to remain open to feedback and learning. Supervisors also assist supervisees in recognizing and overcoming their own internalized authority issues, which may interfere with personal empowerment.

Feminist supervisors are also responsible for examining the power differential embedded in the social structure, such as the vulnerability of supervisees of color working with dominant culture supervisors. Feminist supervisors recognize that neither therapeutic nor supervisory relationships can be removed from broader social contexts. Supervisors examine the ways in which their own privilege may contribute to power abuses or the lack of safety in supervision. Again, this process models for supervisees the process to be initiated in the therapeutic relationship.

Principle 1 covers the use and abuse of power as well as its analysis. Power must be used in the service of the supervisees. This is accomplished by sharing power when appropriate, setting mutually comfortable boundaries, modeling reflexivity and nondefensiveness in supervision, and using self-disclosure in the service of the supervisee. Many of these processes are elaborated in subsequent principles.

Avoiding the abuse of power prohibits acts that are clearly exploitative in the context of power differences, such as sexual contact, providing therapy and supervision simultaneously, or giving the supervisee an excessive workload and too little supervision. Using supervision to meet primarily the supervisor's emotional needs, coercing the supervisee to self-disclose, or forcing a makeover of the supervisee in the supervisor's image constitute boundary violations as well.

Principle 2: Feminist supervision is based on a collaborative relationship, defined as mutually respectful, in which the supervisee's autonomy and diverse perspectives are encouraged.

Feminist supervisors recognize their supervisees as adult learners and foster their autonomy through collaborative, nonauthoritarian relationships. Principle 2 is parallel to the feminist therapy principle that therapy should promote the client's autonomy and independence. Just as clients define their own therapy goals, supervisees remain in charge of their own learning objectives and goals. Supervisors actively collaborate with their supervisees, providing opportunities for informed choices about the supervisory experience, including selecting one's supervisor, developing learning goals and objectives, and choosing client populations with whom to work. Collaboration does not imply agreement. Differences of opinion are also handled in a collaborative, honest manner, where feedback can be used constructively. In providing feedback, supervisors neither invalidate supervisees' interpretation of their experience nor pathologize them.

Collaborative relationships do not imply equal relationships. Supervisors do have the responsibility to evaluate the work of their supervisees, which is discussed later. Collaboration occurs in the context of the boundaries created by recognizing the power differentials outlined in Principle 1. To portray supervisory relationships as egalitarian denies power where it exists and obscures the nature and purpose of supervisory relationships. Moreover, it increases the supervisee's risk of exploitation by creating the illusion of equal responsibility, informed consent, and free choice when boundaries are violated.

Principle 3: Feminist supervisors facilitate reflexive interactions and supervisee self-examination by modeling openness, authenticity, reflexivity, and the value of lifelong learning and self-examination.

Feminist supervisors are committed, engaged, and genuine during the supervisory process. They recognize that the learning that occurs in supervision is the effect of a mutual, honest, and synergistic relationship. They view the supervisory relationship as reciprocal. Supervisors and supervisees have and take responsibility for their actions, feelings, and beliefs. They illuminate the process of self-examination by remaining open and nondefensive during reflexive dialogue and by self-disclosing in ways that benefit the supervisees. Even when the concepts of transference and countertransference are integral to the supervisors' theoretical framework, they do not relegate all of the supervisees' concerns or negative feedback to transferential issues but recognize the interpersonal intersubjective aspects of the phenomenon. In every interaction, they take responsibility for their part in the relationship. Supervisors remain open to exploring their own motives, feelings, and countertransferential issues that may affect the supervisory relationship. They reveal them when appropriate.

Through this reflexive relationship, supervisors model the process of ongoing and lifelong monitoring and self-examination. They create the environment where value is placed on an honest analysis of their strengths, limitations, and continual growth rather than on being right or having the best technique. They monitor their own supervisory behaviors, including the need for outside consultation or therapy, and they continually work to improve their supervisory skills.

Supervisors may discuss the supervisees' personal and interpersonal characteristics when they influence the treatment of clients. Supervisors do so in a nonpathologizing, nonpunitive manner after gaining the supervisees' consent.

Principle 4: Supervision occurs in a social context that attends to and emphasizes the diversity of women's lives and contexts.

Feminist supervisors integrate the theory and therapy consistent with feminist practice into supervision. These core theoretical and therapy constructs are described in previous chapters and are not repeated here. Feminist supervisors facilitate the understanding of diversity, including gender, race, class, ethnicity, sexual orientation, physical disability, and age and the impact of these differences on both the therapist–client and the supervisor–supervisee relationships. Supervisors are reflexive about their own biases, stereotypes, and expectations because of their diverse understandings and experiences. These multiple factors are particularly relevant as they pertain to clients and supervisees and the impact of language on maintaining these structural inequities. Feminist supervisors are aware of their supervisees' own internalized subordination, related either to being a student or to other structural constructs, such as ethnicity, class, or sexual orientation.

Feminist supervisors encourage the awareness and development of personal cultural identities. They establish a process that ensures the supervisees' emotional safety during this process, including lack of punitiveness when supervisees are unable or unwilling to explore their own identity in supervision. Supervisors avoid blaming, shaming, and other processes that negate the supervisees' perceptions of their oppression. Supervisors attend to the impact of multiple oppressions and the privilege inherent in one's current social status or position.

Principle 5: Feminist supervisors attend to the social construction of gender and the role of language in maintaining a gendered society.

Feminist supervisors recognize that the marginalization and trivialization of women's voices, as well as the voices of other oppressed groups, are inherent in the social construction of language, meaning, and relationship. The social construction of all meanings and practices, including gender, family, intimacy, autonomy, and even supervision itself, must be examined. Marginalization may be an inevitable artifact of any relationship or environment in which process is not examined in the context of the social construction of meanings. When the social construction of language and meaning is not consciously addressed, the oppression continues and is denied. Not infrequently, neither the oppressor nor the oppressed see or understand what is happening.

Supervisors model a process of ongoing consciousness raising. They keep up with the literature and monitor their own use of language, biases, and stereotypes as nondefensively as possible. They openly use consultants either when they lack the requisite expertise or when their personal issues may interfere with supervision.

Principle 6: Feminist supervisors advance and model the feminist principle of advocacy and activism.

Feminist supervisors link feminist therapy practice to social change and public service. They are attentive to clients' economic issues or life circumstances and raise these issues with their supervisees. They strive to "demystify" therapy and recognize when education is part of the therapeutic process. They may address groups of women in the community, believing that they have a responsibility to promote education for the public good. They model their beliefs that their clients' health is often tied to public health and social change through their involvement around these issues with their supervisees.

Feminist supervisors model activism by participating in legislative initiatives or providing public testimony around issues important to the mental health of women. Examples might include creating programs to support lesbian and gay youth or reproductive freedom issues.

Feminist supervisors also challenge their supervisees to think about education, advocacy, and social change roles they might find congruent with their own values. Feminist supervisors are more attentive to guiding their supervisees into thinking about their role, power, and responsibility to affect systems. They also remain respectful of the beliefs, values, and boundaries of their supervisees and model this sensitivity. They recognize the delicate balance between imposing their beliefs and being apolitical in supervision. They are ever mindful of the complexity involved in walking this tightrope.

Principle 7: Feminist supervisors maintain standards that ensure their supervisees' competent and ethical practice.

As in traditional supervision, feminist supervisors are accountable for the well-being of their supervisees' clients. They ensure that clients are aware of the supervisory process. They are responsible for preventing harm to clients and for monitoring and evaluating the progress of both their supervisees and the therapy process. Supervisors are responsible for providing direct and honest evaluations and feedback.

Supervisors teach ethical as well as clinical–counseling practices. They help the supervisee to understand the complexity of ethical dilemmas, the potentially serious harm done to a client when ethical violations occur, and the ways to prevent ethical breaches, including ongoing self-monitoring and consultation.

Feminist supervisors are also responsible for challenging the sexist and racist practices of their supervisees, including the negative use of stereotypes and the misuse of diagnoses. They delineate the relationship of sexist or racist behaviors to ethical violations. They view cultural and gender responsivity as core competencies, which they integrate into the teaching, supervision, evaluation, and feedback processes.

When a supervisor has to recommend a supervisee's termination from a training program because of unsatisfactory and unremediable performance, the interaction should still be grounded in feminist process. The supervisor should keep the best interests of the individual in mind and develop ways to act humanely. Reframing the problem as a mismatch between the supervisee and the occupation or securing outplacement counseling for the supervisee are two examples. This process admittedly is difficult in the moment because the supervisee may be unable to recognize anything as humane in the termination process.

Principle 8: Feminist supervisors attend to the developmental shifts occurring in the supervisory process and provide input as a function of the skill level, developmental level, or maturational level of the supervisee.

Supervision is calibrated to the ongoing growth and changing needs of supervisees. In a sense, this principle mediates between Principle 7, emphasizing responsibility, and Principle 2, fostering collaborative relationships. Principle 8 suggests that supervisors foster supervisees' accountability and independence by increasing their autonomy and self-determination as they develop maturity and competencies. Supervisors monitor their own use of condescending and authoritarian supervisory practices.

This principle also implores supervisors to meet supervisees at their own level. This precaution implies that not all supervisees are ready for a collaborative relationship with their supervisor. Some supervisees may desire, or require, more direction. Not providing structure when requested or needed may create feelings of anxiety and incompetence in the supervisee. The context and process of supervision varies with differing levels of skill, self-confidence, political beliefs, or personal awareness.

Principle 9: Feminist supervisors advocate for their supervisees and clients in the educational and training settings within which they practice.

Supervisors challenge the sexist and racist practices of colleagues toward both supervisees and clients. They recognize that the feminist tenet of working for social change may begin in one's own academic or institutional home. They work to create a climate among colleagues that differentiates behaviors that are sexist and abusive from those that are appropriate supervisory acts. They articulate the need for faculty in general to improve their supervisory skills. They model continuous learning and self-analysis. They advocate fair and ethical treatment of supervisees.

The supervisor may need to assist the supervisee in understanding the political and systemic issues of the educational system or profession. In fact, feminist supervisors may need to provide the opportunity and safety for supervisees' exploration of the full range of possible responses available to her in cases of systemic unfairness or abuse within the educational or professional institution. An open discussion of the range of options would include responses such as direct challenge, inaction, and even the role of subversive behavior in attempting to remediate personal mistreatment or to affect institutional change. Once again, the analysis of power and articulation of the ethical issues involved would be prominent in assisting supervisees to understand their experiences and frame their responses.

MAINSTREAMING FEMINIST SUPERVISION

Principle 9 implies that feminist supervisors are committed to improving the supervisory climate for all supervisees and the supervisory skills of all supervisors. We recognize that this "simple" concept is not so simple to implement. To mainstream the principles proposed in this chapter would require commitment on the part of supervisors, as well as their institutions and universities, to elevate the importance of supervision in educational programs. Most of us have witnessed its importance in our own development; most of our supervisees recognize its essential role in their learning; yet most of our academic institutions bestow little status and few rewards on excellent supervisors.

Reducing one's professional isolation and increasing social support may be necessary steps when attempting to transform supervisory practices. Implementing changes in mainstream supervisory practices must begin with feminist supervisors attempting to foster these changes in their current environments. Supervisors require their own support network to accomplish this goal. This network can reach across organizations and agencies to provide education and support and to reduce isolation. Feminist supervisors must lead faculty discussions, bring in speakers, and offer seminars or practicum groups for advanced graduate students. Faculty and students interested in this area could develop a speakers' series and develop a consultation list of supervisors outside of the organization who could provide feminist supervision or could consult on a particular case with the student and her supervisor. Graduate students certainly will be more excited about these offerings than faculty and can be enlisted in changing the supervisory environment of a department or agency.

CONCLUSION

The group's consensus on the principles of feminist supervision appear in the Appendix.

When asked what feminist supervision is, our collective answer may be: "Process, process, process." Many psychologists and clinicians might argue that this definition does not differentiate feminist supervision from other techniques of "good" supervision. We disagree. Perhaps the most distinctly feminist aspect of the supervisory process described in this chapter is the examination of the social construction of all meanings and practices by both supervisors and supervisees and the focus on both activism and reflection, power and oppression. We believe that the feminist principles and standards laid out in this chapter go much further in defining a balanced, collaborative model of supervisory theory and practices than has been done previously. Our concluding definition is as follows:

> Feminist supervision is a collaborative, respectful process, personal but unintrusive, balanced between supervisory responsibility and supervisee autonomy. Feminist supervision emphasizes an open discussion and analysis of power dynamics, and targets the best interests of the supervisee. It is a process that remains focused on the social context of the lives of the client, supervisee, and supervisor.

Many questions and issues remain uncovered in this chapter. We have not described the techniques of supervision—are some techniques and technologies more effective or more conducive than others to feminist supervision? Is there a combination of formats (individual, group, "live" supervision) that promotes the principles described above? How does a supervisor truly monitor supervision and remain empowering and collaborative? How do we help when a supervisor is being marginalized in a department or agency because of her feminist theoretical stance? It may be difficult to determine why someone is being marginalized; perhaps marginalization itself is the issue, whatever the complex cause (e.g., age, status, disability, ethnicity, seniority, or theoretical stance).

Another area not delineated in this chapter is the way in which feminist supervisors integrate theories about men or address specifically the inclusion of male supervisors–supervisees in this process. Some group members have strongly advocated that the growing edge of feminist thinking is, and needs to be, the inclusion of all authentic voices. Snyder (1993), one of the group members, articulated this position in a letter to participants after the conference:

> In our practices, many of us are attempting to reveal and model relationships with boys and men that integrate the assertive (and appropriately aggressive) with the relational, that allows for attentive and compassionate listening side-by-side with authentic, passionate expression. One primary way in which the girls and women who are our clients can claim their voices with men as well as with other women is from watching us do this in family therapy sessions. One primary way in which boys and men can come to better understand the experience of women, while also claiming their own true voices, is through their relationships with a feminist therapist who is learning the interface of speaking one's meanings truthfully and constituting genuine intimacy. (p. 6)

These principles provide a coherent picture of the philosophy, goals, and values of feminist supervisors and feminist supervision. We have taken an important step in codifying feminist supervision theory and practice. However important this first step is, future steps, that respond to these unresolved questions, are crucial.

APPENDIX
PRINCIPLES GUIDING FEMINIST SUPERVISION

Principle	Description
Principle 1	Feminist supervisors are proactive in analyzing power dynamics and differentials between the supervisors and the supervisee, model the use of power in the service of the supervisee, and vigilantly avoid abuses of power.
Principle 2	Feminist supervision is based on a collaborative relationship, defined as mutually respectful, where the supervisee's autonomy and diverse perspectives are encouraged.
Principle 3	Feminist supervisors facilitate reflexive interactions and supervisee self-examination by modeling openness, authenticity, reflexivity, and the value of lifelong learning and self-examination.
Principle 4	Supervision occurs in a social context that attends to and emphasizes the diversity of women's lives and context.
Principle 5	Feminist supervisors attend to the social construction of gender and the role of language in maintaining a gendered society.
Principle 6	Feminist supervisors advance and model the feminist principle of advocacy and activism.
Principle 7	Feminist supervisors maintain standards that ensure their supervisees' competent and ethical practice.
Principle 8	Feminist supervisors attend to the developmental shifts occurring in the supervisory process and provide input as a function of the skill level, developmental level, and maturational level of the supervisee.
Principle 9	Feminist supervisors advocate for their supervisees and clients in the educational and training settings within which they practice.

References

Alonso, A., & Rutan, J. S. (1988). Shame and guilt in psychotherapy supervision. *Psychotherapy, 25,* 576–581.

Dutton Douglas, M. A., & Rave, E. (1990). Ethics of feminist supervision of psychotherapy. In H. Lerman & N. Porter (Eds.), *Feminist ethics in psychotherapy* (pp. 136–146). New York: Springer.

Greenberg, L. (1980). Supervision from the perspective of the supervisee. In A. K. Hess (Ed.), *Psychotherapy supervision: Theory, research, and practice* (pp. 85–91). New York: Wiley.

Hawes, S. E. (1992, January). *Reflexivity and collaboration in the supervisory process: A role for feminist poststructural theories in the training of professional psychologists.* Paper presented at the National Council of Schools of Professional Psychology Conference on Clinical Training in Professional Psychology, Las Vegas, NV.

Lopez, S. R., Grover, K. P., Holland, D., Johnson, M. D., Kain, C. D., Kanel, K., Mellino, C. A., & Rhyne, M. C. (1989). Development of culturally sensitive therapy. *Professional Psychology: Research and Practice, 20,* 369–376.

Newman, A. S. (1981). Ethical issues in the supervision of psychotherapy. *Professional Psychology: Research and Practice, 12,* 690–695.

Pope, K. S., Schover, L. R., & Levenson, H. (1980). Sexual behavior between clinical supervisors and trainees: Implications for professional standards. *Professional Psychology: Research and Practice, 11,* 157–162.

Porter, N. (1985). New perspectives on therapy supervision. In L. B. Rosewater & L. E. A. Walker (Eds.), *Handbook of feminist therapy* (pp. 332–342). New York: Springer.

Porter, N. (1995). Integrating antiracist, feminist, and multicultural perspectives in psychotherapy: A developmental supervision model. In H. Landrine (Ed.), *Handbook of cultural diversity in the psychology of women* (pp. 163–176). Washington, DC: American Psychological Association.

Sarnat, J. E. (1992). Supervision in relationship: Resolving the teach–treat controversy in psychoanalytic supervision. *Psychoanalytic Psychology, 9,* 387–403.

Snyder, M. (1993). Personal letter to some participants, July 26, 1993.

Snyder, M. (1995). "Becoming": A method for expanding systemic thinking and deepening empathic accuracy. *Family Process, 34,* 241–253.

Sterling, M. M., & Bugental, J. (1993). The meld experience in psychotherapy supervision. *Journal of Humanistic Psychology, 33*(2), 38–48.

9

DIVERSITY: ADVANCING AN INCLUSIVE FEMINIST PSYCHOLOGY

BEVERLY GREENE AND JANIS SANCHEZ-HUCLES

WITH MARTHA BANKS, GAYLE CIVISH, SUSAN CONTRATTO,
JOANN GRIFFITH, HOLLY HEARD HINDERLY, YVONNE JENKINS,
AND MARY K. ROBERSON

Feminist theory puts forth a general analysis of societal inequities that are based on gender oppression. It further posits that those inequities are a basic cause of mental health problems in women. Understanding those societal circumstances and their effects is a major focus of feminist therapy and research. The task of unraveling the conundrum of diversity in feminist therapy theory, research, and practice appears deceptively simple, if we assume that gender is the primary locus of oppression for all women. In reality, however, we know that this is not so. In considering the nexus of diversity and feminist psychology on all levels, we are compelled to ask questions that go beyond our understanding of oppression simply as a function of gender. The more that we are aware of the diversity of women's lives and experiences, the more cognizant we become of the need to consider how the intensity and effects of sexism vary or interact with other forms of oppression and privilege experienced by an individual. Our inquiry must also include an examination of the ways that feminist psychology itself can be an instrument, albeit unintended, of oppression. Consequently, we are led first to consider the extent to which current feminist psychology reflects the diversity of women's experiences. When feminist theory and practice are not inclusive, they perpetuate an approach to women's lives as narrow as the traditional psychological approaches assailed by feminist theoreticians. In considering such questions we must first ask what constitutes diversity in feminism and how we define it. The principal of diversity must be defined in a way that always facilitates inclusiveness and works against excluding any group of women. However, the task of defining, even loosely, a construct of diversity is less difficult than the task of operationalizing and implementing it.

This chapter provides an examination of the extent to which diversity is incorporated into feminist psychology. It also charts the course of our group's process. This includes a review of our development as a group and our struggles both with one another and with other working groups at the conference to incorporate diversity across all areas of feminist psychology. This struggle included our attempts to construct a working definition of diversity and a series of recommendations to facilitate greater inclusiveness in feminist psychology.

THE CONTEXT

Sanchez-Hucles (1990) has noted that, although Americans espouse a value of cultural diversity, our institutional culture is insidiously racist and ethnocentric in practice. Its systems have rewarded people for the extent to which they were Anglicized, heterosexual, and similar, rather than ethnic and different. It has idealized White Anglo-Saxon Protestant models and values and devalued other cultural perspectives. Espin and Gawelek (1992) observed that American psychologists typically view human diversity in terms of abnormalities or deficits. In the context of a society that frequently views differences as deficits, those in power have used preexisting biological and social differences between people in a variety of ways. They have created the perception of differences where there are none or where the differences that exist are functionally insignificant.

In other cases, actual differences may be exacerbated or their meaning distorted in the service of creating images and identities of people that facilitate or excuse their exploitation. An obvious example here is the use of actual biological differences between men and women in the establishment of gender hierarchies that deem women inferior to men. This purported biological inferiority of women, with male biology as the norm, is used as the rationale for denying women the same levels of social privilege as men. Actual biological differences are used as evidence, first of the biological and then social inferiority of the group with less social power. Any difficulties encountered by the oppressed group in competing with a dominant and privileged group are used as evidence of the oppressed group's inferiority, circularly reinforcing and explaining the perceived correctness of their subordinate position. Unequal social status is explained as if it were simply the natural order of things. These frameworks minimize the significant roles played by differences in opportunities and access to power between the groups in our society. Similarly, differences in such characteristics as sexual orientation, race, ethnicity, culture, socioeconomic class, ablebodied status, age, physical distinctions, and religion are used to accord or deny social privileges to many women.

DIVERSITY WITHIN FEMINIST PSYCHOLOGY LITERATURE AND RESEARCH

State of the Art

Diverse perspectives are not well represented in feminist psychology literature. Published theory and research in women's psychology are generally based on an overrepresentation of White, middle-class female researchers, theoreticians, practitioners, and populations sampled in studies (Brown, 1990, 1995; Espin, 1995; Espin & Gawelek, 1992; Greene, 1994a, 1994b, 1995; Hall & Greene, 1996; Landrine, Klonoff, & Brown-Collins, 1992; Reid & Comas-Díaz, 1990; Yoder & Kahn, 1993). Although it is more inclusive than traditional psychology, feminist psychology remains ethnocentric and does not well represent the effects of race, culture, ethnicity, socioeconomic class, age, sexual orientation, ablebodied status, and other variables in women's lives (Espin, 1995; Espin & Gawelek, 1992; Graham, 1992; Greene, 1993, 1994b; Hall & Greene, 1996). Almeida (1993) and Hurtado (1989) wrote that feminist theory focuses its inquiry on an exploration of the relational position of White women to White men. However, it does not put forth a similar inquiry or analysis of the relational position of White women to women of color, White women to men of color, or persons of color to White men (Almeida, 1993; Daniel, 1994; Greene, 1993, 1995).

In her analysis of these relationships, Hurtado (1989) described the oppression of White women by White men as one that is characterized by seduction. The oppression of women of color by White men is characterized by rejection, thus creating differences in women's subjective experiences of what it means to be a woman. In Hurtado's schema, women of color have less access to positions of power and privilege than their White counterparts because they are viewed as less attractive and less sexually desirable. It is important to note that this view refers to *public* desirability as is evidenced by the long history of White men's victimization of women of color in forced sexual relationships with them (Greene, 1986, 1994a, 1994b). Almeida (1993) and Greene (1986, 1993) observed that, whereas public work is empowering for White women, private luxury is empowering for women of color; that is, there is a difference between having the opportunity to work and working out of necessity. To fully appreciate the meaning of work for all women, one must include an analysis of the history of different groups of women. For some, public work was neither forbidden nor a novelty—it was burdensome and inescapable.

Work and career are not always synonymous. The woman who works for low wages in a factory, market, or other setting may regard her job as a thankless chore and not as the fulfilling enterprise associated with career status or chosen profession. For some women, work and career create the possibilities of independence and dignity; for many others, their experiences in the workplace are degrading and their treatment harsh. An analysis must include socioeconomic as well as cultural realities of women who are neither formally educated nor middle class. It should also include the difficulties faced by formally educated and middle-class women of color. Education and middle-class status, as measured by income, do not prevent (and, in some cases, actually exacerbate) harassment and other forms of discrimination and degradation (Banks, 1986; Comas-Díaz & Greene, 1994b). Hence, the experience of gender and gender oppression is colored by other personal and group variables and is dynamic rather than static (Comas-Díaz & Greene, 1994a; Espin, 1995; Greene, 1994a, 1994b; Landrine et al., 1992; Reid & Comas-Díaz, 1990; Scarr, 1988).

Effects of White Skin Privilege on Feminist Psychology

McIntosh (1988) attributed the restricted lens from which gender oppression is viewed to the presence of white skin privilege. Espin (1995) expanded the definition of privilege and argued that privileged individuals have the luxury of not seeing anything that does not have to do directly with themselves and tend to define whatever they see as the universal truth. In Espin's view, this myopic tendency ultimately restricts a person's capacity to view reality in an unobstructed manner.

Both Espin (1995) and McIntosh (1988) asserted that current feminist theory reflects the white skin privilege of its creators and, equally important, their subsequent ignorance of that privilege. Espin warned that any theory is limited when it is shaped primarily by members of a society's dominant group. Feminist theory is no exception in that it has both ignored and silenced the experiences of women of color, disabled women (Fine, 1992; Fine & Asch, 1988; Hall & Greene, 1996; Solomon, 1993; Willmuth & Holcomb, 1993), older women (Davis, Cole, & Rothblum, 1993; Hall & Greene, 1996), lesbians (Rothblum & Cole, 1988), religious women (Ochshorn & Cole, 1995; Rayburn, 1982, 1984), poor and working women (Daniel, 1994; Reid, 1993), and others just as men, as dominant cultural beings, silence and ignore the experiences of women. Whereas women of color may represent a more visibly ignored group and are often a greater focus of attention in examples of exclusions in the feminist literature, they are by no means the only women who are not fully represented in the shaping and implementation of feminism and psychology.

Such omissions adversely affect the nature of our knowledge base, leaving it incomplete and faulty (Espin, 1995). Just as the experience of heterosexism, racism, "ablebodiedism," and poverty influence the experience of gender and of gender oppression of those who endure them, they also shape, albeit differently, the experience of gender oppression of those women who do not endure them. For example, when White women presume that their primary experience of gender and gender oppression is a function of their gender alone and not their race, they may incorrectly presume that characteristics of White middle-class women are core to the psychology of all women (Espin & Gawelek, 1992). In such a context, they may not consider that some of these characteristics are actually defense mechanisms used by a specific group of women to negotiate their oppression.

Walker (1995) observed that the minimal differences between White women and women of color in rates of abuse may indicate little about the meaning of violence in the lives of women of color. The impact of violence on women who are discriminated against on levels other than gender alone may be different than it is for their White counterparts. Walker also cited differences in the range and quality of public services available to battered women of color and their White counterparts, their appropriate heightened suspicion of dominant group institutions offering services, and the meaning ascribed to the abuse itself.

Invisibility of Disability and Trauma

Disabled women form another group of women whose special psychological needs are frequently ignored. Banks and Ackerman (1992) highlighted psychological issues for women with disabilities and for women who are full-time caregivers of disabled family members. Banks, Ackerman, and Corbett (1995) examined the lack of access to appropriate assessment and treatment for brain injury caused by accidents, the physical assault that frequently accompanies rape, and other forms of physical assault and battery that often claim women as victims.

Solomon (1993) raised the importance of cultural context in understanding women with disabilities, particularly when these women are challenged by the presence of physical distinctions that accompany their disability. She observed that the estimated 5.8 million women in the United States with disabilities or physical challenges are rarely featured in feminist or traditional mental health literature. Within this group there is virtually no data on women of color with disabilities and physical distinctions. She argued that it is crucial to understand the role of subculture in the development of body image and in its nexus with the dominant culture's negative attitudes toward persons with disabilities. With incisive analysis, she demonstrated that culture plays a major role in what is deemed desirable or attractive and that it is an important part of any analysis in which body image is a factor. A woman's perception of the cultural beauty standard of her group, her perception of how she meets that standard, and her perception of how important meeting that standard is to ethnic group members plays a major role in the development of her sense of body image and her feelings about herself. This dynamic is further complicated for disabled women, whose experience of their gender may be influenced by their disability and its sequelae.

Solomon (1993) defined *disability* as the physical manifestation of a biologically determined (congenital or acquired) abnormality of physiology or loss of an anatomical part or function. The degree to which a disability is handicapping is a function of social, environmental, and cultural factors and societal prejudice as they interact with a woman's physical limitation and as those factors influence how the physical limitation is perceived. Hence, she suggested, even our most basic data on who gets reported as disabled is a function of a cultural context that depends on who considers herself or is considered as disabled or impaired. It is also a reflection of who is doing the counting.

Henderson-Daniel (1994) suggested that the understanding of trauma and recovery in women must be broadened to include racism, political and economic oppression, and colonization. She asserted that the trauma literature comes about primarily from a middle-class, Eurocentric historical perspective that does not incorporate the realities of the history and ongoing danger of racial oppression for women of color raised in the United States. In her analysis, living in environments where racism is ubiquitous (whether or not it consists of physical violence) is stressful and potentially traumatic, and it may have long-lasting psychological effects. For White women as well as women of color, socioeconomic status (SES) is another variable used to determine one's worth to society, and we must pay attention to what happens when it is not factored into an analysis of a woman's condition. As such, SES can play a significant role in altering the context of rape, sexual harassment, and domestic and other forms of violence in ways that can profoundly affect how a woman is treated and even whether or not she is believed.

Who Are the Women in the Psychotherapy Literature?

Hall and Greene (1996) examined the psychological literature on women and psychotherapy from 1990 to 1992 to determine the extent to which the complexion of the growing diversity of psychologists and consumers was represented in that literature. The authors reviewed 789 citations. Thirty-two of these citations focused on older women, 17 on African American women, 17 on lesbian women, 7 on Jewish women (published primarily in one special issue of a feminist journal), and 12 on an unspecified group of women that focused on multiculturalism and diversity issues generically. Most articles did not mention the age of the population studied; however, when articles focused on older women, the content was almost exclusively on the negative aspects of aging. There were two notable exceptions: *The Psychology of Women Quarterly*'s (Fodor & Franks, 1990) special issue on aging ("Women at Midlife and Beyond") and a special issue of *Women and Therapy* (Davis et al., 1993). Both special issues approached the topic of aging from more diverse and affirmative perspectives. On reviewing this material, we wondered whether more culturally diverse samples would have yielded perspectives on aging that were less negative. For example, African American, Native American, Latina, East Indian, Caribbean, and other cultures accord special honor to elder women, and their absence from the literature may result in a limited perspective on the broader experiences of women and aging.

Most studies did not indicate the sexual orientation of their participants, presuming either their heterosexuality or the irrelevance of this variable (Hall & Greene, 1996). However, these studies did not hesitate to generalize their findings to all women. This practice perpetuates the lack of inclusiveness of lesbians in the literature, even though they are represented in the feminist literature to a far greater degree than in the traditional psychological literature. Most articles on lesbians were on problems that they confront and virtually never identified the ethnicity of the lesbian participants. Roberson et al. (1994) proposed that many of the negative thoughts, feelings, and disadvantages experienced by lesbians about being a lesbian occurred in the context of interacting with a heterosexist society, not from the intrinsic experience of being a lesbian. They noted that research with lesbian participants often does not sample large numbers of lesbians who are active in lesbian culture who are otherwise satisfied with their lives. Still, this omission did not prevent authors from generalizing their data to all lesbians or lesbian couples.

Hall and Greene (1996) noted in this review that Jewish women were the only White ethnic group identified, giving an incomplete view of the salience of ethnic identity for other White women. Overall, most studies did not indicate the race or ethnicity of their samples, and theoretical articles did not take any cultural perspective into account when interpreting their concepts or usefulness. Only 43 of the more than 700 articles reviewed address the concerns of women of color. The articles did not address SES differences between women or the impact of poverty as a salient variable in women's mental health. References made to low income women were in citations on women of color. Other populations not well represented included rural women, blue-collar working women, single mothers, working mothers in nonprofessional households, disabled women, retarded women, developmentally or learning disabled women, and bisexual women.

Until a recent special issue of *Women and Therapy* (Ochshorn & Cole, 1995), the role of spirituality and religion, particularly the conflicts many religious women experience about their feminist beliefs or longings, was virtually ignored. (Rayburn, 1982, 1984, was the notable exception.) Poor White women and middle-class women of color were ignored. This bias in sampling perpetuates the dangerous stereotypes that women of color must always be poor and that White women are not. It is yet another example of the critical absence of diverse perspectives and voices required to make feminist theory truly responsive to the needs of all women. Were it not for the special theme issues of two leading feminist journals, the coverage on diversity and multicultural issues, middle-aged women, Jewish women, and others would have been marginal to nonexistent. Even in these journals, authors did not seem to be consistently required to identify a number of salient variables, such as race, ethnicity, sexual orientation, age, class, or physical status, nor were they required to discuss the limited generalizability of research results when they are based on samples where all or the majority of the respondents were White, middle-class, and often educated women.

It is in this charged context of bias and omission that the diversity working group began the task of developing guidelines for diversifying feminist psychological theory, research, practice, and training. We began with both excitement and trepidation as we approached our discussions of those issues that are usually anxiety provoking and often scrupulously avoided in such gatherings for fear of disrupting that illusory but oft-sought-after glow of feminist harmony.

THE PROCESS

Defining the Scope of Our Task

Initial Dynamics: Tensions and Cohesions

The diversity group consisted of nine members: six African Americans (including two student scribes) and three White Americans. An interesting fusion was created in this group because the group leaders were African American, and several of the African American members and one of the White members had previous experiences of working productively with one another. This cohesion helped some of the group members feel a significant degree of comfort and minimized some of the customary awkwardness of meeting new people.

In contrast, the White American members were in many ways the "minority" in this group both numerically and psychologically, and for some, this was an unfamiliar experience. Whereas some people may experience minority status in this fashion as a novel challenge, it can just as easily invoke a kind of apprehension that makes it difficult to participate, feel included, or feel that one's contributions make a difference. One of the members wrote, "A piece of the tension is that some of us are not used to being a group member and a learner. The nature of any conversation about diversity requires this stance regardless of color and life experiences. Every statement of fact, belief and feeling is embedded in culture, politics, history and economics. Therefore, this is a hard conversation to have." Two of the White women verbalized their sense that women of color inherently were more "expert" in a subgroup on diversity in a feminist conference than were women from the majority group. A third White group member recalled, "I always feel everyone is more expert in these groups [meaning diversity groups] because I have not spent a lot of time reading or studying diversity, I just like it."

Concomitantly, there was a less well-expressed tension about being White in a diversity group. Two of the White members struggled to present themselves in a manner that conveyed an understanding of the issues of diversity and a significant interest in learning more. At the same time they did not want to fulfill the stereotype of the "liberal know-it-all feminist" who can be perceived as insensitive to racism and classism. One of the White members shared her 12-year commitment to placing herself in positions of being the minority in certain settings so that she could "observe and learn the heart/mind of those who were different from me" in a range of experiences. She added that as a result of these activities she knew more deeply not only the identities of others who are different but also her own identity. The tensions and cohesions forged by being a part of the majority or the minority group in the diversity working group, at this predominantly White conference, became a significant process issue throughout the conference.

Members introduced themselves, described their areas of expertise, and explained their interest in participating in the diversity group. Several areas of agreement emerged in this initial discussion. All members supported the contention that diversity was a complex issue and that it was virtually impossible for anyone to be an expert on all facets of it. Group members also agreed that the topic of diversity was unique in the conference because it was integral to the focus of all the other working groups, rather than a topic that stood apart from the others. In fact, we felt that the integration of diverse concerns into all other groups and their topics was essential to the development of a feminist therapy that is true to its ideals.

Use of the Self to Shape Understandings of Diversity

We concurred that the first step in promoting our understanding of diversity, which is all too often ignored, was to focus first on self and then look at how historical, social, spiritual, political, and economic realities have affected our psychological development. After self-examination, the next step was to examine how these realities were related to feminist psychology training and practice.

Group members readily acknowledged that the term *diversity* was politically and emotionally charged. We agreed that there has been a tendency in the discourse of psychology to associate difference with hierarchy; that is, if people are different, some are or must be superior to others. As a discipline, psychology has often developed instruments to measure differences and then used these assessment results to rationalize differential treatment of individuals and groups and to maintain power among those in privileged groups.

As we attempted further to explore the issue of diversity, we tried to identify why diversity represented such a sensitive and taboo topic for so many of us. We discussed whether diversity should strive to focus more on commonalities between people. There was a recognition that this approach is usually more comfortable for people with privilege. Those who have power in society are threatened by possible changes in their status. Many members of the dominant culture falsely believe that efforts to diversify society have resulted in the significant loss of jobs and educational opportunities for them. Such perceptions often occur when members of the majority group have enjoyed an unfair advantage that is defined as normative. When change occurs it is not experienced as balancing the scales; rather, it is seen as moving from a fair system to an unfair one. Hence, there is the mistaken belief that affirmative action programs that were designed to encourage and facilitate diversity constitute reverse racism. We therefore concluded that to develop a better understanding of diversity, we must focus less on our commonalities and more on our differences and their meaning because those differences are more likely to be a source of conflict.

As we talked about diversity, we realized how negative values of differences are embedded in the language. For example, it became increasingly difficult for us to find words that reflected differences between people and groups that were not polarized into good and bad, superior and inferior, normal or abnormal. We observed that even as we tried to begin our deliberations by focusing on the self, we were reminded that developmental and self-esteem scholars have indicated that self definitions evolve from comparisons to others. In our society, value is implicitly and explicitly measured with respect to how well one fits the norm of being White, male, heterosexual, and wealthy. How then do those of us who are not defined in those ways develop a healthy self-esteem and positive self-definitions? We know that many people achieve these goals. What was surprising was how little we know about how people who do this successfully evolve those adaptive strategies. Perhaps the simple absence of formal work in this area speaks to our culture's silencing of persons who are not majority group members. This discussion led us to question how communication is fostered between people who enjoy various degrees of privilege or lack of it in our society.

Forging Alliances

We accepted the dictum that the personal is political and that we must first begin with a personal exploration of our own feelings about diversity. We decided that our vision of diversity was egalitarian, not hierarchical, embracing shared privilege and power in society. Hence, to understand diversity one must begin with an examination of personal discomforts, biases, anxieties, and fears and their origins about the meaning of diversity. This process facilitates the forging of fluid and supportive coalitions. We refused to describe any group in terms that were oppositional to us. We resisted the temptation to externalize our frustration and anger by indulging in "male or White male bashing." We believed that acknowledging, staying with, and working through our personal anxieties and tensions as they relate to diversity would create the openness and trust for us to learn how to talk about diversity in new and productive ways. We felt strongly that any discussion of diversity, whether in academic or professional settings, must begin with this initial personal work. Discussions that focus only on the academic and the intellectual are not sufficient to enhance our understanding and appreciation of diversity, nor do they automatically lead to the social change that is a mandate of feminist theory.

Gender as a Primary Locus of Oppression: An Obstacle to Diversity

We were amazed that so little of the initial discussions in this group focused on feminism, although the topic of the conference was on feminist training and practice. What emerged in the very first discussions of diversity in the group was the view that gender and gender oppression are not the primary locus of identity or oppression for all women. We agreed that all women share gender oppression but that they experience this oppression through their individual historical, social, political, economic, ecological, and psychophysical realities. To understand any woman, therefore, one must incorporate an understanding of many different aspects of her, not merely gender. This was easy enough for us to conceptualize, but it proved to be much harder to put this understanding into practice. We realized that an inherent tension accompanied our attempts to develop ways of incorporating the multiple aspects of people into our understanding of them.

Generating the Group's Perspective

A perspective emerged early in the group process. We determined that there is a need to move beyond looking at similarities and differences to an analysis that focuses on complexities. We determined that human beings are complex and that many aspects of their realities interact, overlap, conflict with, and complement each other. This stance opposes attempts to overgeneralize or universalize people's experiences. We believe that simplistic analyses of human conditions are easier to comprehend but produce reductionistic and erroneous theories, policies, and practices.

We made a commitment to avoid the temptation of looking for how women were similar rather than different. As a result, we examined the reasons that psychology and other disciplines emphasize the universalization of experience. It appeared to the group that universalizing people's experiences produced less anxiety, particularly for those with privilege and power. In contrast, the quest for similarities tends to marginalize, render invisible, and disempower those in society with less privilege.

Group members forged early goals to commit ourselves, feminism, and the field of psychology to work through the tension between diversity and the tendency to universalize. We believed that as we succeeded in resolving these tensions, we could achieve personal and professional transformation. The more we embrace and practice diversity, the more we empower feminist psychology to transform itself and the field of psychology.

Another interesting dynamic for the diversity working group was that, with its commitment to incorporate fully the study of differences, there was no significant debate about whether men should be included in a discussion of diversity in feminist practice. We acknowledged that diversity in feminist practice must be completely inclusive, which requires examining all issues of diversity, and we deemed important an awareness of the multiple effects of gender oppression. This awareness includes understanding how racism, classism, and lack of privilege affect groups of men in the society as well. We wanted to avoid the trap of seeing men as the enemy and instead search for and understand the similarities and differences of women's and men's experiences of oppression in our society. We believed that a comprehensive investigation of differences would promote a knowledge base in psychology that would be increasingly comprehensive, representative, accurate, and dynamic. Without a full consideration of difference, psychology offers narrow and distorted perspectives of the world and functions as an instrument of social control. The challenge we adopted was to help psychology realize its potential as a vehicle for promoting advocacy, fairness, and constructive social change.

Defining Diversity and Cultural Competence

After delineating the philosophical bases of the group, attention next focused on the attempt to define diversity. Key elements of the definition included what diversity is and what it is not.

Diversity is

- openness to differences among and between people;
- the cultivation, appreciation, and nurturance of different perspectives;
- receptiveness to and respect for others;
- valuing difference;
- a noun and a verb in which we are all subject and object.

We agreed that what it means to be a woman varies across many dimensions and that data in feminist psychology must reflect all women's experiences and should come from a wide range of sources.

Diversity is not

- affirmative action/equal employment opportunity, pluralism, multiculturalism, tokenism, marginalism, "special" status;
- deficiency, being "underprivileged or culturally deprived";
- an elective;
- just gender;
- passive tolerance but social action;
- assimilation, homogenization, accommodation;
- equal, rather fair treatment;
- an afterthought, an add on, an "add and stir" approach to curriculum issues;
- tolerance and acceptance of hate speech as free speech;
- having a friend who is "one";
- holding minorities responsible for solving the "minority problem."

We felt the need to develop a professional standard for diversity in feminist training and practice. This standard was best expressed by advocating that professionals in the field of psychology be culturally competent. In our view, the term *culture* includes race, ethnicity, gender, sexual orientation, religion, and geographical location, and it allows for other dimensions of persons or groups that are salient to their understanding of the world and of themselves to be incorporated into any analysis. *Cultural competency* is a measurable professional standard that should inform all aspects of practice and that should function in the service of the consumer to facilitate the goals of diversity. It includes goals of diversity that ensure professional services to promote empowerment, openness to and nurturance of differences, respect, and the understanding of multiple perspectives.

Moreover, it encompasses differential historical, political, social, economic, psychophysical, spiritual, and ecological realities and their interaction and impact on individuals and groups.

The session ended with the question of how to make diversity a reality in feminist training and practice given our very ambitious definitions of diversity and cultural competence. We committed ourselves to take the process one step further in the next session and to delineate the process by which feminism becomes more diverse.

Diversifying Feminist Psychology

As we mused about how to diversify feminist psychology, we recognized the enormity of our task. In particular, the African American members of the group commented that, although diversity was already part of their self-definitions, a great deal of their professional time was spent either having to take the responsibility to initiate a focus on diversity issues or on promoting diversity by being assigned "special" tasks or being put on special committees. These assignments reflected the fact that, although these women of color might have some interest in and expertise in addressing issues of diversity, they typically worked for individuals who were much more privileged than they with respect to the power to implement such plans. Being in these positions often left them feeling marginalized or burdened when given this task in addition to whatever their formal job responsibilities entailed. This realization prompted several members to indicate that all too often "diverse people" are seen as both the problem and the vehicle for solving the problem through the disproportionate use of their time and energies.

Through discussion, we concluded that people with less privilege are not responsible for recruiting other people like them or for making people who are included feel more comfortable about excluding others. We concurred that we need to become a society and a professional arena where valuing diversity is the norm, not the exception. We then prepared ourselves to share our conclusions with other working groups and with general conference participants in the plenary sessions.

Adjusting the Lens: Shifting the Focus from Gender to Diversity

Two significant process issues developed after our group reported our deliberations at the plenary and breakout sessions. It became clear that some of the other conference participants were amazed and not pleased that the diversity working group did not make feminism, gender issues, or sexual oppression the central focus of its work. For the African American members of our working group, it felt very natural for them to make diversity and not gender their central focus. Some of them clearly were prepared for the negative reaction to our position. Two commented that they had experienced this reaction to promoting diversity many times before. One, however, reported that she expected greater tolerance in a feminist group and was shocked by the strong negative response.

In contrast, several White members of the group reported feeling anxious, conflicted, and surprised by the negative response of conference members to our group's position. Hence, the first issue for our group was that of observing and then processing the marked differences between African American and White members' reactions to the larger groups negative response to our proposal. One of the White women in our group observed, "I recall that our proposal was initially read by one of our co-leaders . . . when the negative responses came, the African American women in our group sat back and just listened. . . . I spoke up, defensively I'm sure, as did one of the other White women from our group. . . . Afterwards, I asked one of the African American women about her silence. She said that she was tired, that she had heard those same kinds of comments many times before and that she wanted White group members to experience what had been her sense of the defensiveness and unwillingness of many White feminists to engage in a real discussion about these issues. That we could have this conversation at all speaks to the bond of trust and safety that had been forged within our group."

One of the African American members of our group reported, "I am never surprised at this response. In a lot of women's groups, where folks feel isolated or oppressed because of being women or lesbians, these women assume that oppressions are interchangeable. When I point out to them that this is not so and suggest that they must look at themselves and their role as victims as well as perpetrators of oppression, they direct their anger at me! I believe this response is easier for them than experiencing the discomfort that comes from having to subject their own conduct to scrutiny, and perhaps finding it is not consistent with their espoused beliefs. It's like they are angry with the messenger instead of listening to the message and perhaps being dissatisfied with their own conduct. It is as if you get punished for pointing out something that is a daily, inescapable reality for you, and then you are treated as if it is your 'personal' problem rather than a part of a broader social phenomena that is problematic." Another African American member concurred and observed, "It is as if your concerns have to be minimized to get rid of the problems and the questions they raise."

A White member of our group expressed discomfort with feeling treated as if she had betrayed the "club" by suggesting that gender oppression should not be our primary focus. She observed, "I felt very disappointed with the response from the therapy working group who espoused that psychotherapy with women was complicated enough and that what we currently do was all we could handle at this time. I didn't say anything else during the short time we had left. Others from the diversity group entered the conversation but eventually I believe everyone from our group felt silenced. I was busy trying to understand what it means to be a person who by social characteristics is part of one group, but by identity in some ways is not aligned with that group. If it is true that promoting diversity is not the job of those who are less privileged, then how is it that those of us who do have privilege talk to those of our own group about 'misbehaving' without getting ourselves trashed [by them]? I think it is precisely this deep feeling of not being a part of any group but being a part of all groups that is necessary for those with privilege to experience and enact in our lives. While I was anxious after the breakout groups, I felt like I was experiencing something very core and important to the process of furthering the goal of inclusivity in psychology. My real ambivalence came later in the form of fear of speaking out to those outside of the diversity working group."

The second process issue to emerge at this critical juncture was the negative response to our proposal itself. Describing her troubling encounter, a White group member observed, "We proposed that we privilege diversity and that gender be one of the components of diversity in interaction with other components . . . the immediate response to this proposal was hostile. As I recall, people did not want to explore this suggestion but attacked it. I vividly recall one person saying 'If we put diversity on top, we will lose gender . . . women will get lost.' The reception of our proposal by other women at the conference, one that I experienced as hostile, dismissive, and disrespectful, certainly intensified my allegiance to our group."

Another White group member noted, "I recall feeling surprised, as I always am, that feminism isn't about all people, including men, surprised that this isn't the goal. . . . I understand the old guard's fear that the core of theory would be lost in the complexity and that the war [would be] fought on too many fronts."

An African American member of the group recounted her experience: "You could feel the hostility, you could cut it with a knife . . . it was as if we were talking about things that were not nice, that disrupted this sense of harmony, and that those disruptive ideas had to be censored. Well, you can't censor this process and you can't make it nice because it isn't nice . . . it is inherently difficult."

After meeting with women from other working groups, another White woman in our group observed, "I read our definition of cultural competence . . . I remember a lack of reaction at first, kind of stunned silence . . . then came the questions, what about gender? Shouldn't we place female gender at the center of this feminist theory and practice? I tried, as did others, to explain that gender has different salience for different people and groups and to be inclusive of all people we must include gender as one aspect among all sorts of sociological factors. But my words seemed to fall on deaf ears ... our definition of cultural competence was dismissed by some of the women who were dominating the discussion. I want to acknowledge that the group members were not always silenced. One example of enthusiastic response to our group's work was at the first plenary when we shared our definition of diversity. It was met with genuine delight. It was when we moved on to the issue of cultural competence that the going got a little more rough. Just think about it, in one case we are talking about an abstract definition, in the other we are talking about how that might be integrated into psychology in a meaningful way ... it is the difference between embracing an abstract concept and weaving that concept into the process ... into action. When we met as a large group at the last meeting, I could not help but notice that a number of final key point papers posted by other working groups did not have the topic of diversity as an important, explicit conclusion. Yet, it was posted in the final summary of key points that cut across all groups. This was another example of profound intellectual awareness, but something not sinking down or infusing the entire structure."

Our discussions following these events highlighted the fact that historical discussions of feminism not only have marginalized and obscured diversity issues but on some level have considered them a threat to the primacy of gender issues. We agreed that it was important from both a process and a content perspective to make diversity the focal point of our discussion even at a conference whose focus was on feminist training and practice. We recognized that, because many of us do not take the time to explore fully what diversity means to us from an affective as well as a cognitive perspective, people feel intimidated about making diversity a central issue for feminism. Lack of exposure, training, and skills further made many participants unsure of how to integrate diversity issues into their working group topics.

One example of integrating diversity with other working group issues came as a result of several members' interactions with the therapy working group. This group had spent a great deal of time describing how to conduct feminist therapy with women. However, we saw a potential problem with therapists conducting their visions of feminist therapy with women who were not feminists and who might be alienated by the values and principles of a feminist therapy that views gender as the central locus of oppression for women. We felt that we had to examine our own values as therapists, not impose them on others, and work in ways to empower our clients while we honored their values and goals for therapy. We presumed that a significant conflict could develop if feminist therapy operated in a fashion that did not take a range of elements and priorities in a woman's life into consideration. We believed that failing to do this would render a woman unable to function in her current life circumstances and without the psychological or financial resources to function on her own.

We arrived at the conclusion that standards of cultural competence should guide all working groups in their quest to integrate diversity. We argued that in any topic we must first be willing to look at individuals and groups in light of their multiple contexts and not simply through the lens of gender (with respect to our own beliefs and values). We cannot make changes in training and practice without first understanding others in their own voices. We did not feel that we had to choose between focusing on diversity or feminism. Instead, we maintained that authentic diversity, by definition, includes a full consideration of gender issues and oppression from a wide range of perspectives. At present, gender alone is not as inclusive a framework as diversity.

Exploring the Relationship Between Diversity and Universalism

Conference respondents asked us how the diverse fits into the universal. We felt that a focus on universal norms would not best facilitate an inclusive feminist training and practice. Instead, we felt it important to focus on broadening our understandings of current theories, that is, viewing them from multiple perspectives. For example, another working group proposed the trauma of sexism as a possible universal model. We felt that perhaps a more appropriate model in terms of inclusiveness would be the trauma of diversity. We concluded that the trauma of diversity perhaps explained in part (a) the frequent silence about diversity; (b) the chilling of the climate and tension that was produced when diversity issues were raised in our meetings with other working groups; and (c) the difficulty experienced by the diversity working group in communicating clearly and effectively with other participants, who responded defensively and with discomfort. Our personal experiences at the conference reconfirmed our belief that feminists still struggle to understand people who experience trauma from perspectives other than gender.

Role of Guilt and Shame in Integrating Diverse Concerns

In her self-analysis, Holzman (1995) discussed the role of guilt and shame in White women's antiracism work. She observed that "guilt is an immediate, powerful reaction of white women learning about racism" (p. 325) and that its most unproductive form is one that is misdirected or produces immobilizing shame. By contrast, guilt can be productive when it motivates one in the direction of changes in behavior and attitudes.

In situations in which guilt is used to elicit sympathy or ward off anticipated attack, women of color often feel that they are expected to forgive, soothe, or assuage the majority person's guilt (Holzman, 1995). Some of the African American women in our group identified with this position. In her analysis, Holzman observed that when such feelings of discomfort are used to shift the focus from examining racism or oppression to taking care of the person or persons who feel guilt or shame (usually members of the majority), these feelings become impossible to work through. Members of the majority who experience such emotions often project them onto minority members rather than confront the painful discrepancy between their ego ideal and real self (Greene, 1994b).

Many members of our group, African American and White American alike, experienced a reenactment of this scenario and identified with being the bearers of bad news in an environment where it is easier to kill the messenger than hear a painful message. One of our White members wrote, "My sense of our place at the conference was of that pesky little group that couldn't or wouldn't stop being a nuisance. . . . It is also noteworthy that while individual White women apologized to some of us after reacting so strongly to our group's proposals, none of them saw this as a larger problem more significant than particular misspeaking."

Despite the negative response to our proposal that diversity be a major component and overarching theme in any feminist analysis, we felt that we were addressing these issues with well-intentioned and not malicious or evil people. An African American group member remarked, "The discomfort that arises in confronting these issues can be a positive indication; it can be viewed as a challenge or opportunity to either grow or remain stuck. After all, when we are totally comfortable, there is nothing to work on."

Diversity in Research

It is important to remember that the personal struggles inherent in attempts to advance diversity in feminist psychology do not occur simply within the psychotherapy arena. Such endeavors are an active component of research efforts as well.

Gerrard (1995) described her painful experience as a White feminist researcher attempting to do research on women of color. Despite her good intentions, she found herself being treated with suspicion, hostility, anger, and resentment by the women of color whom she attempted to interview for her research. She argued that the feelings engendered in the researcher are important to attend to and can enrich the process while being respectful of the participant. One of the White women in our group noted that her experience of the group's process made her identify with Gerrard's sense of feeling misunderstood. Gerrard wrote that her experience of feeling dismissed, powerless, and hopeless by the women she wished to interview, women that she felt she could assist in some way, helped her instead to understand how these women must feel all the time. Reframing her experience, she came to understand her research participants' resistance to her well-intentioned inquiries and efforts as a part of their resistance to the racism of a White society of which she is member. She encouraged women who do research to begin talking about such painful experiences and admonished them to avoid what she referred to as "research abuse." She defined this abuse as the practice of researchers, a majority of whom are White, "parachuting" into people's lives, stirring up painful, old feelings, and then vanishing, leaving the research participant to address unresolved and painful feelings alone.

Reviewing the Process

Minority group members are usually the ones to challenge, raise, or address issues of diversity because they are often most affected by the absence of inclusiveness. The members of the diversity working group shared this task. When members of minority groups raise these issues and attempt to confront the reluctance of majority group members to incorporate aspects of the minority experience, they may elicit anxiety, discomfort, guilt, shame, and anger from majority group members. Distancing, minimizing the importance of the minority experience and their concerns, and projecting hostility may be observed when such emotions are elicited. We feel that this was characteristic of some of the other working groups' responses to our proposal. This reaction may be heightened when addressing majority group members who view themselves as allies or as having the more highly evolved, more egalitarian social consciousness that is often characteristic of feminists (Brown, 1995).

We believe that the evolution of our group's bonding process was shaped in part by the fact that White women in the group felt that they were treated in the manner that women of color and other members of minority groups are routinely treated. Although some reported that this was an experience they found distressing and unfamiliar, they also found it to be transformative.

Our experiences made us wonder how we could help even well-intentioned individuals minimize their own denial or defensiveness with respect to diversity and help them and ourselves address the different levels and kinds of trauma that may be masked because they do not manifest themselves in traditional hierarchical patterns. We found Holzman's (1995) analysis and personal insights useful in making distinctions between productive guilt and nonproductive guilt. She raised the importance of making rational assessments about the things one has control over and the things one has no control over. For example, rational assessments would include a personal examination of the ways in which a person who is a majority group member derives the "fruits" of White privilege, how one colludes with oppression to harm its targets for one's own benefit, and when a person speaks and behaves in ways that harm oppressed people (Brown, 1995; Holzman, 1995). She observed that this often painful self-inquiry can best be accomplished in a supportive atmosphere where a person's boundaries and stage of readiness to explore these issues are respected, a conceptual framework for understanding them is available, and coping strategies can be developed (Holzman, 1995).

Our fundamental resolution was that cultural competency should be the cornerstone of our educational and training endeavors beginning with this analysis of the self and one's own personal behavior. This is a necessary step toward developing a feminism and psychology that is diverse in positive and affirming ways.

RECOMMENDATIONS

The general recommendations of the diversity working group are presented in the Appendix.

Professional Standards and Research

Members of the diversity working group believed that the American Psychological Association (APA) should play an even more central and proactive role in ensuring that diversity is fully implemented at all levels of our profession. Current standards either are inadequate or are not being implemented in the domains of training, curriculum development, research, licensing, accreditation, and professional guidelines. Current professional guidelines should be clarified and enforced to protect consumers and promote psychological practice in accord with the highest ethical standards.

We expressed concern that many practitioners who attempt to provide services to linguistically and culturally diverse populations have received little or no formal training in such areas and many do not seek it voluntarily. Graduate and internship sites often comply only minimally with diversity accreditation standards. The language in our profession frequently does not conform with the mandate to avoid heterosexist, sexist, ageist, and other insensitive or degrading language.

In a related fashion, research studies whose participants are overwhelmingly White, middle class, heterosexual, and young (frequently of college student age) make generalizations about their findings that go far beyond those in their samples. Furthermore, they are rarely challenged about this practice in professional journals and publications. We are also concerned that ethical standards for the use of assessment and intervention techniques, in the area of diversity, are often ambiguous or ignored.

It is essential that professional psychologists include operationalized standards for diverse practice in their formal professional guidelines. It has been our experience that discussions of diversity trigger denial, minimization, resistance, or only superficial compliance. Diversity is an anxiety-provoking issue; rather than fleeing the anxieties aroused, however, the issues that give rise to them should be examined and discussed. Hence, more stringent guidelines are needed that clearly delineate how diversity standards should be operationalized. Criteria should be developed to define insufficient compliance with diversity requirements, and procedures should be implemented to mandate the suspension of professional activities until appropriate remediation is accomplished.

Roles of Professional Organizations

For APA to become more effective in upholding the standards of diversity, a cadre of committed groups and individuals with skills and a knowledge base in diversity should be identified and empowered to help transform our profession. APA should serve in an oversight capacity and ensure that diversity is mainstreamed throughout the organization. Diversity should be a central focus of all divisions, even those that perceive themselves as less people or consumer oriented. Committees, divisions, and directorates should work together to coordinate and collate information and initiatives. APA can play a critical role in establishing continuing education programs for the profession as it continues to develop, refine, and enforce professional standards throughout the areas of training, curriculum, research, and guidelines for licensing and accreditation.

Curriculum and Training

It is imperative that psychology training programs make diversity a routine and not tangential feature of training. This goal can be accomplished by having separate courses on the effect of cultural and ethnic diversity on the delivery of psychological services and by including relevant materials in all courses. All programs should be able to demonstrate the following: practicum experiences with diverse populations; ability to recruit and retain diverse faculty, students, and supervisors; and the use of didactic and experiential techniques to explore and overcome the biases imposed by privilege, individual worldviews, perspective taking, and other sociopolitical realities.

Training programs must grapple with the difficult issue of encouraging all faculty to assume the responsibility for diversity training and not simply delegating this work to staff members who are members of diverse ethnic and cultural groups. Decisions must be made regarding who is qualified to teach courses according to diversity guidelines and when does an instructor's academic freedom (in terms of content or process) conflict with professional standards for diversity. Adherence to cultural competency standards must begin with undergraduates and proceed through graduate, postdoctoral, and continuing education programs.

An awareness of diversity should be better integrated with research activities in professional psychology. APA has taken steps to make editorial boards and reviewers more diverse, and this should be continued. The diversity working group favored developing and using nontraditional research paradigms, expanding current visions of "scholarship," and ensuring that research goals be of service to consumers. It also is important to examine issues of privilege and the dilemma faced by researchers who are embedded and privileged in the system they are studying. Understanding the relevance of demographic and cultural matches between experimenters and study participants and their effects is another important area of exploration. We also considered the importance of understanding how political factors and agendas determine what research projects are funded and the effect of those factors on shaping the body of knowledge. We believed that psychological research standards should be mediated by addressing and resolving the questions that we raised and any other questions that facilitate diversity by creating appropriate research questions and methodologies and by finding applications.

Licensing, Accreditation, and Professional Guidelines

Our final area of recommendations focused on issues of licensing, accreditation, and professional guidelines. We believed that feminist ethics and professional guidelines for psychologists should be more explicit with respect to diversity both to protect the consumer and to minimize potential lawsuits. As our client base becomes more diverse, and given the realities of managed care, it is imperative that licensing and accreditation boards require practitioners to demonstrate cultural competency. This goal can be accomplished by enforcing guidelines for diversity in the accreditation of training programs, internships, and postdoctoral training and by state boards that require continuing education for those individuals who are already licensed. Material on diversity should be reflected on national licensing examinations and in oral examinations for state boards and professional examinations that confer diplomate status in psychology.[1]

A consistent theme in our deliberations was the recognition that focusing on diversity is perhaps a never ending struggle; there always appears to be an opposing force that seeks to silence those of us who demand to be heard. We are committed to trying to learn and practice any procedures that will help feminism and professional psychology resist the stagnation and inappropriate use of our knowledge and techniques. When we saw that our attempts to expand the discourse of psychology produced resistance

---

[1]Since our meetings, the Massachusetts State Board of Psychology, under the leadership of Jessica Henderson-Daniel, herself a woman of color, has demonstrated leadership in this area by implementing the requirement to demonstrate competence in these areas as a routine feature of licensure.

and denial, we committed ourselves to finding new ways of communicating with others. We found the process and task of the diversity working group to be challenging, painful, and frustrating but ultimately nourishing and renewing. By attempting to practice standards of diversity in our group, we rehearsed the roles that we have adopted as feminist psychologists: We try to speak the truth as we know it while constantly striving to improve our knowledge base, and we continue to raise our voices in opposition to the forces that attempt to silence or distort what we have to say.

We acknowledged that in a feminist paradigm, people with less power and privilege are not responsible for the recruitment of others like them, nor are they responsible for making privileged members comfortable with their presence. Furthermore, we asserted that those who are less privileged should not be expected to feel grateful when they and their needs are appropriately considered. Advancing inclusiveness is an explicit part of the tenets that form the underpinnings of feminist principles. Behaving in ways that further those goals is not a special activity or superfluous effort, it is simply consistent with what feminists seek to do.

SUMMARY

Feminism and Diversity

Although current practice of and literature in feminist therapy does not reflect the full range of diversity among women, it is absolutely consistent with the core goals of feminist therapy to do so. These goals are explicitly reflected in the mandate of feminist therapy to examine the role of societal oppression in the lives of all women. Diversity goals are also reflected in the importance accorded to explicit monitoring of the power dynamics within and outside of the treatment and training process as well as in the emphasis placed on the need to understand the social and cultural context in clients' lives and treatment. Interpretations of this mandate that lead to the privileging of gender as the primary locus of societal oppression for all women is perhaps what is most problematic in making feminist practice sensitive to the diversities of women. Despite the limited practice and interpretation of feminism's mandate, the importance accorded to contextualizing women's lives and the role of societal oppression in them is perhaps most eloquently stated in feminist theory's commitment to a kind of social change that both promotes and supports equality for everyone.

When we consider diversifying clinical training and practice, we understand that we must first acknowledge the inherent tension involved in incorporating multiple aspects of people's experiences and differences into the practices of a large and diverse group. It is far easier to theorize about diversity than to practice it. It is important at this point to ask who does the theorizing and on whose experience that theory is based. In American feminist theory and therapy, the identification of gender as the primary locus of all women's oppression maximizes the importance of gender oppression and minimizes other equally or more important aspects of women's experiences and oppressions. This approach precludes the authentic incorporation of the different realities that constitute diversity. For example, all women share gender oppression, but they do not all experience that oppression in the same way.

Locating Ourselves on the Spectrum of Oppression and Privilege

The experience of oppression and privilege are filtered through the many different lenses and realities that must be incorporated and understood. Hence, universalizing human experience should be carefully scrutinized. It increases disempowerment among those who are marginalized, and it is often used to maintain entitlement and marginalization status quos. Universalizing may also serve to avoid the difficult tensions that disrupt the false sense of harmony and security between women and that fail to give voice to the ways that women may engage in oppressive behavior toward other women both personally and institutionally.

Anyone who holds societal advantage and the power that accompanies it may engage in oppressive behavior. Because of that potential, it is always important in feminist therapy to determine the location of both the client and (perhaps more important) the research scientist, therapist, supervisor, or teacher along the spectrum of oppression and power. People in power must locate and acknowledge their own locus of social advantage and its effect on their view of their clients, students, research participants, or supervisees. This is often anxiety provoking because most people grow up believing in the values of fairness and in the explicit assumption of fairness of our social institutions. Meritocracy is the system that doles out social rewards on the basis of ability and hard work, and it is presumed to represent the system by which people in our society have and continue to receive social rewards. Unfortunately, meritocracy is largely a myth in American culture. Many people may have ability and work hard, but that is not the most salient ingredient in success. Often, social, familial, and political connections with persons in positions of power and influence, good timing, and sometimes just luck are essential. Most people know this on some level and may even articulate it when they are treated unfairly. However, if they are confronted with the ways in which their optimal development is enhanced by factors that are not based on a simple function of ability, hard work, or fairness, but rather, on things they did not earn, they may need to avoid acknowledging that reality. To acknowledge this reality may appear synonymous with minimizing their personal ability and effort. Such denial, however, creates major obstacles in implementing diversity and (in some settings) even in discussing it. In research and psychotherapy theory and practice, avoiding the acknowledgment and understanding of the broad and divergent role of societal privilege and oppression in people's lives is problematic. It ultimately results in an inability to deliver optimal services, whether in clinical treatment or in valid research findings. Therapists who are unable to view themselves and their own position fully will be unable to view clients and their positions fully.

Working through the tension between diversity and the tendency to universalize is necessary to achieve an authentic personal and professional transformation. When we practice authentic diversity we enhance the efforts of feminist psychology to transform the discipline of psychology. We should not, however, confuse tokenism with diversity. Token gestures may give the illusion of practicing diversity under the aegis of feminist practice; however, such gestures do not represent the authentic inclusion of differences required to transform feminist theory. Fully incorporating the study of difference affords us the multiple perspectives needed to provide for an increasingly comprehensive, representative, accurate, and dynamic knowledge base in psychological theory and practice. Incorporating diverse perspectives and concerns in our paradigms should facilitate an authentic understanding of all human beings. Although they may at times fall short of those goals in practice, our theoretical paradigms should at least attempt to do so. Omitting diverse perspectives results in a narrow and distorted view of women's worlds and realities. The inclusion of multiple perspectives, however, can transform psychology from an instrument of social control to a powerful instrument of advocacy and social change. In this paradigm it is no longer necessary to see people as the same in order to treat them with fairness. We stress the importance of making the leap from equal treatment that presumes and requires sameness, to standards of fair treatment that acknowledge and even celebrate the richness of human diversity.

APPENDIX
RECOMMENDATIONS OF THE DIVERSITY WORKING GROUP

1. APA should play a more central, coordinating, and proactive role in ensuring that diversity is fully implemented at all levels of our profession (e.g., in training, curriculum, research, licensing, accreditation, professional guidelines, committees, divisions, directorates, and continuing education).
2. APA should enforce professional standards that mandate cultural competency and training for the provision of services to linguistically and culturally diverse populations. These guidelines should impact practitioners, graduate programs, internship sites, postdoctoral training, state licensure boards, and continuing education programs.
3. All professional discourse in the field of psychology should conform to standards to avoid heterosexist, sexist, ageist, and other insensitive language.
4. Editorial reviews should ensure that generalizations are not made from research studies whose participants are White, middle class, heterosexual, and college-student age.
5. Ethical standards in the use of assessment and intervention techniques should be made more explicit and enforced.
6. Professional standards for diverse practice should be clearly operationalized. When individuals or groups do not meet professional criteria, professional activities should be suspended until appropriate remediation is completed.
7. APA should play a leadership role in empowering individuals and groups to assist in the transformation of our profession.
8. Curriculum, training, and practicum experiences should include diversity as a mainstream focus both by having relevant course materials integrated into ongoing courses and by having separate courses.
9. Training programs should be able to demonstrate experience with diverse populations; the recruitment and retention of diverse faculty, students, and supervisors; and the use of didactic and experiential techniques to explore and overcome the biases imposed by individual worldviews, taking stock of or understanding different perspectives, and other sociopolitical realities.
10. Training programs should ensure that all faculty (not just those who are members of culturally and ethnically diverse groups) assume the responsibility for diversity training.
11. Decisions must be made according to diversity guidelines regarding who is qualified to teach courses and when issues of academic freedom are in conflict with professional standards for diversity.
12. Diversity should be better integrated with research activities in professional psychology. These activities include using diverse editorial boards and reviewers, expanding current conceptions of research and scholarship, ensuring that research be of potential use to consumers, and understanding and changing when appropriate the criteria that determine research funding and the relevance of demographic and cultural matches between experimenters and study samples.
13. Material on diversity should be reflected on national and state oral and written examinations and professional examinations that confer diplomate status in the fields of psychology.

REFERENCES

Almeida, R. (1993). Unexamined assumptions and service delivery systems: Feminist theory and racial exclusions. *Journal of Feminist Family Therapy, 5*(1), 3–23.

Banks, M. E. (1986). Black women clinicians: Survival against the odds. In S. Rose (Ed.), *Career guide for women scholars* (pp. 108–114). New York: Springer.

Banks, M. E., & Ackerman, R. J. (1992). Family therapy for caregivers of brain-injured patients. In J. Chrisler & D. Howard (Eds.), *New directions in feminist psychology: Practice, theory, and research* (Vol. 13, pp. 66–84). New York: Springer.

Banks, M. E., Ackerman, R. J., & Corbett, C. A. (1995). Feminist neuropsychology: Issues for physically challenged women. In J. Chrisler & A. Hemstreet (Eds.), *Variations on a theme: Diversity and the psychology of women* (pp. 29–49). Albany: State University of New York Press.

Brown, L. (1990). The meaning of a multicultural perspective for theory-building in feminist psychotherapy. *Women and Therapy, 9*(1/2), 1–23.

Brown, L. S. (1995). Antiracism as an ethical norm in feminist therapy practice. In J. Adleman & G. Enguidanos (Eds.), *Racism in the lives of women: Testimony, theory and guides to practice* (pp. 137–148). New York: Harrington Park Press.

Comas-Díaz, L., & Greene, B. (Eds.). (1994a). *Women of color: Integrating ethnic and gender identities in psychotherapy.* New York: Guilford Press.

Comas-Díaz, L., & Greene, B. (1994b). Women of color with professional status. In L. Comas-Díaz & B. Greene (Eds.), *Women of color: Integrating ethnic and gender identities in psychotherapy* (pp. 347–388). New York: Guilford Press.

Daniel, J. H. (1994). Exclusion and emphasis reframed as a matter of ethics. *Ethics and Behavior, 4*(3), 229–235.

Davis, N. D., Cole, E., & Rothblum, E. D. (Eds.). (1993). Faces of women and aging [Special issue]. *Women and Therapy, 14*(1/2).

Espin, O. (1995). On knowing you are the unknown: Women of color constructing psychology. In J. Adleman & G. Enguidanos (Eds.), *Racism in the lives of women: Testimony, theory and guides to practice* (pp. 127–136). New York: Harrington Park Press.

Espin, O., & Gawelek, M. (1992). Women's diversity: Ethnicity, race, class, and gender in theories of feminist psychology. In L. Brown & M. Ballou (Eds.), *Personality and psychopathology: Feminist reappraisals* (pp. 88–107). New York: Guilford Press.

Fine, M. (1992). *Disruptive voices: The possibilities of feminist research.* Ann Arbor: University of Michigan Press.

Fine, M., & Asch, A. (Eds). (1988). *Women with disabilities: Essays in psychology, culture and politics.* Philadelphia: Temple University Press.

Fodor, I. G., & Franks, V. (1990). Women at midlife and beyond [Special issue]. *Psychology of Women Quarterly, 14*(4).

Gerrard, N. (1995). Some painful experiences of a White feminist therapist doing research with women of colour. In J. Adleman & G. Enguidanos (Eds.), *Racism in the lives of women: Testimony, theory and guides to practice* (pp. 55–63). New York: Harrington Park Press.

Graham, S. (1992). "Most of the subjects were White and middle class": Trends in published research on African-Americans in selected APA journals 1970–1989. *American Psychologist, 47*, 629–639.

Greene, B. (1986). When the therapist is White and the patient is Black: Considerations for psychotherapy in the feminist heterosexual and lesbian communities. *Women and Therapy, 5*, 41–65.

Greene, B. (1993). Psychotherapy with African-American women: Integrating feminist and psychodynamic models. *Journal of Training and Practice in Professional Psychology, 7*, 49–66.

Greene, B. (1994a). African American women. In L. Comas-Díaz & B. Greene (Eds.), *Women of color: Integrating ethnic and gender identities in psychotherapy* (pp. 10–29). New York: Guilford Press.

Greene, B. (1994b). Diversity and difference: The issue of race in feminist psychotherapy. In M. Pravder-Mirkin (Ed.), *Women in context: A feminist reconstruction of psychotherapy with women* (pp. 333–351). New York: Guilford Press.

Greene, B. (1995). An African American perspective on racism and antisemitism within feminist organizations. In J. Adleman & G. Enguidanos (Eds.), *Racism in the lives of women: Testimony, theory and guides to practice* (pp. 303–313). New York: Harrington Park Press.

Hall, R. L., & Greene, B. (1996). Sins of omission and commission: Women, psychotherapy and the psychological literature. *Women and Therapy, 18*(1), 5–31.

Henderson-Daniel, J. (1994). Exclusion and emphasis reframed as a matter of ethics. *Ethics and Behavior, 4*, 229–235

Holzman, C. (1995). Rethinking the role of guilt and shame in White women's antiracism work. In J. Adleman & G. Enguidanos (Eds.), *Racism in the lives of women: Testimony, theory and guides to practice* (pp. 325–332). New York: Harrington Park Press.

Hurtado, A. (1989). Relating to privilege: Seduction and rejection in the subordination of white women and women of color. *Signs, 14*, 833–855.

Landrine, H., Klonoff, E. A., & Brown-Collins, A. (1992). Cultural diversity and methodology in feminist psychology: Critique, proposal, empirical example. *Psychology of Women Quarterly, 16*, 145–163.

McIntosh, P. (1988). *Understanding correspondence between white privilege and male privilege through women's studies work* (Working Paper No. 189). Wellesley, MA: Center for Research on Women, Wellesley College.

Ochshorn, J., & Cole, E. (Eds.). (1995). Women's spirituality, women's lives [Special issue]. *Women and Therapy, 16*(2/3).

Rayburn, C. (1982). Feminism and religion: What price holding membership in both camps? *Counseling and Value, 27*(2), 83–89.

Rayburn, C. (1984). Impact of nonsexist language and guidelines for women in religion. *Journal of Pastoral Counseling, 1*(1), 5–8.

Reid, P. T. (1993). Poor women in psychological research: Shut up and shut out. *Psychology of Women Quarterly, 17,* 133–150.

Reid, P. T., & Comas-Díaz, L. (1990). Gender and ethnicity: Perspectives on dual status. *Sex Roles, 22,* 397–408.

Roberson, M. K., Malloy, K. A., Powell, J. M., Soderland, J., Thomas, L., & Curtis, E. (1994, August). *Affirmed identities in an oppressive world: Lessons from lesbian subculture.* Paper presented at the 102nd Annual Convention of the American Psychological Association, Los Angeles, CA.

Rothblum, E. & Cole, E. (Eds.). (1988). Lesbianism: Affirming nontraditional roles [Special issue]. *Women and Therapy, 8*(1/2).

Sanchez-Hucles, J. (1990). Biculturalism in American ethnic minorities: A direction for a society that values diversity. *Focus, 42,* 13–14.

Scarr, S. (1988). Race and gender as psychological variables: Social and ethical issues. *American Psychologist, 43,* 56–59.

Solomon, S. (1993). Women and physical distinction: A review of the literature and suggestions for intervention. *Women and Therapy, 14*(3/4), 91–103.

Walker, L. E. A. (1995). Racism and violence against women. In J. Adleman & G. Enguidanos (Eds.), *Racism in the lives of women: Testimony, theory and guides to practice* (pp. 239–250). New York: Harrington Park Press.

Willmuth, M. E., & Holcolmb, L. (Eds.). (1993). Women with disabilities: Found voices [Special issue]. *Women and Therapy, 14*(3/4).

Yoder, J. D., & Kahn, A. S. (1993). Working toward an inclusive psychology of women. *American Psychologist, 48,* 846–850.

10

POSTDOCTORAL TRAINING IN FEMINIST PSYCHOLOGICAL PRACTICE

NORINE G. JOHNSON AND PAMELA REMER

WITH ASUNCION AUSTRIA, ANNETTE BRODSKY,
NATALIE ELDRIDGE, ETHEL MAGIDSON, JANET MATTHEWS,
ROBERTA NUTT, ESTHER ROTHBLUM, AND RECECCA ROY

As psychology readies for the next millennium, feminist psychological practitioners, academicians, and researchers are poised to propose that there be specialty training in feminist psychology. This specialty training should not be limited to feminist therapy; consistent with the conceptualizations of the Boston National Conference, it should include all aspects of psychological practice: therapy with women and men, consultation, teaching, research, supervision, political action, assessment, prevention, and forensics. Training for this specialization in feminist psychological practice could occur in doctoral or postdoctoral training programs or in predoctoral internships.

Postdoctoral training in feminist psychological practice is relevant for both female and male psychologists who have specialized interest in gender or women's issues. This training would be appropriate for psychologists who want to be feminist psychological practitioners or who want to focus on therapy and research issues strongly affected by gendered experiences in society. Although most existing feminist practice training programs primarily focus on women's issues, this postdoctoral training approach would encourage the expansion of feminist applications to men's issues. Most training programs emphasize feminist therapy skill development, but the national conference participants agreed that training must be inclusive of all areas of practice.

Consistent with this vision of a speciality in feminist psychological practice, the postdoctoral working group examined the issues surrounding feminist postdoctoral training and created postdoctoral models for training psychologists to be feminist-oriented practitioners. This chapter summarizes the process and accomplishments of this working group. We begin this chapter by reviewing the existing literature on training in feminist psychological practice. Then, we provide a summary review of the status of psychological postdoctoral education and accreditation. These literatures provided the foundations for our working group's deliberations. We next describe the process and content of the meetings of our working group on postdoctoral training. Finally, we explore a variety of postdoctoral training models, and we suggest future directions for postdoctoral training in feminist psychological practice.

LITERATURE REVIEW

Postdoctoral Education Is a Women's Issue

Almost one quarter (22%) of the 1991 graduates in psychology were employed as postdoctoral fellows or had completed postdoctoral programs according to the American Psychological Association's (APA) Office of Demographic Employment and Educational Research (Kohout, 1991). Of the 1991 doctorates, 62% were women.

The quality of postdoctoral training is important for feminists, not just because of the numbers of women undertaking postdoctoral training, but because of the potential for women to be exploited. Licensing as a psychologist in most states requires a minimum of 1 year of supervised experience after earning a doctoral degree. Women were more likely than men to choose an internship in their community rather than moving to other locations.

In 1997 the APA Education Directorate reviewed the status of internships in Professional Psychology. Jill N. Reich, executive director of the Education Directorate, summarized what was known in a memorandum to the APA Board of Directors. One of the patterns that emerged from annual reports of accredited programs was that faculty and students repeatedly ranked geographic restrictions as the most salient reason for reported unsuccessful internship placements. Women were paid 66% of what men were paid during internship. This situation leaves women at risk for receiving poorly paid, poorly supervised, and poorly organized postdoctoral training as was concluded by the postdoctoral committee of Association of Psychology Postdoctoral and Internship Centers (APPIC) postdoctoral committee in 1985.

In 1985, APPIC surveyed all postdoctoral programs listed in its directory of internship and postdoctoral training programs. At that time, APPIC had not yet promulgated criteria for listing postdoctoral programs. The survey found enormous variability in programs, ranging from programs with funded training positions and quality supervised organized training to programs that offered no funding and required significant service with little supervision. For example, one program had 25 unfunded doctoral psychology trainees, required 30 hours of direct client service, and provided only 1 hour of group supervision. The trainees at that program were all women. Postdoctoral training in psychology is clearly a feminist issue.

Approaches to Feminist Training

Whereas the focus of many books and journal articles over the past 15 years has been on defining the theory and application of feminist therapy, little has been written about how to train feminist psychological practitioners at either the graduate or the postgraduate level. The extant literature has targeted feminist therapy specifically rather than examining the broader concept of feminist psychological practice, which would encompass assessment, consultation, community development, teaching, research, and so on. The central documents that have addressed feminist therapy training stress the importance of both the content and the process of training. In this section, several of these documents are reviewed to identify the most essential underlying foundations for postdoctoral feminist training programs.

Worrell (1980) identified the emergence of a discipline or approach to counseling women. This discipline is based on a new body of knowledge about women, women's issues, and therapeutic techniques designed to meet women's needs. Building on Harway's (1979) training model for gender-fair counseling, Worell called for programs to train psychologists in this specialty discipline for counseling women. She believed these graduate training programs must "disseminate appropriate information, and encourage development of relevant skills and attitudes in counseling women" (p. 481).

Principles Concerning the Counseling/Psychotherapy of Women

The APA Division of Counseling Psychology developed a set of foundational principles for providing therapy to women (Fitzgerald & Nutt,

1986). These 13 "Principles Concerning the Counseling/Psychotherapy of Women" do not directly address the desired nature of training programs, but they do put forth basic guidelines on which feminist training programs can be built. The principles stress the impact of societal sexism on female clients and the need for therapists working with female clients to be aware of their own values and to be knowledgeable about biological, psychological, and social issues that affect women. These principles have been endorsed by most of the practice-oriented divisions of APA.

National Council of Schools of Professional Psychology Conference on Women's Issues in Professional Psychology

In 1991, the National Council of Schools of Professional Psychology held a conference on women's issues. The conference participants issued a set of 15 resolutions that were to be included in all professional psychology training programs, all of which are relevant to feminist practice training programs. Some of these resolutions called for member schools (a) to amend their organizational policies and structures to include women's experiences and to aid women's professional development, (b) to make students knowledgeable about the needs and issues of female clients, and (c) to develop a flexible training model (e.g., part-time programs and internships to accommodate the needs of women and other special groups). Although some training programs offer half-time internships, the number of such offers is estimated to be still significantly below the expressed interest of psychology interns in part-time programs.

An Empowerment Training Model

Worell and Remer (1992) proposed a model of training for feminist therapists that gives attention to the knowledge, attitudes, and skills needed to implement a feminist practice perspective. This model was designed primarily for graduate-level training, but it can be applied to postgraduate training as well. In designing a training program, Worell and Remer encouraged a focus on attitudes and values and on a structure that is supportive of a feminist perspective.

Development of feminist values in trainees is an important goal of this training program. The model includes trainers who have attitudes and beliefs consistent with feminist perspectives and support faculty who must hold nonsexist and nonracist values. Prominent among these beliefs and attitudes were the following: (a) Many of women's problems come from living in a society that discriminates against them and places them in a subordinate power position; (b) women and men differ primarily because of differential gender-role socialization; (c) all forms of oppression (racism, ageism, heterosexism, etc.) must be eliminated; (d) female perspectives must be given equal weight to male perspectives; and (e) egalitarian relationships are valued (Worell & Remer, 1992).

Professional female trainer and supervisor role models are viewed as crucial in the development of feminist psychology practioners. Elimination of sexist language in training materials, gender-fair equitable distribution of monetary resources, and enforceable sexual harassment policies are important elements in the structure of the program. A feminist training program includes specialized courses related to feminist theory and practice, but it also must infuse gender and women's issues into all courses and educational activities in the program. For example, a research design course should include nonsexist and feminist criteria, such as those suggested by McHugh, Koeske, and Frieze (1986).

Worell and Remer (1992) pointed out that feminist therapy perspectives are essential for effective supervision of practice. Trainees need to be exposed to cases in which a feminist perspective is the most appropriate approach. Therapy goals, assessments, definitions of pathology, and theoretical orientations must be evaluated for their compatibility with feminist practice values. Feminist site supervisors in a variety of practica and internship sites specializing in women's issues are crucial for trainee practice experience. Supervision should help trainees focus on the external as well as the internal sources of clients' issues. Egalitarian supervisory relationships which respect and build on trainees' strengths are valued. Trainees need to have a support structure from both trainer–supervisor role models and peers.

Furthermore, according to Worell and Remer's model, a feminist psychological practice program should include training in development outreach and prevention programs related to women's issues. Trainees must be taught skills for bringing about institutional change, and they must be encouraged to become involved in social change activities. For example, trainees might attend workshops on date rape and sexual harassment. They might interview a director of a battered women's shelter with an emphasis on the organizational, financial, and political structures deemed relevant to the functioning of the shelter. Worell and Remer have implemented an adaptation of this model within their Counseling Psychology Graduate Program at the University of Kentucky. Doctoral students in this program may choose to develop an expertise in feminist psychological practice.

Feminist Practice Training: An Application

In a personal communication, Rothblum (1994) described how she implemented feminist practice training into a graduate clinical psychology program at the University of Vermont. Key feminist elements in this program include teaching methods for both surviving in and changing a patriarchal institution. Students work with mentors who support feminist professional development. Students are trained about publication strategies and encouraged to publish and present their research. Rothblum emphasized the importance of designing flexible training programs that accommodate women from different professional backgrounds and for different training needs.

Identification of Existing Training Programs in Feminist Practice

In their preparation for the APA National Conference on Postdoctoral Education and Training in Psychology, Wiens and Baum (1995) surveyed 229 postdoctoral programs and compiled a list of specialty areas in postdoctoral training. Two of these specialties, trauma treatment and traumatic stress, have significant implications for women and feminist psychology. Of significance for women is the absence of programs that specialize in women's issues, feminist psychology, or gender issues.

Scattered predoctoral and postdoctoral training programs in feminist practice are available in the United States, but at the time of this writing, there was no systematic listing of such programs. Prospective students must learn which programs offer a feminist practice focus by networking and writing for application materials. APA's Division 12, Clinical Psychology, recently established a special committee to survey and collect information to develop a listing of training programs with a focus on women. If feminist training programs are to be available to trainees, trainees must be able to identify them.

POSTDOCTORAL TRAINING IN PSYCHOLOGY AND EMERGING SPECIALTIES

In the past 7 years, postdoctoral education for professional psychology has generated considerable interest within organized psychology (e.g., National Council of Schools of Professional Psychology National Conference on Women, held in Tucson, Texas in 1991; National Conference on Postdoctoral Training in Professional Psychology, held in Ann Arbor, Michigan, in 1992; National Conference on Postdoctoral Training and Education, held in Norman, Oklahoma, in 1994). Psychology has grappled with the mission of defining excellence in psychological education. Postdoctoral education has been defined as a lifelong process, and multiple models are acceptable. Various committees, divisions, and directorates have sponsored conferences, conducted research, written policy papers, and revised criteria in an attempt to define quality postdoctoral education in training (e.g., *Report of the Joint Council on Professional Education in Psychology*, Stigall et al., 1990; *Report*, Joint Interim Committee on Identification and Recognition of Specialties and Proficiencies, 1994; *Guideline and Principles for*

Accreditation of Programs in Professional Psychology, Committee on Accreditation, 1996).

Accreditation is one way a profession has to recognize training programs that meet a promulgated set of criteria designed to establish standards of quality and excellence. Psychology has accredited doctoral training programs and internships, but only recently, in 1994, was the scope of accreditation expanded to include postdoctoral training.

The guidelines and principles established by the APA Committee on Accreditation (COA; 1995) had two major principle and value changes. The first is that each program will be evaluated by its own education and training philosophy, model, goals, objectives, and methods. The second is that the accreditation review process will emphasize outcomes of the program's training efforts. The move away from a single model of training to a multimodel approach is consistent with the feminist postdoctoral groups' ambivalence about the old APA criteria.

A footnote in the APA guidelines and principles (COA, 1995) states that a program's model of training may be one identified through a national conference of psychologists, from which guidelines for professional education and training have been approved by conference delegates. This suggests that a doctoral program, internship training program, and postdoctoral training program could state that it followed a feminist training model by identifying the guidelines for professional education and training approved by the National Conference on Feminist Education and Training in Practice. The training program must delineate how its goals, objectives, and methods are consistent with the feminist model and to provide outcome measures for how it met its goals.

A few of the other elements of the APA postdoctoral guidelines and procedures (COA, 1995) that are consistent with articulated feminist training values are as follows: (a) The provision for half-time as well as full-time training; (b) the explicit requirement that each program "engages in regular and systematic actions that indicate respect for and understanding of cultural and individual diversity" (p. 53); *cultural and individual diversity* refers to age, color, disabilities, ethnicity, gender, language, national origin, race, religion, sexual orientation, and social economic status (p. 5); (c) the inclusion of mentoring in the listing of modalities to foster socialization into the profession of psychology; and (d) the addition of a domain that stresses mutual respect and courtesy in the relations between students, interns, or residents—supervisors.

Between 1985 and 1994, several emerging specialties (e.g., neuropsychology, forensic psychology, and family psychology) took the lead in developing their own standards for postdoctoral training in their areas of specialization. The APA's Joint Interim Committee on Identification and Recognition of Specialties and Proficiencies (JCIRSP) standards and procedures for the identification and recognition of specialties has been accepted as policy by the APA Council of Representatives. JCIRSP recommended that each defined specialty in professional psychology contain four elements: (a) core scientific foundations in psychology, (b) a basic professional foundation, (c) advanced scientific and theoretical knowledge germane to the specialty, and (d) advanced professional applications (JCIRSP, 1994, p. 4).

A review of the identified principles suggests that feminist psychology might be in sufficient compliance to be considered for recognition as a new specialty. For example, feminist psychology has a core scientific foundation that can be related to general and specialized professional practice and could specify standards for the acquisition of advanced scientific knowledge and professional applications in the practice of feminist psychology. Feminist psychology also is in compliance with the principles of the parameters of practice. Feminist psychology can specify the populations serviced by the specialty; the psychological, biological, and social problems addressed; and the procedures and technologies used. This book, which contains the expanded discussions, conclusion and consensus of the National Conference on Feminist Training and Education, could provide the background for a petition for recognition as a new specialty. Again, feminist psychology is in the forefront of the changes in psychological education, allowing feminist training programs a myriad of options.

POSTDOCTORAL WORKING GROUP

Each of the 10 women in the postdoctoral working group came with her own agenda and her own study. Each woman expressed her interest in, if not commitment to, adding a dimension to training that offered postdoctoral experiences from a feminist perspective. The women worked in a variety of settings: general psychology departments, counseling psychology departments and clinics, professional schools, women's colleges, teaching hospitals, and private practice. There was a range in age, years of experience in the field, and lifestyle. The group included Asian American and lesbian members but no African American or Hispanic women. We speculate that many women of color who were conference participants were drawn to other working groups, such as the one on diversity. The postdoctoral working group missed this diversity of input in the small group discussions. However, cultural diversity was provided in the triad discussion groups.

Process

Day 1

From the beginning the postdoctoral training group assumed task pressure to develop a document that outlined the basic format and requirements of a postdoctoral training program in feminist psychological practice. The push to develop such a document by the end of the conference was felt throughout our deliberations.

At our first meeting each member introduced herself and told about her current work situation and her reasons for choosing this group. The group was bimodal in terms of interest in postdoctoral training. Many group members were already involved in some aspect of postdoctoral training. By contrast, a few members had not listed postdoctoral training as their first choice and expressed concern about their ability to contribute. The introductions established that all members' contributions were needed and respected.

Three major areas were addressed the first day. First, we brainstormed a list of possible questions to discuss and answer by the end of the conference. Answering these questions became the focus of our work together. Second, we discussed the major underlying issue of our committee work. We debated whether formal postdoctoral training programs were compatible with a feminist practice perspective. Using a feminist perspective, we generated a list of pros and cons. Consensus was reached through lively discussion and a creative compromise that maximized the advantages and minimized the disadvantages of postdoctoral training for feminists. The group voted to develop several models for postdoctoral training in feminist practice, including one or more that would fit the APA's criteria for accreditation as a postdoctoral training program.[1]

Finally, we developed five "General Principles for Postdoctoral Training Feminist Practice" that are presented in the next section of this chapter. Although the group's overall energy was lower this first day than later, we accomplished several major tasks and began to coalesce. Active participation was encouraged and solicited from all group members, and no group member dominated the discussions. As the student observer recorded our deliberations, she took an active role by challenging us to be clear and specific about our consensus and our disagreements. She became an integral and crucial member of our discussions. The use of collaborative brainstorming and the reaching of the multiple model compromise allowed us to respect one another's input and avoid an impasse that could have polarized the group.

Day 2

On Day 2 we divided into subgroups and joined triads composed of other working groups' members to discuss issues that cut across groups. When our group reconvened, we commented on how much our group had accomplished the first day and how much we liked the collaborative, fem-

---

[1]The new guidelines and procedures described earlier were accepted 2 years after the Boston National Conference.

inist process we had been using. Our triad work resulted in a sense of pride in and identification with our group. The energy level of our group meeting increased. We also realized that our decisions about feminist practice post-doctoral training would have important implications for predoctoral training as well.

Our next major task was to focus on developing minimal competency and exit criteria for feminist practice postdoctoral training (e.g., explicating the attitudes, knowledge, and skills needed for competent feminist practice). We defined *exit criteria* as outcome criteria a program might use to evaluate the effectiveness of its own feminist training model. As we discussed the exit criteria, we wrestled with several significant issues, such as the role of diagnosis and pathology-based perspectives and the impact of postdoctoral training programs on existing predoctoral internships. We debated the importance of the training process versus the outcome criteria.

We finally agreed that the process of the training methods was as important as the exit criteria. Defining the content of the basic competencies needed for feminist practice was an arduous process. We brainstormed all possibilities on paper charts and had each person mark the ones she felt were crucial. The student member was included in the collaborative and active process. Again, we achieved tangible products through lively debates and collaborative consensus. We gave feminist process as much value as our product.

Day 3

On Day 3, knowing our time together was ending, we began listing tasks and issues that remained to be addressed, such as the integration of didactic and service components and the role of men as feminist practitioners and as clients. We reasserted our position that multiple training models were valuable and listed some possible types. Desired time and length of the programs were fervently debated, but no consensus was reached.

The main focus in this session was on consolidating previous sessions' work and discussing the remaining issues so that we could issue our final report, which is detailed in the next section. We continued our collaborative brainstorming and use of lists generated by the entire group to track our work.

Throughout our deliberations, we had achieved a collaborative, feminist process where all members participated and were respected. Although we debated issues that threatened to polarize us, we found common ground for producing a document that would form the basis for the development of multiple models of feminist practice postdoctoral training programs. We had coped with the task pressure and maintained our commitment to feminist process.

General Principles of Feminist Training

The group felt our process allowed us to address significant issues regarding feminist training. The content of the sessions ranged from raising questions to defining principles. Some of these questions were as follows: What would a feminist postdoctoral training program look like? Are there one or more models of postdoctoral education and training? How do we develop a diversity of models? What training structures, formats, flexibility, and boundaries would be most congruent with feminist practice? What is taught to whom? How? When? Where? Why? What should be the minimum generic competencies? What do we envision postdoctoral graduates doing? How can we think about power in the feminist postdoctoral training program? Where do attitudes and values fit in? How do we integrate multicultural perspectives in education and practice?

After listing the pros and cons of developing formal postdoctoral training models in feminist practice, the group reached consensus that the reasons for developing such models qualitatively outweighed the reasons against them. We decided to recommend that a postdoctoral specialty in professional feminist psychological practice be developed. At a later plenary session the conference participants indicated their acceptance of this recommendation.

Discussions during the second day resulted in the acceptance of five principles:

1. The postdoctoral learning environment incorporates principles of feminist pedagogy, including (a) the provision of a feminist collegial environment; (b) small, face-to-face, regularly scheduled peer support group(s) and learning group(s); (c) individual mentor(s); and (d) national support groups, such as the Division of the Psychology of Women.
2. Changing attitudes and values is as central to training as the acquisition of skills and knowledge base.
3. Diversity is a necessary component of feminist practice (a) as reflected in personnel (trainees, faculty), curriculum, and client populations; and (b) with focused attention to the cultural richness as well as the oppressive experiences of diverse groups.
4. Training includes assessment of and intervention in micro- and macro-systems.
5. Feminist perspectives on theory, assessment and diagnosis, therapy–interventions, curriculum, pedagogy, supervision, research, and diversity must be integrated into the training program. Examples of these perspectives can be found in the principles of the nine working groups of the National Conference on Education and Training in Feminist Practice.

Issues Discussed

The discussion on the final day addressed remaining questions and topics. Five topics were addressed: exit criteria, supervision, models for length of programs, and nomenclature. A fifth topic, men's issues, received less time.

Exit Criteria

We reached consensus on some exit criteria for postdoctoral training in feminist practice. The postdoctoral training program should focus on developing attitudes and values, knowledge, and skills for sound professional feminist psychological practice. At the end of the program, trainees must have a knowledge base in the following areas: (a) foundations of feminist theory; (b) diversity; (c) women's issues, such as harassment, rape, and violence; (d) women's socialized reactions (e.g., a tendency to internalize rather than act out); and (e) models for and strategies in feminist practice, such as Worell and Remer's (1992) empowerment model. Furthermore, trainees would demonstrate skills in applying this knowledge base to feminist psychological practice with diverse populations and a variety of women's issues.

Supervision

The discussion on supervision led to three conclusions:

1. Postdoctoral training programs in feminist psychological practice must include training in feminist supervision, and supervisees must experience being supervised by a feminist psychologist.
2. Postdoctoral training programs must acknowledge the power differentials between supervisor and supervisee. They minimize hierarchical structures by using a collaborative process.
3. Feminist supervisors are mentors and role models.

Length of Training

The discussion of options for the length of programs evoked a spirited discussion related to what to do if the model of feminist postdoctoral training conflicted with parts of the APA accreditation criteria. The general feeling was that consistency with our feminist values was most important and that the promulgation of a feminist model of training could influence the APA process.

The group reached consensus on part-time programs as an option for postdoctoral training in addition to full-time programs. We decided that an essential element that must remain in part-time feminists' programs is face-to-face, small-group experiences. We did not believe this requirement could be met through sporadic meetings, such as a 2-day retreat once a month.

Disagreement remained about the amount of flexibility to be given part-time programs. The group reached consensus that exit criteria were more important than rigid time lines. We acknowledged that trainees would probably have differing skill levels on entry to a postdoctoral program and that these initial differences could result in varying levels of skills at the end of a postdoctoral program. We agreed that having minimal standards for exit criteria would ensure competency while allowing for individual variations.

Titles

The language to be used in training evoked concern, especially about titles such as *resident* or *fellow*. The consensus was that *trainee* was the most neutral and least androcentric and could imply a lifelong learning process. Consensus was not reached about the title for trainers. Those who preferred *supervisor* felt it was important to stress the appropriate differentiation of power in training. Those who preferred the title *preceptor* were primarily in research settings where they felt this title represented the feminist principle of equality better than *supervisor*.

Men's Issues

We tacitly agreed that feminist perspectives were important to therapy with male clients; however, our focus remained on training models on women's issues. We considered men as feminist trainees, recipients of feminist psychological practice, and providers of feminist practice. We avoided debating whether men can be feminist psychological practitioners and spent little time on the male therapist–client issue, which had caused some dissension in other working groups.

Summary

Throughout the conference, the postdoctoral working group felt creative tension. On the one hand, we wanted to define a mainstream model of postdoctoral training that would be fully funded and accredited and that would influence national psychology. On the other hand, we deliberated the equally stimulating prospect of defining our own model regardless of the constraints of the establishment. In other words, we experienced the feminist dilemma and were stimulated by it. We achieved consensus on most issues and resolved to continue the group after the conference until a prototype model of formal feminist postdoctoral training was developed.[2]

DIVERSITY AND CROSS-CULTURAL PERSPECTIVES

Incorporating diversity and cross-cultural perspectives into feminist psychological practice was highly endorsed by all the conference participants. The postdoctoral working group concluded that integrating diversity perspectives into the curriculum should occur at all levels of training, including postdoctoral training. As the face of America changes, there is a growing realization of the importance of diversity. American society is rapidly becoming diverse: One out of every five North Americans is of African, Asian, Native, or Latin American descent. Race, gender, ethnicity, age, sexual orientation, religion, and geographical location are salient variables in understanding human behavior.

Postdoctoral training should provide an advanced psychological understanding of the issues of diversity for psychologists. The foundations of feminist psychology and practice are consistent with valuing diversity. We consider three component areas in which diverse perspectives are important: curriculum transformation, research and practice, and the selection and retention of faculty and trainees.

Curricular Transformation

Preparing postdoctoral students means providing them with a knowledge base about cultural diversity. Common, but limited, approaches to curriculum inclusiveness include changing the reading lists, changing the course structure, and adding a program or a course (e.g., Asian Studies). However, these approaches can bring about token changes without addressing adequately the issues related to diversity.

Another approach to including diversity is curricular transformation. This approach calls for infusion and full integration of diversity into the curriculum to reflect unity and inclusiveness. Curricular transformation begins with an understanding that race, ethnicity, gender, and class form the basis of our human identities (Butler & Walter, 1991). It calls for weaving themes about cultural diversity and inclusiveness throughout the courses, choosing texts that incorporate differences, encouraging trainees to conduct research and write papers that fully explore diversity issues, and adopting teaching methods to reflect respect for the range of trainees' backgrounds and cognitive styles. Curricular transformation celebrates diversity as differences are identified and similarities are affirmed.

---

[2]A group within Division 35 continued this work, and the Executive Committee voted at its 1997 midwinter meeting to develop a specialty petition for feminist psychology.

Training in Research and Practice

Postdoctoral trainees must have adequate training to provide services and conduct research with diverse populations. Exposure to various populations enhances the trainee's awareness and sensitivity to different learning styles and to the development of innovative research methods, diverse perspectives in drawing research conclusions, appropriate assessment and diagnosis, and relevant practice strategies.

Faculty and Trainees

Enhanced recruitment and retention of diverse faculty and trainees are needed in our profession (Williams, 1990). *Visions and Transformations: The Final Report of the APA Commission on Ethnic Minority Recruitment, Retention, and Training in Psychology* (Commission on Ethnic Minority Recruitment, 1996) underscored the need for increasing the number of ethnic minority doctoral-level psychologists. The report stated that from 1976 to 1993 only 3,833 ethnic minorities were awarded a doctorate in psychology. This represents only 7.6% of all psychology doctorates during that period. Although progress has been made, it is slow. In 1993, ethnic minority psychology doctorates were only 9.4% of the total. Additional monies are needed for scholarships and training stipends. Furthermore, the environment must support diversity through mentoring; networking collaboration; and regularly scheduled, substantive interactions between trainees and faculty.

In summary, it is the goal of the feminist training program to develop in its participants increased awareness and understanding of ethnicity, race, gender, age, sexual orientation, religion, geographical location, and class issues. Ultimately, feminist researchers and practitioners incorporate this knowledge base in providing effective and culturally appropriate mental health services to the entire society.

MODELS FOR POSTDOCTORAL TRAINING IN FEMINIST PSYCHOLOGICAL PRACTICE

The postdoctoral working group recognized the need to develop (a) mainstream models of postdoctoral training that could be fully funded and accredited and would influence national psychology and (b) less formal models that were not bound by the constraints of the establishment. The models that are presented in this section are examples of both formal and informal types.

Scientist–Practitioner Feminist Training Model

In a world of managed care, tight budgets, health care resource rationing, and service evaluation by outcome data, new models of training are examined closely for their contribution to the bottom line. Feminist training models historically have been more focused on egalitarian process and fairness to culturally diverse clients than on the cost effectiveness of treatment or selection of the most needy. Thus, rather than creating another method that considers feminist psychological practice as a specialty in its own right, this model considers applying feminist process, philosophy, research, and treatment to existing professional specialty or proficiency training programs in psychology.

What would this integrated model look like? For inpatient programs, the forms for admission, evaluation, treatment plans, and discharge would consider women's roles in the culture. This could be done by including information on caretaking expectations, such as family support of the client and substitute support for those for whom the client has been the primary caretaker. Realistic inclusion of the client, as well as the professional team, in treatment planning would be taught and modeled. The role of abuse in client histories would be explored, and trainees would be challenged to include consideration of these histories in arriving at diagnoses. Client passivity and deference to the professional would be anticipated and discouraged to enable client independence. Research would compare differences in gendered responses or would focus on women-prevalent disorders.

Developing a proficiency in feminist treatment perspectives could be accomplished within existing professional psychology postdoctoral programs by adapting feminist principles and processes to existing client populations and by having the trainee seek an emphasis on cases within a particular population that exemplify feminist issues. For example, the postdoctoral fellow in a behavioral medicine program who wants a feminist concentration experience would seek and treat clients with pelvic pain, women athletes with sport injuries, or ovarian cancer patients and conduct research on a feminist issue, such as the role of therapy in enhancing survival for breast cancer patients. The trainee could work with a designated feminist mentor–supervisor, complete specific feminist readings, lead a feminist group, and receive didactic training in women's or gender issues, perhaps joining with other feminist postdoctoral fellows from other specialty or proficiency programs in the institution or from other community agencies. Trainees would be encouraged to discuss and debate the implications of applying feminist perspectives to such treatment and training issues as diagnostic categories, prescription privileges, and universal health care coverage.

Exit criteria for evaluating expertise in feminist knowledge and techniques could be applied to the particular proficiency area by the feminist supervisors–mentors who are experts in the clinical specialty or proficiency. The final product would be a certificate in feminist therapy, in addition to certification in the proficiency–specialty of the postdoctoral program.

A Model for Postdoctoral Training of Experienced Clinicians

A program could be designed to focus on the development of feminist practice among experienced clinicians trained in various disciplines and treatment modalities. Applicants should hold the highest degree in their discipline (e.g., Ph.Ds. for psychologists, M.S.W.s for social workers, or M.D.s for physicians). In addition, applicants would be required to have at least 3 years of clinical experience and to be practicing psychotherapy either privately or in a group or institutional setting. The general training model would be a 3-year, part-time program. All seminars, group meetings, and supervision would be scheduled 1 day a week from September through May. Core clinical training faculty and supervisors would be practicing clinicians. Many also would hold teaching positions in graduate programs in various disciplines. Faculty would be diverse in race, ethnic background, sexual orientation, age, cultural and religious backgrounds, and clinical training. Visiting scholars would be a regular part of the program, allowing a national perspective and network to develop. The program would be approved by APA to offer Category I Continuing Education for psychologists and by the National Association of Social Workers to offer Category I Continuing Education for social workers. Depending on the professional discipline of the participants, every effort would be made to offer a program that would meet the continuing education requirements for other disciplines, such as nursing.

First Year

The first year's focus would be on learning the foundations of feminist theory and its application to assessment and diagnosis, therapy styles, intervention, and research on women. The diversity of women's experience would be a major theme woven throughout this material. This first year might be waived for those with comparable training in the psychology of women and training–supervision in feminist practice.

On entering the program, each participant would become part of a small discussion group with other participants who entered the program at the same time. In the second semester of the first year, this group would be encouraged to function as a peer-supervision group, providing opportunities to present current cases from their work in other settings. Participants would also be paired with a third-year participant for guidance in negotiating the training program.

Second Year

The second year would focus on the treatment of various presenting problems common among women, including depression, career development, childhood sexual abuse, reproduction problems, eating disorders, relationship violence, rape, and substance abuse. Arrangements would be made for each participant to work with women in two specialized treatment programs and to be supervised by faculty from the postdoctoral program. Clinical supervision from the faculty would begin in the second year and would continue throughout the program in a group format (two to three supervisees meeting with one core faculty supervisor). Supervisors would serve as role models and mentors.

Third Year

In the third year, the participant would continue supervised practice, provide a seminar in clinical supervision, and supervise a therapist coming to the program for feminist supervision. In addition, each third-year participant would have an independent project involving a plan for instituting feminist practice beyond the psychotherapy room. Examples might include political advocacy around feminist issues, promoting feminist administrative policy and practice in an organization, or developing a feminist consultation service. This requirement supports a systemic view and sense of the broad responsibilities of feminist practice.

Postdoctoral Practitioner Model

Training in Feminist Practice

The postdoctoral program would provide advanced education and training in feminist practice. It would be a multifaceted program exploring issues concerning the integration of gender, race, class, culture, and sexuality through clinical practice, theory, and research–scholarship. This practitioner-oriented program would provide training with a primary focus on application, defined broadly to include areas such as clinical practice, program development, teaching, management, consultation, and supervision. The program would examine the experiences of women and men as a result of psychological, social, and historical factors that influence their lives. The content, methods, and assumptions of psychology would be reconsidered and revised in light of feminist scholarship.

Integration of Theory and Practice

In the practitioner model, particular emphasis would be given to the integration of theory and practice. This integration would be evident not only in the content of the education and training but also in the structure of the programs and the processes of teaching and learning. Part-time programs would be expected to allow women time for developing career paths and integrating career with the requirements of family life. Training and course work would be integrated at every level, to make practice meaningful and to facilitate the acquisition of skills, knowledge, and attitudes for feminist practice. Similarly, attention would be paid to the process, with collaborative models of learning, female role models, and mentors to facilitate women's processes in learning. In a practitioner model, research might be used as a foundation for knowledge and practice, rather than for developing competence in conducting formal research.

Fulfilling Licensure Requirement Models

State's Requirements for Licensure

Nearly 90% of states in this country require some type of postdoctoral professional experience before granting licensure (Texas State Board of Examiners of Psychologists, 1992). In most of these states this requirement is fulfilled in 1 year (variably defined as 1,000; 1,500; 1,600; 1,750; 1,800; 1,900; 2,000; or 2,060 hours); in a few states the requirement is 2 years. The postdoctoral experience is usually further defined by requirements such as minimum 1-hour per week face-to-face supervision. The supervisor must be a licensed psychologist in the state in question, competent in the areas of expertise being supervised, and ultimately responsible for the cases being supervised. These specific requirements vary greatly across states.

The Model Act for Licensure of Psychologists developed by the Association of State and Provincial Psychology Boards (ASPPB, 1992) offers the general principle that

> an applicant for licensure must demonstrate that he/she has completed two years of supervised professional experience, one year of which shall be predoctoral internship, and one year of which shall be postdoctoral. Both years of supervised experience must be acceptable to the Board and comply with the specific guidelines set out in the Board's rules and regulations. (p. 76)

The ASPPB's aim is to move toward the standardization of licensing acts across the United States and Canadian provinces.

A trainee–resident–fellow who wanted to use a feminist postdoctoral training experience for licensure would, of necessity, be subject to the requirements developed in her or his particular state or province. It would be very important to gain a working knowledge of the specific requirements of the state or province in which the postdoctoral experience is offered and those of any state or province in which the trainee might choose to live at a later time.

A Feminist Licensure-Sensitive Model

This discussion of supervised postdoctoral experience required for licensure falls under the mainstream model. The feminist postdoctoral training program that incorporates the licensure model would understand and value the need for trainees' experience and curriculum to meet state regulatory guidelines. The program would specify clearly what offerings met state regulatory guidelines and would assure that each trainee met those requirements within the program.

Using a feminist model of collaboration, the program would help each interested trainee to find out the requirements for licensure in other relevant states. The program would ensure that supervisors were experts in feminist psychological practice so that the trainee met the licensure requirement of competency in areas of declared expertise. The licensure-sensitive program would resemble other feminist postdoctoral training programs in all other areas as delineated earlier in this chapter.

RECOMMENDATIONS FOR THE EXPANSION OF FEMINIST PSYCHOLOGICAL PRACTICE

As has been documented throughout this book, feminist practice has undergone a revolution in the past 20 years. As an outgrowth of the women's movement's critique of psychology's mistreatment of women, feminist perspectives on psychology and therapy have grown into a legitimate, complex discipline. Today, feminist psychological practice includes not only therapy with women and men but also research, consultation, supervision, assessment, education, public service, prevention, political action, and forensics.

Despite the diversity and complexity of feminist psychological practice, the participants in the 1993 National Conference on Education and Training in Feminist Practice were able to unanimously agree on many core beliefs and principles that characterize feminist practice. (See Appendix A: "Final Plenary Session Common Themes," p. 249.) These resolutions form a common foundation on which postdoctoral training in feminist psychological practice can be built.

Furthermore, as has been documented throughout the chapters in this book, feminist researchers have generated important and relevant data that have enhanced our understanding of women's issues and our treatment of women who are coping with these issues. We believe this knowledge and the common feminist psychological practice beliefs endorsed by the participants of this conference create an ideal foundation for working with gender and diversity.

Despite advancements in and expansion of feminist practice in psychology, feminist psychological perspectives are not mainstream in graduate training programs. Feminist research and treatment approaches are given little or no attention in graduate and postgraduate training programs. Although training programs in feminist psychological practice do exist at the predoctoral and doctoral levels at several universities, it is clear that these programs alone cannot successfully meet the challenge of training sufficient numbers of practitioners. Additionally, the current trend within psychology is for specialty training to occur at the postdoctoral level. Thus, the development of postdoctoral training programs in feminist practice is a logical and important progression.

Our initial charge was to consider the development of formal postdoctoral training programs in psychological feminist practice; however, an additional outcome of our discussions was an awareness of the need to articulate models and guidelines for doctoral and predoctoral training in feminist psychological practice as well. We believe the five training guidelines developed by our committee as well as the core beliefs and principles agreed on by all the conference participants apply to all psychologists and their treatment of women.

We believe it is important to develop postdoctoral specialties in feminist psychological practice, but feminist practice should not be relegated only to the postdoctoral level. All psychology training programs must integrate the knowledge generated by feminist practitioners into existing curricula to ensure that their students are competent to work with women clients.

SUMMARY

When we ended our deliberations, we were all aware that our task was not finished. As this book goes to press, Norine Johnson, past president of Division 35 (Postdoctoral Training Task Force), continues the work begun here. Our intention is to generate a feminist model for postdoctoral training in women's mental health issues for use by institutions wishing to offer such a formal postdoctoral program. Furthermore, our model could serve as a standard for training feminist practitioners in general.

We remain committed to generating and refining alternative models for both postdoctoral training and continuing education in feminist psychological practice. We anticipate that having the models for postdoctoral training in feminist practice will stimulate Division 35 to define basic requirements for predoctoral training for working with female clients. The time has come to establish minimum competency standards required for all psychological practitioners who want to do therapy with women. The establishment of postdoctoral standards is an important first step.

We envision a future where a student interested in receiving feminist psychological training can ask during the initial interview with the predoctoral training educator or with the internship director or with the postdoctoral training director, "Does your program espouse the model of training put forward at the National Conference on Education and Training in Feminist Practice?"

REFERENCES

Association of State and Provincial Psychology Boards. (1992). *The Model Act for Licensure of Psychologists*. Washington, DC: American Psychological Association.

Butler, J. E., & Walter, J. C. (1991). Praxis and the prospect of curriculum transformation. In J. E. Butler & J. C. Walter (Eds.), *Transforming the curriculum: Ethnic studies and women's studies* (pp. 325–330). Albany: State University of New York Press.

Commission on Ethnic Minority Recruitment, Retention and Training in Psychology. (1996). *Visions and transformations . . . The final report*. Washington, DC: American Psychological Association.

Committee on Accreditation. (1996). *Guidelines and principles for accreditation of programs in professional psychology*. Washington, DC: American Psychological Association.

Fitzgerald, L. F., & Nutt, R. (1986). The Division 17 principles concerning the counseling/psychotherapy of women: Rationale and implementation. *Counseling Psychologist, 14*, 180–216.

Harway, M. (1979). Training counselors. *Counseling Psychologist, 8*, 8–10.

Joint Interim Committee on Identification and Recognition of Specialties and Proficiencies. (1994). *Report*. Washington, DC: American Psychological Association.

Kohout, J. (1991). *1991 doctorate employment survey: Office of demographic, employment, and educational research*. Washington, DC: American Psychological Association.

McHugh, M. C., Koeske, R. D., & Frieze, I. H. (1986). Issues to consider in conducting nonsexist psychological research. *American Psychologist, 41*, 879–890.

Stigall, T. T., Bourg, E. G., Bricklin, P. M., Kovacs, A. G., Karsen, K. G., Lorion, R. P., Nelson, P. D., Nurse, A. R., Pugh, R. W., & Wiens, A. N. (1990). *Report of the Joint Council on Professional Education in Psychology*. Baton Rouge, LA: Joint Council on Professional Education in Psychology.

Texas State Board of Examiners of Psychologists. (1992). Agenda book. Annual meeting of delegates, Memphis, TN. Unpublished manuscript.

Wiens, A., & Baum, C. (1995). Characteristics of current postdoctoral programs.

In Education Directorate (Ed.), *Education and training beyond the doctoral degree: Proceedings of the American Psychological Association national conference on postdoctoral education and training in psychology* (pp. 27–49). Washington, DC: American Psychological Association.

Williams, J. E. (1990). Synthesis. In L. Bickman & H. Ellis (Eds.), *Preparing psychologists for the 21st century: Proceedings of the national conference on graduate education in psychology*. Hillsdale, NJ: Erlbaum.

Worell, J. (1980). New directions in counseling women. *The Personnel and Guidance Journal, 58,* 477–484.

Worell, J., & Remer, P. (1992). *Feminist perspectives in counseling women: An empowerment model for women.* Chichester, England: Wiley.

11

FEMINIST STUDENT VOICES

BAKER'S DOZEN

This conference provided us with a unique and invaluable opportunity to reflect on the ways in which student experience can improve the application of feminist principles to training in psychology. As feminist students, we felt our point of view to be a crucial component, so we were inspired as a group to let our voices be heard by making a proposal to the conference planning committee. We proposed that a chapter written by student participants be included to enable us to comment on the content and process of the conference by examining the interplay between the construction of a theory of feminist training and its application to students. Collectively, we wrote this chapter through experimentation with the feminist process. Along with a discussion of the experience of the feminist student and our personal experiences of attempting to work within a feminist framework, our purpose is to reflect on the potential of the feminist student–psychologist interaction in the training of feminist principles in a way that truly reflects those same principles.

Members of the Baker's Dozen, in alphabetical order, are Peggy Bell, Susan R. Chamberlin, Theresa Ferns, Colleen J. Gregory, Joann Griffith, Holly Heard Hinderlie, Laura Johnsen, Anna Maria Laurenti, Lisa Rocchio, Rebecca M. Roy, Nicole Simi, Beth Simpson, and E. Alice Van Ormer. We chose to use this collective name to reflect the collaboration of our 13 members and to avoid the hierarchy of traditional authorship.

Our group of 13 women was composed of 4 master's and 9 doctoral students of varying ages, ethnicities, and sexual orientations from Boston College and the Universities of Rhode Island and Kentucky. Two of us were international students, from Belize and Malta; the remaining students represented the New England, Midwest, and West Coast regions of the United States. Many of us met for the first time at the conference, and seven students from out of town stayed together in college housing.

WOMEN'S EXPERIENCES OF TRADITIONAL EDUCATION

The purpose of this chapter is to discuss our experiences as graduate students in training for feminist practice. It is important, however, to place our experiences within the context of the United States's educational system and the way in which it treats girls and women. In its extensive review of 35 education reform documents, the American Association of University Women (AAUW; 1992) delineated the educational biases and barriers that shortchange girls from preschool through high school. Worell and Remer (1992) concluded that "through the sex-biased attitudes and behaviors of school personnel, lack of non-traditional role models, sex bias in educational materials, sexism in the administrative hierarchy, and differential patterns of encouragement for achievement, our educational systems are a major source of sex-role stereotyping and institutionalized sexism" (p. 261). The Project on the Status and Education of Women (Hall & Sandler, 1982, 1983, 1984) corroborated that such biases and barriers continue at the college level. It identified the "chilly climate" that exists for most undergraduate women and described both the subtle and the flagrant ways in which female students are devalued, discouraged, and barred from academic success.

Female graduate students face similar problems (Sandler & Hall, 1986), one of which is the difficulty of obtaining mentors (Gilbert & Rossman, 1992; Women Students' Coalition of Harvard University, 1980). Among the reasons cited are the lack of female faculty (Hall & Sandler, 1983; Sandler & Hall, 1986; Women Students' Coalition of Harvard University, 1980) and the less formal contact that male faculty have with female students than they do with male students (Sandler & Hall, 1986). Finding a mentor is especially problematic for African American women (Moses, 1989) and other women of color who have even less access to informal contact with advisors. Many potential mentors are unfamiliar with ethnic as well as gender issues and are therefore unable to relate to the particular needs of minority women students.

Other difficulties faced by female graduate students include having research interests related to women discouraged and devalued (Six Spoke Collective, 1991) and being viewed as "outsiders" or as less committed, promising, or capable than male graduate students (Sandler & Hall, 1986). For women of color, certain biases (such as being viewed as outsiders and having research interests related to minority women's issues disregarded) are exacerbated (Moses, 1989). Women college students are also dependent on male faculty for admissions, grades, recommendations, committee memberships, and financial and research opportunities (Schneider, 1987) and face both subtle discrimination (Sandler & Hall, 1986) and sexual harassment (Rubin & Borgers, 1990; Schneider, 1987). This lack of a supportive college culture results in isolation (Mallinckrodt & Leong, 1992; Sandler & Hall, 1986).

Women interested in feminist psychology encounter additional barriers that serve to block their professional development. These barriers exist for two main reasons. First, as Faludi (1991) meticulously documented, a feminist backlash is underway. MacKinnon (1991) illuminated the reality of how socially and legally institutionalized patriarchy suppresses and punishes those who dare to name women's subordination. Tavris (1992) recounted psychology's bias against women; Faludi (1991) exposed the media's biased attention to and interpretation of research. Tavris (1992) concurred that "the far better evidence that fails to conform to the dominant beliefs about gender is overlooked, disparaged, or ... remains unpublished" (p. 53).

Second, one of the traditional purposes of education has been the social reproduction of privilege, the reproduction of the culture's gender, race, and class hierarchies in the next generation (Holland & Eisenhart, 1990). The United States's educational system is based on the history of the dominant group, which is White, middle class, heterosexual, and male. Through this system, we internalize the values of the culture and thereby perpetuate the continued oppression of other cultures and nondominant groups (Brown, 1993). Any movement, such as feminism, which runs counter to the dominant group's norms will be resisted in an effort to silence it as well as to dismantle its legitimacy. In part because of these forces, no comprehensive training exists for feminist practice, leaving feminist students to be trained in an unsupportive environment. As Brown (1992) observed, "Training to be a therapist is a seduction into the ways of patriarchy; we are 'professionally socialized' in the words of the criteria by which the American Psychological Association accredits doctoral programs, into a world view which is essentially sexist, racist, heterosexist and otherwise oppressive" (p. 249).

OUR EXPERIENCES OF FEMINISM

As may have been expected, many of the 13 graduate students who participated in the conference were already self-identified feminists and looked forward to the chance to immerse themselves in an atmosphere with a shared feminist identity and worldview. Several of the students described a long-standing commitment to feminist ideals and principles. For one student, feminist ideals and principles were so intrinsically expressed in her educational community that only recently did she discover that feminism was something that could not be assumed. Another student described her experience in her masters program as providing validation for the "closet feminist" in her.

Although all of us maintained that our values were consistent with feminist principles, some hesitated to label themselves *feminist*. Some described their initial exposure to feminism as antithetical to their indoctrinated worldviews, "rocking [their] beliefs and convictions to the very root." Given the scarcity of feminist role models and mentors, it is not surprising that some of the students in our group identified themselves as feminists only a few months prior to the conference. Two hypotheses may be advanced to explain why some of the students struggled to identify themselves as feminists: (a) Because of the frequent misinterpretation of the feminist label, public identification as a feminist involves the risk of professional and social alienation; and (b) the educational system is designed to maintain the status quo, and therefore the absence of feminist ideas and scholarship in education logically follows.

When the development of a feminist identity itself is fraught with various societal obstacles, any attempt by the feminist graduate student to integrate a feminist identity with her professional development may be risky. We were perhaps different from other graduate students in that we were exposed to feminist scholars in our programs. Those of us who had nurtured our feminist identities described a strong sense of passion, excitement, and commitment for the feminist worldview and identified it as a connecting link among the many parts of our lives. Yet, educational and clinical institutions have frequently done little more than acknowledge the relevance of feminism to the field of psychology. Consequently, exposure to feminist scholarship has been almost nonexistent, and training for feminist practice at the graduate level remains rare.

This neglectful atmosphere has implications for all graduate students, and especially those with feminist identities. Specifically, opportunities to explore the feminist dimension of formal education and professional practice have not been encouraged. Students may have had an occasional opportunity to convene with feminist psychologists at symposiums and conferences, such as the American Psychological Association's (APA) Division 35 (Psychology of Women) or the Association of Women in Psychology (AWP), as a way to receive feminist training. More frequently, however, feminist graduate students have had to rely on their own initiation and motivation (e.g., reading journals on the psychology of women and feminist practice in addition to their regular course load; writing papers in "mainstream" courses from feminist perspectives; doing "independent" feminist studies outside of class).

Students are also greatly affected by the institutionalized patriarchy in higher education, which may have even more impact than the lack of feminist faculty. Feminist training in academic institutions has usually been found where one or two feminist professors are on the faculty. That the normative criteria used to qualify a department as feminist has been the presence of only one or two feminist faculty members is a commentary on the sad state of the integration of feminist scholarship into training.

In addition, feminist students have also been confronted with the risk of limiting their potential range of practical, research, and other professional opportunities if they choose to disclose their feminist identities or interests. The absence of feminist mentors for students may have contributed to the difficulty in making these types of important decisions. Psychologists-in-training may have felt compelled to resolve this dilemma by choosing between a feminist agenda and social acceptance from the larger academic community. When these two professional issues are in conflict, the frequent result is that one is unequivocally compromised when the other is chosen.

Consequently, most feminist students have learned to gauge the safety level of a particular situation and have had enough sense of self-preservation not to jeopardize their positions unnecessarily. In a poignant article by the Six Spoke Collective (1991), the group of feminist graduate students noted that "to succeed in our graduate program, our feminist convictions frequently must be denied" (p. 103). This lack of institutional support has often led to feelings of isolation. Perhaps this is why feminist graduate students have often found themselves seeking a community of peers and forming collaborative networks.

The important question gets asked again and again: To what extent are feminist graduate students willing to compromise their feminist values to obtain opportunities for optimal professional development? We compromised to various degrees in our educational and professional lives; some of us silenced ourselves to avoid censure, whereas others have not compromised on principles but struggled with the positive and negative repercussions of that decision.

OUR EXPERIENCE OF THE CONFERENCE

Not surprisingly, much of what brought us to the conference reflected the neglectful atmosphere noted in our programs of study. Most of us came to the conference hoping to gain a sense of community, to learn about feminism and its practice, and to enhance our professional development. Evident in our reflections and experiences was the intense desire to overcome isolation by making connections with others who shared a feminist worldview. This community of "kindred souls" provided the safety to explore and embrace personal feminist identities among many of the very feminists whose work had been inspirational.

Our Role

The conference coordinators presented us with the opportunity to participate in the conference by fulfilling the role of observer–note taker, and one of us assumed the role of event coordinator. Although we were not invited to participate verbally, the conference planners hoped we would benefit from having the opportunity to meet and witness the discussions among some of the foremost women in feminist psychology in the United States. This conference was to be a "working conference" where the participants came together to define and delineate feminist practice in psychology. Note taking was seen as an important aspect; the daily recording of proceedings provided the documents from which participants worked. In this way ideas could be built on or reviewed and revised as the conference progressed. We chose groups according to our interests, and each working group had one or two note takers. The definition of the student role had been accepted prior to the conference but presented a problem in the context of the conference and feminist principles.

Experiences of Inclusion and Exclusion

Practical and theoretical concerns were raised by the student role from the very beginning. As indicated in previous chapters, theories of feminism emphasize the importance of acknowledging power differentials in professional relationships (e.g., teacher–student, therapist–client) as a step toward the prevention of the exploitation of power. However, some viewed the role of silent note taker as an exploitation of the power differential between the conference participants and the students. One participant acknowledged to a student, "the students have the most difficult job because the gag rule has been imposed upon you. It will be exceedingly difficult to record what is being said and not be allowed to participate." Some of us were even encouraged by our own feminist peers not to attend because the conference structure would involve a patriarchal use of silence, where those in power instructed those without power not to speak. We were aware of these issues and curious about just how feminist principles would be applied within the conference itself.

The various ways in which the student's role was dealt with in each of the nine groups produced a heterogeneity of experiences among us, which seemed to fall on a continuum between being included in group discussion on one pole and being silenced and excluded on the other. A few of the groups directly invited students' contributions, whereas those of us in other groups remained primarily observers. Most of us had experiences that fell between these two extremes.

One student who was actively encouraged to participate wrote of her group, "Their feminist process was so open and inclusive, within the first day they welcomed critical feedback from the students and encouraged us to actively help them frame, conceptualize and organize a draft report. . . ." Another student wrote, "the women in my group picked up on my non-verbal messages, and before the second session began they invited me to participate. This I did when I was not too busy taking notes, and my opinions were welcomed and respected. I felt accepted as one of the group."

Although many of us did not enjoy such active participation, several of us wrote about the ways in which we were invited into the group or active in the group process. One student was active by pacing the discussion and working with the participants to clarify, synthesize, and refine their ideas so that she could document them accurately. Although she did not offer much opinion, she felt like a very important and acknowledged group member. Another was included when her working group broke up into dyads or triads. Two other students enjoyed personal interactions with two of the participants during which the participants shared "their own histories [and] how they became involved in the psychology of women. The stories were a way of understanding the history of feminist psychology and a way of mentoring."

Many felt acknowledged and appreciated but not included in the group discussion. "I felt attended to in my group [but] I even found it difficult to speak with these women outside of the meeting room because of the role I had assumed of silent recorder," one student admitted. Another reflected that "there were times when opinions expressed did not appear completely representative, lacking the student viewpoint."

A number of us were not included around the discussion table but sat separately from the group. These experiences represented the excluded end of the continuum. Observing stimulating discussion all day but not being explicitly afforded the freedom to participate made some of us feel silenced and ignored. It seemed appropriate to most of us that the active participants were to be doctoral-level psychologists with years of experience and that we would have a lesser role. However, a sense of contradiction arose during the deliberations because of our limited role. One student described this experience in these words: "They were very concerned with ensuring that every group member's voice was heard during this processing, but it [didn't seem] to occur to them that we had voices! The resulting invisibility was extremely uncomfortable." All agreed that being silenced was a peculiar experience in an atmosphere that strives to hear all voices.

In addition to the structural power inequities, some of us silenced ourselves at times for reasons relating to both individual and group dynamics. Some of us were confident enough to be assertive in our groups, and some participants were more persuasive than others in their invitations to the students to speak. Some students knew at least one participant in their group, or had close ties to other conference participants or organizers, and therefore may have felt more comfortable speaking out or asking questions than students who knew no one in their working group. Students who agreed with what was being said or who had more exposure to feminism may have felt freer to speak when invited. In acknowledging the potential role of self-silencing on the part of the students, however, it is important to keep in mind that there were significant power differentials between students and participants, and those power inequities were institutionalized in the very construction of the conference.

Note Taking

The responsibility of taking notes in the group discussions and later editing the notes to provide a comprehensive document of the day's proceedings quickly became overwhelming for many of us. Much more work was involved than had been expected. The importance of the work coupled with our undefined status created further conflicts. As one student explained, "I felt overwhelmed by the responsibility of my job. Renowned women were speaking and it was up to me to record it so that the rest of the feminist and psychological community could share it for years to come . . . such a lot of responsibility with such a lack of power." Although many may not have realized it at the time, the students actually had a great deal of power—the "power of the pen," as labeled by one conference coordinator. One student acknowledged the need to monitor judiciously this power: "As student recorder, I was aware of my own biases. Certain group members I found more interesting than others, and some opinions made more sense to me than others. Perhaps the most difficult part of my job was trying to be objective in my note-taking and summarizing, giving everyone's ideas the same importance."

The enormous task of documenting lively group discussion was alleviated for one student when a participant brought in her laptop computer for note taking. Such gestures of acknowledgment and recognition from the participants for the arduous workload were greatly appreciated. One participant asked if we were getting paid for our work. After learning that our accommodations were free and included the Thursday night dinner, she conceded that room and board were valid forms of pay but thought it important for planners of future conferences to budget in salaries for student workers. She put it in these words: "There is something significant about women being paid for their work."

Reflections

The general consensus of the student group was that it was exciting to be at such a conference. However, as another student wrote, it was painful to observe that "even at such a conference, it requires diligent self-awareness to transcend the hierarchies that women find themselves shelved upon by society at large." The need for active resistance of such hierarchies is eloquently highlighted in Brown's (1993) discussion on racism, in which she asserted that one can be racist or anti-racist, but "there is no such category as non-racist; one cannot be neutral or value-free, but rather is a participant in the problem or is engaged in some manner in resisting" (p. 84). The difficulty arises in the impossibility of perpetually maintaining the energy required for diligent self-awareness and active resistance. When the energy for this lapses, individuals and groups inadvertently fall back into previously learned ways of being. We students at the conference witnessed this almost cyclic process of surging ahead (implementing feminist principles) and falling back (reverting to hierarchy, ignoring power differentials).

Identification With the Student Group

At the APA-sponsored banquet dinner held on the first night, most of the students arrived late, having been immersed in the compilation of notes after the day's work. One student reported, "My feelings regarding sitting around the table among the other students was that I was sitting there because we had all worked late and had missed the opportunity to mingle with the participants during the reception. It was at *their* tables that I really wanted to be [identification with the dominant group]. I had not yet identified with the students or recognized the benefits of identifying with them." That evening, as the students began to share their individual experiences in fulfilling the note taker role at the conference, a common experience emerged. Up until this time, each student was unaware that many of the others felt as isolated and unheard as she did.

For most of the group, it was perhaps the huge task of accurately compiling the day's notes that was initially unifying. As we began to recognize the power differential that was at work at the conference and how it affected our feelings about our note taker role, a new group identity was forged. The support network that developed helped us to cope with the discomforts cited. Out of this support and group identity came strength. For some, it was the strength to speak up in the working groups. For others, there was empowerment in simply knowing that they were not alone.

Not all of us identified with the student group, however. Some identified more with their working group because their experiences of inclusion in those groups were extremely positive. One student with strong feminist convictions freely engaged in the discussions and felt exhilarated by the exposure to the range of diversity within feminism. Another student agreed, stating, "For the first time I was able to learn and expand my feminist thought by witnessing and experiencing rather than educating others or defending myself." At times, these students felt isolated from the student group because their experiences were so dissimilar to those being expressed.

The degree to which we felt included or excluded seemed to correlate directly with the degree to which we identified with either the working group or the student group. However, neither extreme of inclusion or exclusion represented the majority of the group. Regardless of group identification, all of us agreed that there was a contradiction between the feminist principles, as defined and promoted at the conference, and the experiences of isolation, voicelessness, and lack of agency. This contradiction brought the hierarchical structure into focus. Rather than being defeating, we felt empowered because we were then able to consider ways in which we could respond to this awareness and take action.

OUR OBSERVATIONS ON THE CONFERENCE PROCESS

Language

This conference represented an unorthodox approach to thinking about psychology. Participants struggled with the interpretation of words and acknowledged the limitations of the English language in expressing concepts from a female-oriented perspective. In one group, the student noted that, "on the whole, consensus was reached on major issues, but where it wasn't, it was hung up on points of semantics."

Conflict and Consensus

In the working groups, processing seemed to be a metaphor for the struggle to incorporate feminist principles into practice. This struggle took place not only within the dynamics of the group but probably also within each participant herself. As one student observed, "Each strong-minded, well-informed woman struggled to remain true to her own thoughts, feelings, and beliefs, while in the feminist spirit she also tried to give equal value and consideration to the ideas of others." This student was not prepared for the amount of disagreement and, at times, inflexibility that she witnessed. Another student appreciated the positive aspects of such debate by commenting, "it was so great to see participants working to hear others dialogue from a variety of feminist perspectives. Witnessing the critical thinking among feminists was so powerful and transformative in and of itself."

Yet, at times, the feminist collaborative process was experienced as cumbersome and as hindering progress. Hearing all voices occasionally resulted in tangential and lengthy discussions. Conflict was sometimes avoided and consensus sought even in the face of passionate disagreements. One student queried, "In the effort to insure that all voices were heard and all points of view validated, were legitimate disagreements and conflicts smoothed over?" She was inclined to think so and felt that, although it is necessary for us, as feminists, to cooperate, "something important is lost when conflict is stifled." The difficulty in finding a balance between conflict and consensus exemplified the struggle between the theoretical and applied forms of the feminist process.

Power and Voice

Several students noted power differentials among the participants. At times the reputations of the participants preceded them; those women more published or better known or whose age or years of feminist involvement gave them status were more frequently invited to speak, more likely to speak, and more attended to when they spoke. Participants who were more assertive, more vocal, or simply spoke louder often enjoyed more power and influence than those who spoke more quietly or who were less likely to demand attention. Groups varied in their composition, and a couple of students observed that the voices of the lesbians or participants of color were sometimes less attended to than others. The student note takers were also susceptible to such influences and described needing to be aware of the potential for selective recording.

Diversity

Some of the groups brought up several issues related to diversity. One student from the diversity working group wrote, "The issue of using and defining the term *diversity* appeared to be of paramount importance because it signified a shift in focus in defining the parameters of race, culture, class, sexuality, and other aspects of the human condition. Putting gender first may be masking the importance of these other facets of selfhood for a person. Therefore, is gender the most salient feature for a feminist perspective, and if so, is the feminist process lost if boys–men are included?" In the opinion of another student, "The real issue is not gender per se but gender as one of the categories along which power is distributed. Does focusing on gender contribute to our ignoring other power inequities such as race?"

The other significant observation concerning diversity was in regards to its place at the conference. One student expressed it as follows: "the issue [of diversity] seemed to be [segregated]. Minority members [isolated themselves through self-selection to] one group, which diluted the minority voice in other groups and maintained its separateness within the conference. Although all nine groups were commissioned to consider issues of diversity, the minority perspective was still less salient in those groups without participants of color."

The dilemma here illustrates a parallel process with the segregation or integration of feminism into mainstream education. Ideally, the history, achievements, developmental theories, and perspectives of women and minorities would be integrated into mainstream curriculum, not just in a course on women or minorities. How will this happen when diversity issues are the responsibility of one group (or class) and not the responsibility of all? Similarly, when postdoctoral training programs are established, will they attract and isolate feminist voices instead of spreading them around to affect more departments?

Parallel Process and Transformation

In the struggle to apply the feminist process, the participants attempted to use experience to inform theory. "I have never been to a conference in which personal experience was processed in the way it was in this one," one student stated. These linkages between personal experience and theory are integral to feminist practice and exemplify the concept of "parallel process," which was ubiquitous at the conference. There was a parallel process between the *content* of the nine working groups and the *process* that the participants and students engaged in and experienced. For example, one group proposed that some of the essential components of postdoctoral training in feminist practice would be small-group interaction, collaboration, peer support to minimize isolation, networking, feminist role models, and mentors. Every one of these components was present at the conference and experienced by participants and students alike. Furthermore, a parallel experience of transformation occurred in both the working groups and the student group. This transformation seemed to result from *experiencing* the feminist process.

One student described this transformation as resulting from the process of arriving at the conference as isolated individuals and, over the course of 3 days, becoming a part of a cohesive and powerful group. For the working groups, this process was fueled by long hours of arduous discussion, debate, and negotiation to produce a document that would become part of the foundation for feminist practice in psychology. As one group's document began to solidify, and as the groups gathered in triads to share their works-in-progress, the student note taker sensed a group identity being forged.

> In the members of my group, I witnessed a sense of pride in what we had accomplished, an identification with the other members of our group, and a sense of responsibility in representing the group. Back in our home groups everyone seemed vibrant and alive, as if they felt excited by the triad process but even more excited to come *home* and share it with each other. What I was witnessing was the power of *feeling* a part of a group.

The members of the student group experienced a parallel process, either within their working groups or within the student group (or both). The feminist process was so transforming and empowering for the students that they were able to recognize the contradiction of their voicelessness and to seek to make their voices heard.

OUR GROUP AS AUTHOR

From Joke to Proposal

As the conference progressed, we began to gather to joke, support one another, and explore our own "groupness." When we learned that the conference would be producing a book and using our notes for the framework, we began to joke about writing the last chapter. We joked that our chapter could be titled *Labor* because "what comes after nine months of pregnancy (or the nine working groups) but before the baby (the product of those groups, the book)? The labor, that's us!" Humor was important; it allowed us the chance to relax and create productive ways to decrease our defensiveness and act more as agents in our own growth and development. We used our group as a place to reaffirm our self-worth and remind ourselves that we have important ideas and valuable insights. In the safety of the student group, we could move beyond "just getting through" the conference to empowering ourselves to contribute something valuable. Our confidence increased, and we challenged one another to take greater risks; we did not have to hide in silence. The fact that half of us were rooming together for the conference helped us tremendously in this 3-day transformation from individuals to a group.

One of the conference coordinators was very supportive of the work that we were doing and saw the truth in our joke about writing a chapter about our experiences. She encouraged us to make a proposal to the planning committee. We began tentatively asking one another, "Are we really serious? Would we really like to write the 11th chapter of this book?" We were aware that if we were truly to address the implementation of the feminist process, we would have to illuminate both the convergence and the contradictions to what we saw as optimal and to attempt to implement the process ourselves.

We gathered together to assess our commitment to writing such a chapter and brainstormed a proposal to present to the conference planning committee. We designated three speakers to present our proposal and encouraged the rest to chime in if they had something to add. Our proposal went approximately as follows:

> Given that the goal of the conference was to frame and define feminist thinking across a diverse group of areas, with attention to implementation, we believe it will be valuable to incorporate our unique perspectives as feminist students, into a process which would enable all our voices to be heard. The feminist principles that are being defined and integrated have played themselves out in our group process and have furthered the development of our collective identity as feminist students. For example, principles such as networking, mentoring, modeling, collaboration, and egalitarian relationships have become clearer through this experientially based learning opportunity. The inclusion of a student written chapter will enable us to comment on the content and process of this conference by examining the interplay between the construction of a theory of feminist training and its application to students.

Our approach to the conference leadership was one of respect; our intentions were to practice the principles of feminism; and our hope was that if nowhere else, here, within the community of feminist psychologists, we would be heard. On the third day of the conference, the planning committee heard and enthusiastically supported our proposal, and we began our life as a task-oriented group. This chapter is our voice, a voice from within a community that values attending to all voices.

Process of Writing the Chapter

Our first hurdle was deciding on authorship: Who would do the primary work of writing and earn the rewards that come with authorship? After discovering that each of us wanted this primary role, the question immediately became "can a chapter be written by 13 people?" and then "how can we do it?" Our decision to use a collective name for authorship arose out of our commitment to the collaborative spirit of the work; we thank Six Spoke Collective (1991) for their example. This decision, however, came with a price: Without a hierarchical form of authorship, our work is currently inaccessible through electronic databases. Our second hurdle was deciding what we had to say. We brainstormed six questions to which we each responded in writing, articulating our experiences both as feminist students and at the conference. Quotes from this body of writing enabled us to interweave our voices throughout the chapter.

We delineated and volunteered for the tasks, roles, and committees necessary to write the chapter and plotted a time line for the year that was allocated from conference to publication. We were a group of busy graduate students who had come together amidst the pressures of "too many tasks," yet days later we were happily volunteering for tasks galore over the course of a year. This apparent contradiction is important and can be resolved if one sees us as transformed. Initially, our work was dictated by the external structure of the conference. The decision to contribute a chapter fostered intrinsic motivation for our efforts. In addition, the exposure to feminist principles, awareness of power and voice issues, and support from our collective group was empowering and transforming.

Like the conference participants, we had to be diligent in our attention to the equalization of power between us. Like them, we experienced lapses in this awareness, which led to power shifts and imbalances. While writing or reviewing parts of the chapter, some students felt as though they had less voice because of their physical distance from the others. For example, a majority of us lived near Boston and therefore may have found it easier to communicate with one another rather than those living far away. This resulted in the experiences and ideas of the majority enjoying more exposure and documentation compared with those living at a distance or whose experiences differed from what became the "norm."

Self-silencing clearly had a role in the distribution of power among us. We differed in the amount of time we were willing or able to commit to the chapter writing. Those of us who were willing to devote more time were able to exert more influence than those who did not attend all of the student meetings. Moreover, those of us who felt that our experiences differed significantly from what was being written at times hesitated to voice a different viewpoint.

Throughout the process, various students became aware of the ways in which we had fallen back and (within the feminist spirit of our work) sought to point this out and ensure that all experiences and perspectives were represented. This is another example of the parallel processes of both the student experience and the conference experience. Although power differentials can be minimized and attended to, lapses in their equalization may be inevitable when dealing with multiple persons with various experiences, strengths, and struggles. Acknowledging the lapses without defensiveness seems to be the first step toward working through the barriers to collaboration.

We do not present our solutions as the only right way to develop a collaborative project; rather, we hope that by sharing how we struggled, we can help to lessen the isolation of others grappling with similar issues. The more we talk, the less isolated we are, and ultimately the more power and options we discover we have. We hope that readers are able to see how we have fallen back and to move forward by learning from our experience.

REFLECTIONS AND RECOMMENDATIONS

As illustrated in this chapter, feminist psychology is unique in its concentrated attention to themes of power. In particular, feminist psychologists are in tune with power inequity and the potential for the exploitation of power. The conference participants and the students grappled with ways to transcend the power differentials in their professional lives and specifically in the material discussed and explored at the conference. Considerable attention was devoted to the power imbalance between dominant group members and groups who lack social and political power because of their gender, ethnicity, social class, age, sexual orientation, or religion; however, participants and students struggled with power issues themselves. Issues of power were noted in three main areas: (a) between the conference participants and the students, (b) among the conference participants themselves, and (c) among the students themselves.

Like other fields or businesses, psychology has its virtues and vices. Nothing is sacrosanct or inherently enlightened about the personalities, motivations, or behaviors of psychologists, including feminist psychologists. As the student who served as the event coordinator noted, "this conference was no easier or more difficult to organize than any other." That perspective makes one pause to think about human nature, specifically the nature of power and control. It may not be unrealistic to champion the general concept of equality, but is it asking too much of human nature and of psychology to seek to neutralize power differentials and foster collaboration? In the course of writing this chapter, we, too, had difficulty maintaining diligent awareness of the differentials in voice and power that emerged over the course of a year.

Recommendations for the Second Conference

The role of student note taker should be reconsidered. The idea to include note takers in the conference came directly from an earlier conference on postdoctoral training, attended by one of the coordinators; it is fairly safe to assume that feminist principles were not considered when it was organized. The re-definition of note taker could result from examining the role in light of the principles of collaboration and participation. As student note takers, we recommend that the following steps be taken in future feminist conferences to incorporate the unique perspective of feminist students into a process that would enable all voices to be heard: (a) explicitly invite student participation from the beginning; (b) increase the number of student note takers, at least two per group, to improve the distribution of work and allow for more student participation; (c) provide laptop computers to each student dyad; (d) include students in scheduled social events, allowing them the opportunity to network with potential mentors; and finally (e) give monetary compensation to the students.

Feminist Restructuring of Academia

Numerous proposals have been made regarding a feminist restructuring of academia, and some have already been implemented (Paludi & Steuernagel, 1990; Worell & Remer, 1992). From our collective experience at the conference and as feminist students, we propose that graduate programs consider incorporating the feminist ideal of the collaborative process by encouraging faculty to formulate at least some course work according to the particular interests and needs of students. This type of collaboration between students and teachers may be one of the most realistic applications of this feminist principle. As our work on this chapter demonstrates, the work, the meaning of the work, and its rewards become enriched when it is borne out of one's own needs, design, and passion. In this way, students are encouraged to pursue the meaning and development of their unique voices and to share those voices with others.

Collaborating with students to design course work would credit students with the knowledge and capabilities with which to do so, reduce the power differential between faculty and students, and provide the context for a mentor relationship. Isolation would also be reduced for both student and faculty member. Most important, a tradition of open communication of ideas, both confirming and challenging, would reinforce the examination of the current hierarchical system as well as prevent feminists from replacing the old hierarchy with one of their own.

REFERENCES

American Association of University Women. (1992). *How schools shortchange girls: The AAUW report: A study of major findings on girls and education.* Washington, DC: Wellesley College Center for Research on Women.

Brown, L. S. (1992). While waiting for the revolution: The case for a lesbian feminist psychotherapy. *Feminism & Psychology, 2,* 239–253.

Brown, L. S. (1993). Antidomination training as a central component of diversity in clinical psychology education. *The Clinical Psychologist, 46,* 83–87.

Faludi, S. (1991). *Backlash: The undeclared war against American women.* New York: Doubleday.

Gilbert, L. A., & Rossman, K. M. (1992). Gender and the mentoring process for women: Implications for professional development. *Professional Psychology: Research and Practice, 23,* 233–238.

Hall, R. M., & Sandler, B. R. (1982). *The classroom climate: A chilly one for women?* Washington, DC: Project on the Status and Education of Women, Association of American Colleges.

Hall, R. M., & Sandler, B. R. (1983). *Academic mentoring for women students and faculty: A new look at an old way to get ahead.* Washington, DC: Project on the Status and Education of Women, Association of American Colleges.

Hall, R. M., & Sandler, B. R. (1984). *Out of the classroom: A chilly campus climate for women?* Washington, DC: Project on the Status and Education of Women, Association of American Colleges.

Holland, D. C., & Eisenhart, M. A. (1990). *Educated in romance: Women, achievement, and college culture.* Chicago: Chicago University Press.

MacKinnon, C. (1991). To quash a lie: A feminist legal scholar tells what it takes to resist the invisible law to keep silent. *Smith Alumnae Quarterly,* Summer, 11–14.

Mallinckrodt, B., & Leong, F. T. L. (1992). Social support in academic programs and family environments: Sex differences and role conflicts for graduate students. *Journal of Counseling Psychology, 70,* 716–723.

Moses, Y. T. (1989). *Black women in academe: Issues and strategies.* Washington, DC: Project on the Status and Education of Women, Association of American Colleges.

Paludi, M. A., & Steuernagel, G. A. (1990). *Foundations for a feminist restructuring of the academic disciplines.* Binghamton, NY: Haworth Press.

Rubin, L. J., & Borgers, S. B. (1990). Sexual harassment in universities during the 1980's. *Sex Roles, 23,* 397–411.

Sandler, B. R., & Hall, R. M. (1986). *The classroom climate revisited: Chilly for women faculty, administrators, and graduate students.* Washington, DC: Project on the Status and Education of Women, Association of American Colleges.

Schneider, B. E. (1987). Graduate women, sexual harassment, and university policy. *Journal of Higher Education, 58,* 46–65.

Six Spoke Collective. (1991). Feminism and psychology: A dangerous liaison. *Women and Therapy, 11,* 103–110.

Tavris, C. (1992). *The mismeasure of woman.* New York: Simon & Schuster.

Women Students' Coalition of Harvard University. (1980). *The quality of women's education at Harvard University. A survey of sex discrimination in the graduate and professional schools.* Cambridge, MA: Author.

Worell, J., & Remer, P. (1992). *Feminist perspectives in therapy: An empowerment model for women.* Chichester, England: Wiley.

12

AFTERWORD

NORINE G. JOHNSON AND JUDITH WORELL

AFFIRMING OUR VISIONS

The women who gathered at Boston College during July 1993 had a shared vision of transforming the discipline of psychology. To move this vision toward reality we brought together the foremothers of feminist psychology and their daughters to develop a framework for the future education and training of feminist practitioners. We collectively envisioned graduate school programs, internships, and postgraduate offerings that would embrace the tenets of feminism, allowing a new generation expanded opportunities to select psychology training programs that can be clearly identified as feminist. For many of us, the vision included focusing on women's strengths in our feminist practices and in our education and training of feminist practitioners as Worell and Remer (1992) exemplified.

What changed as a result of our coming together? What did we learn? We learned what we already knew but had never acknowledged in such a unified way. We learned that feminist psychology is a broad theoretical approach that assists in the scientific exploration of the impact of the social construction of gender on human lives.

We learned that we can investigate this impact through a myriad of feminist research approaches. We learned that the teaching, training, and

245

supervision of feminist psychological principles have their own breadth of techniques, skills, and attributes. We learned that the psychological practices of feminist therapy and assessment have a variety of techniques and tools, many of which have been empirically validated for specific populations.

We affirmed that a basic tenet of feminist psychology is the recognition and respect of diversity. Feminist psychology means exposing the aversive effects of all the "isms," promoting social transformation, recognizing that the personal is political, stressing the strengths of women, and accepting the challenge of embracing diversity. We learned the challenge of enduring the inherent tension in incorporating multiple aspects of people's experiences. Finally, we acknowledged the danger that when gender is identified as primary it minimizes other aspects of experiences and excludes authentic diversity. To achieve our goals, we learned, we must continuously engage in the feminist process of self-evaluation, monitoring our beliefs and our biases.

FEMINIST DIALOGUE

As we discovered, dialogue was critical to the success of our endeavor. Dialogue can occur on many levels—between theoretical paradigms, between therapists and researchers and academics, between foremothers and daughters of feminism, between teachers and students, within and between groups, and among groups. The most important means for feminist psychologists to advance an inclusive feminist psychology is through dialogue that respects the process delineated throughout this book and that illuminates a vision of the future.

Following 3 days of intensive dialogue within the nine working groups, the final day consisted of a plenary session in which all the groups came together. This day began with each group presenting the final set of principles and themes that were articulated for their content area during their 3 days of work together. After each group presented its thoughts, the collective group of women decided by consensus which themes were common across the nine working groups and which were unique themes to explore. The common themes agreed on by all of us are in Appendix A. The themes to explore are in Appendix B.

Dialogue presents challenges as well as strengths. In valuing the complexity of dialogue, we support the feminist tenet that all voices be heard, encouraged, and valued. However, one of the challenges of using dialogue as a method to advance the discipline is to move the dialogue to the level of action. In arriving at the decision to use consensus as a method of moving toward action, we considered three possible risks of consensus. First, it may be that consensus would be reached only on "safe issues" and that more controversial issues that might move the discipline forward would not reach consensus. A second risk with using consensus is that some may choose not to express their dissent and, therefore, that the consensus would be illusionary. A third risk is that a solitary voice might be sufficiently strong to drown out the possibility of consensus. In the end the group decided to trust the consensus process because the process throughout had been one of consensus building.

Obviously, dialogue has many forms—face-to-face discussions, large conferences, the Internet, or scholarly publications, and our combined dialogue used all these means. The face-to-face discussion was the culmination of the e-mail chats, the scholarly publications, the conventions and conferences, the newsletters, and the multiple and exhaustive ways a profession puts forth its ideas, research, knowledge, and theory. The dialogue within and among the nine working groups, however, was unique in that it followed a feminist process to move the discipline of psychology forward. This dialogue recognized all voices, valued all voices from the beginning, and responded at each group meeting to requests for change and inclusion. The process became a fluid, seamless living dialogue with a shared mission to communicate our past, present, and future.

COMMON THEMES

As we looked at our themes, the recognition and valuing of diversity emerged as a primary theme. As one group stated:

> Diversity is the inclusion of multiple perspectives. Diversity includes empowerment, openness to differences among/between people, appreciation, cultivation, nourishment of different perspectives, recognition of the value in difference, receptiveness, and respect.

The impact of power was another common theme. One group brought it together for all of us by saying that fundamental to feminist pedagogy is a consciousness of and explicit attention to differential power, privilege, and oppression that promotes an analysis of power dynamics in theory and practice. The discussions about power and oppression led naturally to an emphasis on the importance of empowerment in many of the working groups.

Of all the common themes in the groups, the most prominent was how the social construction of gender affected our lives. The view of the participants paralleled the social constructionists' assertion that gender is not a trait of individuals, but a construct that identifies particular transactions that are understood to be "appropriate" to one sex. Feminists, such as Kessler and McKenna (1978), Unger and Crawford (1992), and Hare-Mustin and Marecek (1988), argued that gender is constructed and maintained by social interactions. Our consensus affirmed that gender is not resident in the person but exists in those interactions that are socially construed as gendered. Therapy, assessment, supervision, pedagogy, and curriculum decisions follow naturally from assertions such as Stewart's (1994) that we cannot understand a woman unless we understand her underlying conception of gender and the conceptions current in the social world.

We talked about the importance of developing a social and political action for feminist psychology and enacting this agenda in education, training, research, and practice: to be proactive and visionary.

WOMEN'S STRENGTHS AS A FOCUS OF RESEARCH, TEACHING, AND PRACTICE

Johnson's (1995) focus on women's strengths rather than deficits, envisioning women's behaviors as efforts to respond adaptively, was clearly articulated across the groups. She shared a vision of feminist psychology where research explores women's strengths, where practitioners focus on the strengths that women bring to all aspects of society, and where our feminist education and training influence all psychologists.

Feminist psychology is a broad theoretical approach that assists in the scientific exploration of the impact of social construction on all human lives. It is imperative that we meet the challenge to educate and train psychologists in all aspects of feminist practice.

REFERENCES

Hare-Mustin, R.T., & Marecek, J. (1988). The meaning of difference: Gender theory, post-modernism, and psychology. *American Psychologist, 43*, 455–464.

Johnson, N.G. (1995, August). *Feminist frames of women's strengths: Vision for the future.* Presidential address for the Division of the Psychology of Women presented at the 103rd Annual Convention of the American Psychological Association, New York, NY.

Kessler, S. J., & McKenna, W. (1978). *Gender: An ethnomethodical approach.* New York: Wiley.

Stewart, A. J. (1994). Toward a feminist strategy for studying women's lives. In C. E. Franz & A. J. Stewart (Eds.), *Women creating lives: Identities, resilience, and resistance* (pp. 11–35). Boulder, CO: Westview.

Unger, R., & Crawford, M. (1992). *Women and gender: A feminist psychology.* New York: McGraw-Hill.

Worell, J., & Remer, P. (1992). *Feminist perspectives in therapy: An empowerment model for women.* Chichester, England: Wiley.

APPENDIX A
FINAL PLENARY SESSION COMMON THEMES

Feminist Practice
>   Includes therapy/intervention, teaching, political action, consultation, writing, scholarship, research, supervision, assessment and diagnosis, administration, and public service
>   Promotes transformation and social change
>   Assumes that the personal is political
>   Embraces diversity as a requirement and foundation for practice
>   Includes an analysis of power and the multiple ways in which people can be oppressed and oppressing
>   Promotes empowerment and the individual woman's voice
>   Promotes collaboration
>   Promotes the value of diverse methodologies
>   Promotes feminist consciousness
>   Promotes self-reflection on a personal, discipline, and other levels as a life-long process.
>   Promotes continued evaluation and reflection of our values, ethics, and process, which is an active and reflective feminist process.
>   Asserts that misogyny and other inequities are damaging
>   Encourages demystification of theory and practice
>   Views theory and practice as evolving and emerging

The process of feminist practice is part of the content of feminist practice.
The contextual framework that looks at the psychological and political is important.
Learning integrates thoughts, knowledge, feelings, and experience.

APPENDIX B
FINAL PLENARY SESSION THEMES TO EXPLORE

Feminist practice is unique in that it can be defined.
Feminists need to discover a common feminist language.
Feminists are concerned with the notion of subversion.
Postdoctoral standards should be considered.
Consensus can be a way of silencing.
Women are viewed as active agents.
Reality is complex, requiring inclusive and multiple models and methodologies.
The context of relationships is important.
Working through collaboration and connection is important.
Gender is a significant locus of oppression, but it is not primary for all women.
Feminist practice is strength oriented rather than deficit oriented.
Our constructions are limited by patriarchy.
We are circumscribed by scientific paradigm.

AUTHOR INDEX

Numbers in italics refer to listings in reference sections.

Rodeheaver, D., 96, *119*
Roffman, E., 7, *14*
Rogler, L. H., 43, *55*
Romney, P., 4, *14*
Rooks, L., *115*
Root, M. P. P., 17, *33*, *39*, *54*, 102, *116*
Rose, S., 131, *144–145*
Rosen, R. C., *143*
Rosenburg, J., *144*
Rosenkrantz, P., 60, *69*
Rosewater, L. B., 17, *35*, 42, 46, *55*, 58, *71*
Rosnow, R. L., *144*
Rosser, S. V., *119*
Rossman, K. M., 99, *117*, *243–244*
Rothbart, M., 46, *55*
Rothblum, E. D., 176, *200*, *202*, 207
Rowe, W., 97, *118*
Rubin, L. J., 229, *244*
Russell, K., *140*
Russell, M. G., *144*
Russo, N. F., 1, *14*, 22, *35*, 107, 111–112, *118–120*
Rutan, J. S., *170*
Ryan, M., *144*

Sackett, P. R., 46, *55*
Sadker, D., 107, *120*
Sadker, D. M., *144*
Sadker, M., 107, *120*
Sadker, M. P., *144*
Salas, E., 5, *13–14*
Sampson, E., 26, *35*
Sanchez-Hucles, J., 174, *202*
Sanchez, J., 111, *120*
Sandler, B. R., *144*, 228, *244*
Santos de Barona, M., 40, 42, 46, 53, *55–56*
Sarachild, K., *144*
Sargent, A., *144*
Sarnat, J. E., 160, *171*
Sattler, J. M., 42, *56*
Sauter, E., 58, *70*
Scanion, J., *144*
Scarborough, E., 77, *90*
Scarr, S., 176, *202*
Schlib, J., *144*
Schmitz, B., 111, *120*
Schneider, B. E., 229, *244*
Schneidewind, N., 7, *14*, 122, *145*
Schover, L. R., 155, *170–171*

Schram, P. J., 111, *116*
Schulman, B., *145*
Schuster, M., 111, *120*, *145*
Scott, P. B., 110, *118*
Sears, D. O., 4, *14*
Seltzer, R. A., *115*
Sherif, C., 77, 83, *90–91*
Shor, I., *145*
Shrewsbury, C. M., 122, 130, *145*
Sieber, J. A., 25, *35*
Silverstein, L. B., 58, *71*
Simon, H. A., 37, *54*
Simon, R. I., *142*
Six Spoke Collective, 228, 231, 240, *244*
Slavin, R. E., 135, *145*
Smith, A. J., 39, *56*
Smith, B., 110, *118*
Smith, P., 20, *34*, *145*
Smithson, I., *140*
Snoek, D., *145*
Snyder, M., 161, 169, *171*
Snyder, R., 133, *139*
Soderland, J., *202*
Solomon, S., *176–178*, *202*
Sommers, C. H., 85, *91*
Spanier, B., 111, *120*
Spelman, E., 25, *35*
Spelman, E. V., *145*
Spender, D., 111, *120*, 121, 137, *145*
Stacey, J., 80, *91*
Stake, J. E., 131, *145*
Steele, R., 82, *90*
Sterling, M. M., 160, *171*
Steuernagel, G. A., 111, *119*, *243*, *244*
Stewart, A., 73, *91*
Stewart, A. J., 248, *250*
Stigall, T. T., 208, *224*
Stiver, I. P., 18, 27, *34–35*
Stone, L., *145*
Stuernagel, G. A., 2, *14*
Sugar, J., *146*
Surrey, J., 27, *34*, 82, *89*
Sussewell, D. R., 97, *120*
Svinicki, M., *146*

Tangri, S. S., *115*
Tanner, L. B., 142, *146*
Tarule, J., *143*
Tarule, J. M., 39, *53–54*, 136, 138, *146*

SUBJECT INDEX

Diagnosis, feminist critique, 46–47
Disability, invisibility, 177–178
Diversity
    among and between women, 61
    definition, 185
    feminist pedagogy, 148–153
    postdoctoral training, 216–217
    recognition and respect, 246
    student observations, 237–238
    use of the self to shape understandings,
      182–183
    see also Feminist psychology
Diversity working group, 180–181, 237
    forging alliances, 183
    generating group's perspective, 184
    interaction with therapy working
      group, 189
    minority group members raising issues,
      192
    negative response of conference mem-
      bers to group's position, 187

Education
    institutionalized patriarchy, 231
    traditional, women's experiences, 228–
      229
Empowerment, 61, 69
    of client, 39
    curriculum development, 99–100
    as goal of feminist therapy, 60
    skills, 99–100
    students, 130–131, 148–153
    as therapy goal, 60
    training model, 206–207
    see also Feminist student voices
Enlightenment, as therapy goal, 60
Epistemology, 41
    transformations, 83
Equality, establishing in classroom, 125–
    126
Ethics
    feminist research, 79–81
    feminist supervision, 160–161
Experience, personal, linkage with theory,
    238

Faculty, postdoctoral training, 217
Feminism, diversity and, 196–197
Feminist bio–psycho–social model, 29

Feminist consciousness, 23
Feminist dialogue, 246–247
Feminist intellectual heritage, 18–19
Feminist pedagogy, 121–137, 148–153
    acknowledging our power and author-
      ity, 126–127
    departmental lives of feminist academ-
      ics in psychology, 133
    developing principles and strategies,
      127–131, 148–153
    establishing equality in classroom,
      125–126
    experience of feminist teachers, 131–
      135
    issues of power and authority, 125–127
    personal experience of being a feminist
      teacher, 128
    power and authority, 129–130, 148–
      153
    questions, 123–124
    reaching goals, 131
    recognizing power of language, 126
    rewards, 134
    risks, 132–134
    using process to
      confront diversity, 130, 148–153
      empower students, 130–131, 148–
      153
Feminist political theories, 23
Feminist practice
    consensus decision, 8
    developing an agenda for, 3
    development in grass root manner, 17
    focus on solution of practical problems,
      17–18
    future, 10–11
    honoring personal experience, 8
    lack of guiding theory, 16–19
    leadership, distribution, 7
    promoting social change, 8
    responsibility, distribution, 7–8
    skills required
      collaboration, 103
      complex models, 102–103
      empowering skills, 99–100
      integrative perspectives, 106
      multicultural competence, 97–98
      self-determination, 101
      self-reflection, 1–5
      social action, 104
      structure for diversity, 6–7
      training, 220

valuing all voices, 8
women's strengths as focus, 248
Feminist practice training, 207–208
Feminist practitioner, defining, 19
Feminist process, 233
  formulating, 3–4
  framework, 6–9
  model, 13
  supervision, 158–160
Feminist psychology
  barriers for students, 229
  context, 174–175
  current status, 1–2
  defining task, 180–181
  diversifying, 186
  diversity incorporation, 173–199
  effects of white skin privilege, 176–
    177
  feminism and, 196–197
  gender as primary locus of oppression,
    183–184
  invisibility of disability and trauma,
    177–178
  licensing, accreditation, and profes-
    sional guidelines, 195–196
  literature and research, 175–180
  locating ourselves on the spectrum of
    oppression and privilege, 197–
    198
  professional standards and research,
    193–195
  recommendations, 199
  relationship with universalism, 190
  research, 191–192
  role of guilt and shame in integrating
    diverse concerns, 190–191
  shifting focus from gender to diversity,
    186–192
  women in the psychotherapy literature,
    178–180
Feminist research, 73–89
  content, 76–78
  definition, 76–79
  diversity within, 175–180
  ethics, 79–81
  future, 87–88
  land mines and obstacles, 84–87
  methods and epistemological debates,
    78–79
  politics, 86–87
  relation to feminist therapy, 76–78
  researcher's feelings, 86

responsible methodological approaches,
    80
  transformations
    epistemologies or conceptualizations
      of knowledge, 83
    traditional psychology, 82
    women's lives, 83–84
Feminist student voices, 227–243
  conflict and consensus, 236–237
  diversity, 237–238
  experience of
    the conference, 231–236
    feminism, 229–231
    inclusion and exclusion, 232–233
  group as author, 239–242
  identification with the student group,
    235–236
  language, 236
  note taking, 234
  parallel process and transformation,
    238–239
  power and voice, 237
  recommendations for the second con-
    ference, 242–243
  reflections, 235
  role in conference, 232
Feminist supervision, 155–170
  advocacy for supervisees and clients,
    167
  collaborative relationship, 163–164
  definition, 161, 168
  developmental shifts occurring, 166–
    167
  ethical issues, 160–161
  facilitate reflexive interactions and su-
    pervisee self-examination, 164
  feminist process, 158–160
  guiding principles, 170
  literature, 158–161
  mainstreaming, 167–168
  principle of advocacy and activism,
    165–166
  principles guiding, 162–167
  proactive, 162–163
  social construction of gender and lan-
    guage, 165
  social context, 164–165
  sociocultural factors, 159
  standards, 166
  themes, 156–157
Feminist supervisors, characteristics, 161–
    162

Feminist theory
  application, 29–30
  authorizes voices of oppressed, 25–26
  develops out of experience, 24
  foundational concepts, 23–29
  leads to expanded notions of identity
      and multiple subjectivities, 26–
      27
  multicultural model, 40
  need for, 19–20
  paradoxes, 21–22
  perspective on assessment, 40
  power imbalance in gender and diver-
      sity, 24–25
  psychological practice and, 15–32
  recommendations, 30–31
  reformulated understanding of psycho-
      logical distress, 28–29
  social transformation toward develop-
      ment of feminist consciousness,
      23–24
  tenets, 32
  theory working group, 16
  transformative function, 28–29
Feminist therapist, lack of criteria, 20
Feminist therapy
  coherent system of concepts and prac-
      tices, 63–64
  core tenets, 66–69
  empowerment and enlightenment as
      goals, 60
  gender, centrality, 59–60
  group processes and themes, 61–66
  key questions
    for researchers, 65
    related to teaching, 65–66
  limitations, 62
  literature, 58–60
  relation to research, 76–78
  role of self-disclosure, 62, 64
  sociocultural and intrapsychic perspec-
      tives, 60
Fulfilling licensure requirement models,
    221–222

Gender
  centrality, 59–60
  power imbalance, 24–25
  primacy of issues, threatened by diver-
      sity issues, 189

as primary locus of oppression, 183–
    184
  shifting focus from, 186–192
Graduate level, curriculum development,
    108–109
Group process, feminist perspective, 6
Groups
  stages of development, 5–6
  small, attributes, 4–5
Guilt
  productive and nonproductive, 192
  role in integrating diverse concerns,
      190–191

Health beliefs, 44
High school, curriculum development,
    107
Historical factors, feminist supervision,
    159

Identity, expanded notions, 26–27
Informed consent, 20
Integrative perspectives, curriculum
    development, 105–106

Language
  creating new concepts and words, 83–
      84
  negative values of differences embed-
      ded in, 182
  paradoxes, 22
  recognizing power of, 126
Leaders, types, 5
Leadership, distribution, 7
Learning, cultural views, 45
Lesbians, in literature, 179
Licensing
  guidelines, diversity, 195–196
  requirements, fulfilling, 221–222
Literature
  bias in socioeconomic groups, 180
  diversity within, 175–180
  feminist supervision, 158–161
  feminist therapy, 58–60
  postdoctoral training, 204–208
  women in, 178–180

Mentors, 228

Meritocracy, 197
Model Act for Licensure of Psychologists, 221

National Council of Schools of Professional Psychology, Conference on Women's Issues in Professional Psychology, 206
Note taking, 234

Oppressed, authorizing voices of, 25–26
Oppression
  locating ourselves on the spectrum, 197–198
  by White men, racial differences, 175–176

Parallel process, 238–239
Patriarchy, 82, 228–229
  image of woman-as-selfless caregiver, 27
  social and political context, 18
  theories, connecting feminist theory with, 21
Pedagogy working group, 122–123
Personality disorder diagnoses, critique, 46–47
Personality instruments, concerns, 43
Postdoctoral training, 203–223
  approaches to feminist training, 205–208
  curricular transformation, 216
  development of feminist values in trainees, 206–207
  diversity and cross-cultural perspectives, 216–217
  empowerment training model, 206–207
  exit criteria, 214
  expansion of feminist practice, recommendations, 222–223
  faculty and trainees, 217
  feminist licensure-sensitive model, 222
  fulfilling licensure requirement models, 221–222
  identification of existing training programs, 208
  integration of theory and practice, 220–221

length, 214–215
literature, 204–208
men's issues, 215
model for experienced clinicians, 218–220
models, 217–222
practitioner model, 220–221
principles, 213
psychology and emerging specialties, 208–210
research and practice, 217
scientist-practitioner feminist training model, 218–219
supervision, 214
titles, 215
as women's issue, 204–205
Postdoctoral working group, 210–216
  principles of feminist training, 213
  process, 210–212
Postgraduate level, curriculum development, 109
Power
  differentials among participants, 237
  feminist pedagogy, 126–127, 129–130, 148–153
  issues of, 125–127
Privilege
  locating ourselves on the spectrum, 197–198
  White skin, 176–177
Professional guidelines, diversity, 195–196
Professional organizations, roles, in diversity, 194
Psychological distress, reformulated understanding, 28–29
Psychological testing
  feminist critique, 42
  modifications, 47
Psychology
  mainstream, integration of feminism, 2
  traditional, transformations, 82
Psychotherapy, of women, principles, 205–206

Religion, role, 180
Research
  abuse, 192
  diversity in, 191–192
  nontraditional paradigms, 195
  postdoctoral training, 217

ABOUT THE EDITORS

Judith Worell received her PhD in clinical psychology from Ohio State University. She is currently a professor in and the chairperson of the Department of Educational and Counseling Psychology at the University of Kentucky. She is past president of both the Kentucky Psychology Association and the Southeastern Psychological Association. In the American Psychological Association, she is a fellow of Divisions 9, 12, 15, and 35; chairperson of the Publications and Communications Board; and incoming president of the Division of the Psychology of Women. She is a former editor of *Psychology of Women Quarterly* and a member of several editorial boards, including *Psychological Assessment, Sex Roles,* and *Women and Therapy.* She is the author of numerous journal articles and six books; her most recent book (with Pam Remer) is *Feminist Perspectives in Therapy: An Empowerment Model for Women.* Her research interests center on gender in close relationships, feminist identity development, and the assessment of process and outcomes in feminist therapy.

Norine G. Johnson, PhD, is co-chair of the American Psychological Association's (APA) Presidential Task Force on Adolescent Girls. She is the senior volume editor of *Adolescent Girls: Strengths and Stresses,* which will be published by APA in 1998. Dr. Johnson is a member of the APA Board of Directors and past president of the Division of the Psychology of Women. She has a private practice and specializes in adolescent girls' and women's issues. She is a clinical assistant professor in Boston University Medical School, Department of Neurology. Dr. Johnson was the director of psychology at Franciscan Hospital for Children in Boston, Massachusetts, where she developed a national training program for working with children and adolescents with neurological and learning disorders. Dr. Johnson's theoretical and clinical approach to adolescents and their fam-

265

ilies is to focus on the strengths, challenges, and choices of adolescent girls today. She has written and delivered more than 75 publications and presentations in the area of child and adolescent psychology. She received her doctorate in clinical psychology from Wayne State University and did her postdoctoral work in the 2-year Program for Mental Health Planners/Administrators sponsored by Harvard Medical School.